An Atonal Cinema

An Atonal Cinema

Resistance, Counterpoint and Dialogue in Transnational Palestine

Robert G. White

BLOOMSBURY ACADEMIC
NEW YORK • LONDON • OXFORD • NEW DELHI • SYDNEY

BLOOMSBURY ACADEMIC
Bloomsbury Publishing Inc
1385 Broadway, New York, NY 10018, USA
50 Bedford Square, London, WC1B 3DP, UK
29 Earlsfort Terrace, Dublin 2, Ireland

BLOOMSBURY, BLOOMSBURY ACADEMIC and the Diana logo are trademarks of Bloomsbury Publishing Plc

First published in the United States of America 2023
Paperback edition published 2025

Copyright © Robert G. White, 2023

For legal purposes the Acknowledgements on p. viii constitute an extension of this copyright page.

Cover design: Eleanor Rose
Cover image: "Texas Theatre, Palestine, Texas 0903111439" by Patrick Feller is licensed under CC BY 2.0.

All rights reserved. No part of this publication may be reproduced or transmitted in any form or by any means, electronic or mechanical, including photocopying, recording, or any information storage or retrieval system, without prior permission in writing from the publishers.

Bloomsbury Publishing Inc does not have any control over, or responsibility for, any third-party websites referred to or in this book. All internet addresses given in this book were correct at the time of going to press. The author and publisher regret any inconvenience caused if addresses have changed or sites have ceased to exist, but can accept no responsibility for any such changes.

A catalog record for this book is available from the Library of Congress.

ISBN: HB: 978-1-5013-8501-8
PB: 978-1-5013-8498-1
ePDF: 978-1-5013-8499-8
eBook: 978-1-5013-8500-1

Typeset by Newgen KnowledgeWorks Pvt. Ltd., Chennai, India

To find out more about our authors and books visit www.bloomsbury.com and sign up for our newsletters.

In memory of Edward Said and Jean-Luc Godard

Contents

Acknowledgements   viii

Introduction   1
    Writing back: Edward Said, contrapuntalism and the 'Image of Palestine'

1   Between here and elsewhere: Godard, Genet and the resistance of image in contemporary Palestinian cinema   29

2   Between presence and absence: Remnants and revenants in the cinema of the interior   59

3   Between diaspora and exile: Palestine, Chile and the cinema of Miguel Littín   87

4   Between Basilicata and Bethlehem: Pasolini, Palestine and the non-European   113

5   Towards a post-Palestinian cinema: Imagining states of being beyond the status quo   143

Notes   161
References   173
Index   185

Acknowledgements

This book, like any academic or creative project, took a village. The ideas within have been shaped with the support of friends and colleagues over a number of years. I thank Kingston University colleagues past and present for their thoughts, feedback and generous critique. Most notably, my thanks go to Dr Hager Weslati and Dr Corin Depper, the latter for his generous time and keen eye.

Beyond Kingston, the project has been developed through conferences, conversations with and invaluable feedback from colleagues and friends too numerous to mention. Special mention goes to Alex Marlow-Mann, Richard Rushton, Anna Ball and Henrik Gustafsson; to everyone involved in the London Palestine Film Festival and the Shubbak Festival, whose rich and collegiate environments are essential and have sparked conversations, ideas and friendships; to Marshall Marcus and Saeed Taji Farouky. My thanks also go to the filmmakers featured in this book for access to their films and for shaping the book with their own cinematic reflections on refracted Palestinian-ness.

This book as it now stands has been guided by some trailblazers in my field who have laid the foundations upon which I could build. Special mention goes to Nadia Yaqub, Ella Shohat and Gil Hochberg. An earlier version of Chapter 2 was published in *RCL*, Number 53, 2020, by ICNova, Lisbon. An earlier version of Chapter 4 was published in the *Journal of Italian Cinema and Media Studies*, 10(1), 2022, by Intellect, Bristol.

I'd also like to extend my gratitude to everyone at Bloomsbury for their support in overseeing this from proposal to publication, with particular thanks to my editorial team, Katie Gallof and Stephanie Grace-Petinos, for their support and encouragement.

Finally, my loving thanks to my family. To my parents, Carole and Paul, whose support has been, as ever, unwavering. And of course, to my wife, Gaia, whose love, infinite patience, support and fine editing eye were, and are, invaluable.

Introduction

Writing back: Edward Said, contrapuntalism and the 'Image of Palestine'

In the 2010 postscript to her landmark 1989 text *Israeli Cinema: East/West and the Politics of Representation*, Ella Shohat, reflecting on the emergence of new cinematic voices in Palestine-Israel,[1] draws on the structure of polyphony to situate such a cinema – in her own words – 'relationally' (Shohat 2010: 273). Shohat frames the 'liminal zone' of the cinema of Palestine-Israel as a sound territory, moving between Hebrew and Arabic, home and exile. This framing of cinema through the language of music appears to implicitly draw on Edward Said's own thinking of polyphony which, alongside atonality and – most comprehensively – counterpoint, informs both his cultural criticism and his thinking of Palestinian and exilic subjectivity. Said's thinking of counterpoint comes in the wake of a defining text in Postcolonial Studies examining imperial processes and cultural production, *The Empire Writes Back: Theory and Practice in Post-Colonial Literatures* (Ashcroft, Griffiths and Tiffin 2002 [1989]). This theoretical work was itself influenced by Said's work on filiation and mimicry as an internalized disciplining process of marginalized writers in *The World, the Text, and the Critic* (1983). While Said is cited as a hugely influential figure within Postcolonial Studies, it is in fact his aversion to systems (or by his own definition a thinker of *affiliation* rather than *filiation*)[2] which puts him in relation with another towering figure who looked to music as a way to reveal the world: Theodor Adorno. It is Said and Adorno's thinking of atonality and counterpoint to which this book looks as a framework for understanding a contemporary movement within Palestinian cinema, which I term an 'atonal cinema'. This is a movement which doesn't necessarily seek resolution and harmony but embraces difficulty, dissonance and a complex, contrapuntal relationship with cinematic and literary texts which have, in the past, spoken for it. This contemporary *resistance of image*, in constructing critical dialogue with texts which have a tendency to form either a totalizing *Image of Palestine* or *Image of Resistance*, plays a timely political and aesthetic role in decentring both colonial and nationalist narratives. The notion of 'double vision' will be crucial to situating the films and filmmakers in this book. This way of seeing is one Said posits as constitutive of the exile's perspective, explicitly terming this 'plurality of vision' '*contrapuntal*' (Said 2000: 186; emphasis in original). What might be termed a 'proximate distance' articulates the here/there counterpoint these atonal filmmakers conduct with Palestine as both a place and an idea.

Perhaps fortuitously, this book arrives at a time of renewed critical interest in the intellectual legacy of Edward Said. Nearly twenty years after his death, the last two years have seen two major texts reflecting on Said's life and thought: *On Edward Said: Remembrance of Things Past* (Dabashi 2020) and *Places of Mind: A Life of Edward Said* (Brennan 2021).

The latter is the first comprehensive biography of Said, and engages at some length with Said's late style and a turn to music to structure his thinking in his final decade. As Said's relationship with the Palestinian leadership began to deteriorate in the aftermath of the Oslo Accords, which Said (1995: 7) referred to as 'Palestinian Versailles', Brennan notes that 'with Said largely sidelined by the PLO, music took on an even greater prominence in his life' (Brennan 2021: 291). Brennan (ibid.) cites Said's later texts, particularly *Culture and Imperialism* (1994) and *On Late Style* (2006), as developing a sustained spatial musical vocabulary in texts which were not ostensibly about music. While Brennan's recognition of a musical structure to Said's late thought – one which also occurs sporadically in his earlier work – is enlightening, he is not alone in missing the influence music had on a neglected text: Said's photo-essay with Jean Mohr, *After the Last Sky* (1986). This text, as I argue in this chapter, in fact deserves far closer critical attention as it displays a formative engagement with Adorno, atonality, counterpoint and cinema that will underpin Said's late style. This introductory chapter will first trace Said's contrapuntal method, then situate his thinking of atonality and its relationship with Adorno, before conducting an analysis of Said and Mohr's *After the Last Sky* (1986), from which, I argue, emerges the skeleton for a theory of cinema – one from which my own book evolves.

Edward Said: A contrapuntal method

The musical concept of counterpoint occurs throughout Edward Said's oeuvre, if not always explicitly as a method, then perhaps – as Said himself has alluded to – a motif which recurs throughout his writing. It is a central enough feature of his work that his friend, Mahmoud Darwish, dedicated a poem, 'Counterpoint: For Edward Said', to Said's passing in 2003. The ninth and thirteenth stanzas of the poem express Said's own East/West filiation/affiliation counterpoint, expressed in Darwish's dialogue with his departed friend. In the ninth stanza, we hear Darwish listen to his interlocutor:

> He says I am from there, I am from here,
> but I am neither there nor here.
> I have two names that meet and part,
> and I have two languages, I forget
> with which I dream.
>
> (Darwish 2009 [2005]: 185)

The thirteenth stanza links the contrapuntal to the atonal, referring to a discordant out-of-placeness that is neither a centre nor a periphery:

> Here is a periphery advancing.
> Or a center receding. The East is not completely East
> and the West not completely West,
> because identity is open to plurality,
> it isn't a citadel or a trench.
>
> (ibid.: 186)

Said the critic was something of a nomadic polymath, moving between literary and music criticism, postcolonial theory and political writing. In his book *Reflections on Exile*, Said identifies the plurality of vision prompting these movements as the contrapuntal condition of exile: a double consciousness both inside and outside, part of and separate from the West; a form of non-belonging which constructs 'contrapuntal juxtapositions' (Said 2000: 148), which move between past/present, actual/virtual and here/elsewhere as a mode of critical practice. Said's engagement with counterpoint as method is most sustained in *Culture and Imperialism* (1994), in which he discusses the musical technique as a mode of critical reading.

Broadly speaking, counterpoint in music is the interaction of more than two tones (or voices) in a composition, often harmonically interdependent yet independent in rhythm and pitch. This lack of hierarchy[3] means the focus is on the interaction *between* independent voices rather than their effect as a whole. As such, Said transposes the musical form to a mode of reading for its thematic democracy, noting that 'in the counterpoint of Western classical music, various themes play off one another, with only a provisional privilege being given to any particular one' (Said 1994: 51).[4] The theme of double-consciousness/vision again emerges in Said's first mention of this 'different kind of reading and interpretation' (ibid.: 50). Elaborating on this different methodology, Said suggests that one reread the Western cultural archive '*contrapuntally*, with a simultaneous awareness both of the metropolitan history that is narrated and of those other histories against which (and together with which) the dominating discourse acts' (ibid.: 51; emphasis in original). Such a reading, as Said (1994, 2003) returns to in the case of Joseph Conrad, depends on seeing both the critical virtues and limitations in the original text. As Said (1994: xviii) recognizes, Conrad can be both critical of the ambitions of Imperialism and write 'as a man whose *Western* view of the non-Western world is so ingrained as to blind him to other histories, other cultures, other aspirations' (emphasis in original). These blind spots Said identifies are crucial to understanding the temporality of his reading against the grain, which, in the spirit of Walter Benjamin, involves treating the time of the text not as a static past but rather a past 'blasted out of the continuum of history' (Benjamin 2006: 395). As such, a text should be opened not just beyond the limits of its author's milieu but beyond the limits of its historical context. A reading of Camus's *L'Etranger*, therefore, must include 'the whole previous history of France's colonialism and its destruction of the Algerian state, and the later emergence of an independent Algeria (which Camus opposed)' (Said 1994: 67).

It is important to emphasize this element of temporality in Said's method, as he is often (and quite accurately) framed as a spatial thinker. By his own admission, he sees himself in the 'spatial tradition' of Gramsci (Said 1994; Said and Mitchell 1998). In discussion with W. J. T. Mitchell, Said (1998: 26) defines the function of narrative in *After the Last Sky* as 'speaking from a place'. This primacy of the spatial has opened Said up to criticism, particularly in relation to its counterpoint. In his article 'The Contrapuntal Humanisms of Edward Said' David Bartine (2015) offers a twofold, interrelated critique of Said's writing that there is an overemphasis on spatiality at the expense of temporality, and that this in turn leads to predominance of the visual register over the sonic. However, as Bartine focusses almost exclusively on *Culture and Imperialism*, his critique has some blind spots to Said's wider use of context. In its opening of historical texts to future readings beyond their temporal and cultural milieu, I would argue that rather than neglect the temporal, Said's approach occasions a thinking of both *spatial* territories but *temporal* moments and historical currents, creating contrapuntal dialogues which both spatially displace and temporally disjoint the source texts. Regarding this alleged neglect of a sonic register for a visual one, Said in fact draws on the non-representational register of music, notably *atonal* music, to confront the problem of the Palestinian image in his most ostensibly 'visual' book, *After the Last Sky* (1986). Said first discusses the problem Palestine poses for discourse on account of having no 'one central image' and being ontologically decentred, or: 'Without a center. Atonal' (Said 1986: 129). As will be discussed shortly, the atonal (as thought by Adorno) resists the transposition of affects into images. In discussion with W. J. T. Mitchell over the composition of *After the Last Sky*, Said again returns to the register of non-representational patterns and 'listening' for a musical motif:

> I felt I was actually doing it in a kind of abstract way. That's to say, I was really working according to principles that are much easier for me to deal with within the non-representational art of the Islamic world. You know, where there were certain kinds of patterns that you could see that were not representational in the sense, you know, that they had a subject, but they had some motif and rather a musical motif. (Said and Mitchell 1998: 16)

This thinking of abstraction and listening for motif, rather than visual representation, puts Said's concern for the overcoded regime of Palestinian images – a key thematic concern in *After the Last Sky*, which makes that text crucial in the genealogy of an atonal, contrapuntal reading of contemporary Palestinian cinema – in sharp focus.

After the Last Sky is conspicuously absent from discussions of Said's conceptual use of counterpoint; no mention is made in Bartine's article nor in Kiyoko Magome's (2006) essay 'Edward Said's Counterpoint'. It is very briefly mentioned (Telmissany and Schwartz 2010: xvii) in *Counterpoints*, but only as one of his 'political positions in support of the Palestinian Cause'. This neglect of a foundational early text which develops Said's atonal contrapuntal aesthetic and anticipates Said's own late career engagement with Adorno has, I will argue, led to a misunderstanding of Said's method and a diminishing of the importance of atonality within it. This reassertion of atonal counterpoint as a method for challenging both the limits of representation and the preservation of the political status quo will underpin my approach throughout this book. Indeed, the prominence of atonal counterpoint in Said's methodology has both been neglected (Magome 2006) and criticized for its lack of rigour and slippage with tonality (Bartine 2015). However, I argue that both these readings downplay the influence of Adorno on (particularly, but not exclusively) late Said as a thinker of the atonality of exile. Before examining Said's atonality, some examination of Adorno's philosophy of atonality and its relationship with his dialectics is needed.

Theodor Adorno and the ethics of atonal counterpoint

Said's reading of the atonal both follows and marks a break with Theodor Adorno, who situates atonality at the threshold of traumatic subjectivity and modernity. Adorno's *Philosophy of New Music*, written in 1949, situates 'the new' as a break with historical understanding and, crucially, resolution. Within the context of a shattered post-war Europe, Adorno's philosophy saw a break with the traditions of tonal music as concurrent with a more authentic historical experience. The book is predominantly focussed, in two sections, on the work of Arnold Schoenberg and Igor Stravinsky. It is through the study of Schoenberg that Adorno develops his atonal aesthetics, which in turn will have an influence on Said's cultural critique.

The focus on Schoenberg's atonality requires some contextualization as to what it is being framed against. From the Renaissance up to the twentieth century, Western classical music was broadly tonal. That is, there would be a hierarchy, a tonal pitch that forms the centre – or home – of the composition. While there will be modulation, a piece will usually end in the key in which it began, giving resolution and finality to the listener. This sense of resolution is crucial to tonal music, even as it evolves and becomes more complex and experimental. So, while dissonance emerges in tonal music, in Bach and notably in Beethoven, it is considered unstable and in need of resolution to consonance. By contrast, atonal music is composed without a 'home' key, and therefore narrative return to harmonic resolution through a return to the tonic of the key is absent. While dissonance is a feature of both tonal and atonal music, in the latter the tension that dissonance provokes remains unresolved. For Adorno, the instability seen as intolerable to tonal music in fact reflects the authentic nature of the traumatized historical subject, as he explicates in the following description of Schoenberg, worth quoting at length:

> The genuinely revolutionary element in his music is the transformation of the function of expression. Passions are no longer faked; on the contrary,

undisguised, corporeal impulses of the unconscious, shocks and traumas are registered in the medium of music. They attack the taboos of the form because these taboos submit the impulses to their censorship, rationalize them, and transpose them into images. (Adorno 2006 [1949]: 35)

The question of image, or rather *imagelessness*, is crucial to understanding Adorno's articulation of a language of shock and trauma which irrupts into psycho-social life, beyond the register of the verbal and visual. Adorno's writing draws on not only Hegel and Marx but also Freud in modern music's expression of the unconscious – particularly the repressed trauma of the post-war subject. Indeed reading Adorno contrapuntally, with his articulation of music as the shocks and traumas which lie beyond the limits of representation, invokes the Lacanian register of the Real, particularly its early manifestation in his writings on Freud, as *das Ding*.[5] The dissonance of atonal music reveals (in fragments) the repressed pain and horror of modern subjectivity rather than concealing them in a regime of false images. It is just such a regime, argues Adorno, which tonal music upholds, reinforcing the totality of romanticism, which, by extension, asserts the principles of absolute idealism. It is thus important to read Adorno's thinking of atonality in the context of his later work *Negative Dialectics* (1966). For Adorno, atonality denotes the expression of authentic historical consciousness foreshadowing his own negative dialectics, which he defines (in a critique of Hegel's dialectics) as 'the consistent sense of nonidentity' (Adorno 1996 [1966]: 5). This is expressed in atonal music's relationship with time:

> By virtue of this nonidentity of identity,[6] music achieves an absolutely new relationship to the time within which each work transpires. Music is no longer indifferent to time, for in time it is no longer arbitrarily repeated; rather it is transformed. Yet music does not thereby fall prey to mere time, for in this transformation it indeed persists as identical to itself. (Adorno 2006 [1949]: 47)

The break with the tonal tradition and romanticism is also a break with teleology underpinning Hegel's dialectics (in which the tension between opposites resolves into the whole towards absolute knowledge). Adorno inverted Hegel's positive dialectics, by turning an identity of identity and nonidentity into a *nonidentity* of identity and nonidentity. Nonidentity is both that which resists or exceeds thought and that which cannot be resolved into a unified absolute. In resisting the deterministic nature of Hegelian idealism, it moves from necessity to contingency; as such, it presents trauma, shock and dissonance as challenges to the status quo. The above quote, and its reference to 'mere time', puts Adorno in conversation with Walter Benjamin and his notion of a Messianic caesura interrupting historicism's deterministic 'chain of events' (Benjamin 2006: 392), allowing for contingency to break open the past and present and imagine the future otherwise; or, as Adorno puts it in his own reading of Benjamin, allowing for 'a coming out of the spell' of the mere time of historicism (Adorno 1989 [1964]: 90). It is just such a 'coming out of the spell' Said will invoke in what he terms the 'problem' of the Palestinian present, in which attempts to represent it in narrative form occur as rupture, instability and slippage. Such formal instability manifests in a contemporary Palestinian cinema's resistance of image, a cinema which produces itself but in complex, opaque images resistant to cliché and commodification.

Said and Adorno: Exile and atonal contrapuntal aesthetics

Said makes no attempt to hide his kinship with Adorno, particularly in his late style. Famously, in an interview with Ari Shavit for *Ha'aretz* in 2000, when being told he 'sounds Jewish' in his scepticism to the idea of a redemptive homeland, he responds,

> Of course. I'm the last Jewish intellectual. You don't know anyone else. All your other Jewish intellectuals are now suburban squires. From Amos Oz to all these people here in America. So I'm the last one. The only true follower of Adorno. Let me put it this way: I'm a Jewish Palestinian. (Said 2005: 458)

Despite this Adornian invoking of exile as a philosophical homelessness, the way in which atonality links their thought is somewhat neglected. Said drew on Adorno's atonality as a mode of dialectical thinking, which informed his own contrapuntal method in *After the Last Sky* (1986), *Culture and Imperialism* (1994) and *On Late Style* (2006), allowing a mode of critical practice that remained productively out of place.

Towards the end of *Culture and Imperialism*, Said summarizes the contrapuntal approach to reading he has taken throughout the book with an explicit reference to atonality as the model of critique:

> But this global, contrapuntal analysis should be modelled not (as earlier notions of comparative literature were) on a symphony but rather on an atonal ensemble; we must take into account all sorts of spatial or geographical and rhetorical practices – inflections, limits, constraints, intrusions, inclusions,

prohibitions – all of them tending to elucidate a complex and uneven topography. (Said 1994: 318)

The appeal to an 'atonal ensemble' which comes in the latter chapters of *Culture and Imperialism* has opened Said up to criticism, particularly with regard to the lack of precision in his use of musical terminology. Bartine's article in particular takes Said to task for referring to Western counterpoint quite broadly and the 'concert and order' of its polyphony (ibid.: 51), seemingly referring to tonal counterpoint in that instance. This centralized order/decentralized ensemble dichotomy, Bartine argues, should 'lead to Said's providing a further distinction between two types of counterpoint, tonal and atonal, but it does not' (Bartine 2015: 78). While there is some truth in Bartine's critique of Said's imprecision, his analysis lacks, as it were, a contrapuntal reading of Said. While the article acknowledges Said's discussion with Daniel Barenboim (2004) of the parallels between atonality and homelessness, and mentions (albeit only once) Adorno, the influence Adorno's thinking of atonality had on Said is, I believe, greatly neglected. The relationship between Said and Adorno is explored in far greater detail in Magome's (2006) essay 'Edward Said's Counterpoint', albeit in the complete absence of any discussion of atonality. Thus, these two pieces have two major blind spots. On the one hand, there is a discussion of atonal counterpoint and Said which fails to mention Adorno; on the other, there is a discussion of Adorno and Said's counterpoint which fails to mention atonality. This missed connection between the exilic, dissonant thinking of Adorno and how Said would return to it again and again (particularly in his 'late' style) is puzzling. Adorno appears in the introduction to *Reflections on Exile* (2000) as a figure of musical philosophy who sets 'an impossible example to follow' (Said 2000: xxxii). In that volume's titular essay, Adorno is again invoked as a model of philosophical homelessness: 'In short, Adorno says with a grave irony, "it is part of morality not to be at home in one's home." To follow Adorno is to stand away from "home" in order to look at it with an exile's detachment' (ibid.: 147). A thinking of exile that is at once both spatial and temporal is, as will be seen, crucial to understanding Said's thinking of atonal counterpoint. In addition to the aforementioned discussion of 'atonal' Palestinian culture in *After the Last Sky* (1986), Said quotes from Adorno's late essay 'Resignation', citing Adorno's words on the persistence (and resistance) of critical thought as 'another way of phrasing the Palestinian dream: the perfect congruence of memory, actuality, and language' (Said 1986: 75). The same Adorno quote appears twenty years later, in Said's final text *On Late Style: Music and Literature Against the Grain* (2006). The first essay deals at length with Adorno's late style and quotes again, this time at greater length, from 'Resignation'[7]: 'What once was thought cogently must be thought elsewhere, by others: this confidence accompanies even the most solitary and powerless thought' (Adorno 2005 [1969]: 293). In this essay, Said frames Adorno as an 'untimely, scandalous, even catastrophic commentator on the present' (Said 2006: 14), and late style as '*in* but oddly *apart* from the present' (ibid.: 24; emphasis in original). This notion of a temporal sense of exile from one's own time – a standing apart – is how Moustafa Bayoumi (2005) frames Said as a disjointed contemporary in the tradition of Adorno, particularly focussing on his post-Oslo political critique. Indeed, this double consciousness of exile as both being out of place and out of time, in which Said finds kinship with Adorno, is crucial to understanding the lateral connections between Said's 'political' works and 'literary/aesthetic' works. Viewing these works as a continuum of his atonal contrapuntal thinking, rather than in isolation, avoids missing these atonal threads across Said's intellectual oeuvre in the manner witnessed in this chapter (Telmissany and Schwartz 2010; Bartine 2015). Indeed, a truly contrapuntal reading of Said would situate *Culture and Imperialism* in the historical context of Said's post-Oslo critique of the political status quo, and recognize the untimely force of *After the Last Sky* (1986) as anticipating Said's growing engagement with Adorno, atonality and late style.

Said, contemporaneity and the problem of the present

The first chapter of *Culture and Imperialism* opens with a discussion of T.S. Eliot and tradition in relation to historical consciousness. More accurately, as is throughout his wider work, Said's focus is on contemporaneity, that is, on the artist's (and the critic's) relation to their time. For Said, the contemporary (and contemporaneity), rather than a historical marker, signifies a critical relationship with one's time. In his essay 'Arabic Prose and Prose Fiction after 1948', Said credits Constantine Zurayk's *Ma'na al-nakba* (The meaning of the Disaster) (1948) as understanding both the criticality and the complex temporality of contemporaneity. The contemporary, Said recognizes, much like Roland Barthes, is neither the past nor the present, but rather the *untimely*, in that it denotes a critical disjointedness with one's own time.[8] The untimely retains a political force with which the past can be excavated to reveal the contingency of the present (and future). Interestingly, Said was writing over thirty years before Giorgio Agamben would deal with the question of contemporaneity in a strikingly similar manner in his 2008 essay *What Is the Contemporary?*, identifying it with a breaking open of one's time so as to understand it critically. In other words, the contemporary is that which both unhinges time and attempts to recouple it. Said (2000 [1974]) sees Zurayk's work as performing a double movement between past and future, and sees the problem of the present as constitutive of that which the Palestinian intellectual must interrogate. When writing of Zurayk's contemporariness – his relationship with his time – Said writes,

> The paradox is that both these observations hold, so that at the intersection of past and future stands the disaster, which on the one hand reveals the deviation from *what has yet to happen* (a unified, collective Arab identity) and on the other reveals the possibility of *what may happen* (Arab extinction as a cultural or national unit). The true force then of Zurayk's book is that it made clear the problem of the *present*, a problematic site of contemporaneity, occupied and blocked from the Arabs. (Said 2000: 47; emphasis in original)

The 'problem of the present' is key to Said's thinking of the contemporary as critical practice. As well as identifying it with Zurayk's thinking of the Palestinian Nakba of 1948, Said also reflects on the formal instability of the present, and as such a challenge to representation, in *After the Last Sky* (1986). For Said, the formal fragmentation is indicative of 'the elusive, resistant reality it tries so often to represent' (Said 1986: 38). For Said then, when Palestinian *reality* is an overcoded regime of images which trap Palestinians within the frame, the Palestinian *Real* is that which resists representation. The challenge of the contemporary, therefore, is 'the almost metaphysical impossibility of representing the present' (ibid.). Much like Said before him, Giorgio Agamben theorizes the contemporary as a fracture, a break within time, a caesura that opens a space of critique. For one to be contemporary, claims Agamben, a critical distance is required:

> Contemporariness is, then, a singular relationship with one's own time, which adheres to it and, at the same time, keeps a distance from it. More precisely, it is *that relationship with time that adheres to it through a disjunction and an anachronism*. (Agamben 2009b: 41; emphasis in original)

This disjuncture manifests itself more dramatically in Agamben's reading of a 1923 Osip Mandelstam poem, 'The Century'. Agamben views the poet as the contemporary par excellence in that he sees his time as always already broken.

The poem frames the century, and thus the poet's time as a beast with a broken back. The poet, Agamben (ibid.: 42) tells us, 'insofar as he is contemporary, *is* this fracture, *is* at once that which impedes time from composing itself and the blood that must suture this break or this wound' (emphasis in original). The untimeliness of the contemporary is precisely this breaking and attempting to heal time, to recognize the problematic site of the present, a time that 'is in fact not only the most distant: it cannot in any way reach us' (ibid.: 47). Much like Zurayk's double movement that articulated his experience of a *disastrous* contemporaneity, for Agamben the contemporary grasps their time 'in the form of a "too soon" that is also a "too late"; of an already that is also a "not yet"' (ibid.).

A contemporary and friend of Said, Mahmoud Darwish, articulates a similar untimeliness in what he sees as the duty of the poet to exercise a contemporary critical distance, this in fact being his natural stance. When writing of his complex relation with the Palestinian leadership, he states, 'I encouraged the leadership in its time of weakness. Now that they are strong, I'm allowed not to applaud. If a Palestinian State is established, I will be in opposition. That is my natural position' (Darwish 2012: 64). Perhaps the most recognizable figure of contemporary Palestinian cinema, Elia Suleiman expresses a markedly similar position of critical resistance with regard to the question of institutional power and statehood. Reflecting on what he sees as his national identification, as opposed to identity, Suleiman is cautious as to the direction potential statehood may take:

> Let's say the Palestinian state raised the flag, built the borders, and we had a certain amount of freedom, a certain amount of less oppression – what if this state is not necessarily the kind of state we'd adhere to, in terms of justice and democracy, even though it achieved a liberation of some sort? Will I still be supporting a Palestinian state? No I will not. If it becomes another oppressive authority, I will be fighting to lower the flag. (Suleiman 2010: 4)

The political force and (un)timeliness of the contemporary cinema under study in this book is this multifaceted thinking of resistance. On the one hand, it responds to what John Collins (2011: x) identifies as 'a Palestine that is globalized and a global that is becoming Palestinized' by resisting the globalized 'Image of Palestine' as cliché and locating traces of Palestine in transnational conditions of subalternity. On the other, its complex, dense images perform a double critical deconstruction of the Israeli state and Palestinian Authority: both for their respective empty signifiers of oppression and resistance, and their bureaucratic management of the status quo. This critical contemporaneity produces a distance which allows for an imagining of the political otherwise, beyond the pessimism and East/West binaries which sustain the status quo. It is a contrapuntal movement between here and elsewhere that both structures this book and also underpins the critical movement in the films under study within it. Just such a structure draws on Said's proto-cinematic text of atonal counterpoint, *After the Last Sky*.

A contrapuntal reading of the 'Image of Palestine': Edward Said's *After the Last Sky*

Said's (1986) photo-essay *After the Last Sky*, written in dialogue with the photographs of Jean Mohr, occupies a curious and somewhat neglected position within his intellectual biography. As discussed, it is often framed as a political text, and seen as a diversion from his development as a cultural thinker, rather than a text where political, philosophical and aesthetic concerns converge. In fact, its untimeliness lies in its resonance with the aesthetic concerns of contemporary Palestinian cinema, and its anticipation of the disappointments of the post-Oslo stasis which would increasingly see Said occupy the late-Adornoian position of an untimely commentator on the present, in a similar manner to his friend and contemporary, Mahmoud Darwish. The book is structured in four sections, entitled 'States', 'Interiors', 'Emergence' and 'Past and Future'. Seeing the images and territories of Palestine as elements of a topological field, discrete but interconnected, Mohr's photographs documenting Palestinian lives are often conceptualized as tools to unpack philosophical and political problems.

Said's reading of the atonal in *After the Last Sky* builds on both what will become a lifelong engagement with Adorno and his philosophy of music, and also a debt (by his own admission) as a Gramscian spatial thinker who sees the territories and images of Palestine as situated within the same plane. In fact, Said's thinking of the atonal can not only be interpreted spatially, through the decentred and non-hierarchical, but can also be temporally read as discordance, a going-against-the-grain. Perhaps what is most striking, in what is primarily unsaid between the written commentaries and their corresponding photographs, is that Said sees a musical structure as imperative to composing the four chapters of the book. In the aforementioned conversation with W. J. T. Mitchell about arranging Mohr's photographs, Said clarifies that there is an insufficient equivalent discourse that he could draw on from narrative theory or philosophy. Of the former, that is, the problem of thinking narrative in Palestinian terms, he situates the lack of finding space in which to speak from as concurrent with the lack of territorial place, therefore language itself can produce 'a territorial object' (Said and Mitchell 1998: 26). This framing of narrative as a lateral act of positioning, as a relation between language and space, subject and object, interior and exterior, further evokes Adorno's thinking of language providing a home in exile. However, it also resonates in how Elia Suleiman views the Palestinian image. This is not a stable image with a subject, but rather a 'de-centred' and 'de-authored' image, what he terms 'decentralization of viewpoint, perception and narration' (Suleiman 2000: 97).

Said's construction of *After the Last Sky* follows a Gramscian spatial narrative – its chapters almost resembling interconnected territories of Palestinian history – which both problematizes and opens up Palestinian-ness onto the tangled temporalities of past and the future in conversation with a fossilized present absolute, echoing his thinking of narrative as an act of positioning. Said's thinking of atonality in *After the Last Sky* occasions a series of unresolved 'contrapuntal' double movements he sees in exile, from burden to liberation, subjection to subjectivity, exterior to interior. These positions are set up and deconstructed throughout the book, as Mohr's images are read contrapuntally.

The book is essentially an attempt to decentre the framing of Palestinian experience and preserve, in an Adornoian sense, the nonidentity of Palestinian life as a means of resisting totalizing forces which, throughout the book, Said recognizes both over-determine a positive identity and also reinforce a negative identity. The former comes through the constant requirement to show proof that validates Palestinian existence or the existence of the Palestinian subject, the latter in a series of negations: the other Arab in other Arab nation-states, the non-Jew of Israel and the non-citizen of an inexistent Palestine. Edward Said writes 'to', rather than just about, Mohr's photographs, while constantly striving to move beyond their frames. The primacy of the visual in *After the Last Sky* is a clear departure from his earlier work as a literary theorist. That being said, Said's literary background comes through the text, notably in its references to Bartleby and Habiby, the latter a recurring figure in his later work, not to mention the allusion in the title of the book to Mahmoud Darwish's poem.[9]

Perhaps what is most pertinent, both for Said's book and its underlying spatial themes which resonate in contemporary Palestinian cinema, is a blurring of the categories of inside and outside, dislocation and hemming in, the everywhere and the nowhere. This notion of being trapped within but also abandoned to the outside permeates Said's conversation with Mohr's photographs and it can be similarly drawn from the framing of space in contemporary Palestinian cinema.

This notion of being hemmed in and being on the outside is articulated again towards the end of 'States', when Said reflects on a long shot of a village scene outside Ramallah. The image is striated by tiers of terraces and houses horizontally, and vertically by thick trees and stairs. It is a relatively innocuous, pastoral scene on the surface, but Said soon discerns something else in its grid-like composition:

> As for those terraces and multiple levels: do they serve the activities of daily life or are they the haunted stairs of a prison which, like Piranesi's, lead nowhere, confining their human captives? The dense mass of leaves, right and left, lend their bulk to the frame, but they too impinge on the slender life they surround, like memory or a history too complex to be sorted out, bigger than its subject, richer than any consciousness one might have of it. (Said 1986: 48)

This reflection on the hidden and haunted, paths, passing time, bodies and objects that uncannily appear or terminate everywhere and nowhere, lurking both within and outside the frame, can render a seemingly innocuous photograph something more sinister and oppressive. A similar approach to the framing of a space suspended between the totality of the everywhere and the negation of the nowhere is prominent in the cinematography and mise en scène of Kamal Aljafari's two features *The Roof* (2006) and *Port of Memory* (2009). The roof and port evoked in the titles of the films are respectively the unfinished roof of Aljafari's mother's house in Ramle, and the port of Jaffa.

In *The Roof* Aljafari, in a similar way to Said, speaks to the frozen frames of moving images. After opening the second scene with an establishing shot of Ramle, which tracks slowly from right to left across the cemetery while Aljafari narrates a history of dispossession, the film then sets up its thematic inversion. The past, the foundations and origins are not hidden in the ground where one might expect, but rather above, in the unfinished roof of the title, abandoned in 1948 and now lying above, burying the house below it. The beautiful skeletal roof acts as a burden of memory and holds the characters captive in the space below. A similar spatial language is at work throughout *Port of Memory*, where walls and windows striate the 'exterior shots' of Jaffa, compartmentalizing the screen into a grid and giving the sense of open confinement that Said recognizes in the pastoral scene in *After the Last Sky* (ibid.).

'States' is also largely a reflection on notions of the nation-state, the competing and tangled claims to the space that is Palestine, and the question of nationalism. More specifically, it deals with the question of Arab nationalism or, perhaps more accurately, deconstructs the myth of pan-Arabism. Speaking of the various negations of Palestinian identification, Said writes,

> We all know that we are Arabs, and yet the concept, not to say the lived actuality, of Arabism – once the creed and the discourse of a proud Arab nation, free of imperialism, united, respected, powerful – is fast disappearing, cut up into the cautious, relatively provincial Arab states, each with its own traditions – partly invented, partly real – each with its own nationality and restricted identity. (ibid.: 34)

Later in the same chapter, Said (ibid.: 35) recognizes the inclusive exclusion that Palestinians experience as Arabs, when he states, 'thus we are the same as other Arabs, but different. We cannot exist except as Arabs, even though "the Arabs" exist otherwise as Lebanese, Jordanians, Moroccans, Kuwaitis, and so forth.' The exclusion that the Palestinian experiences in the midst of Arab nations – who simultaneously identify with, and speak in the name of, 'the Palestinian cause' as an emblem of resistance and Arab nationalism – is a theme prominently dramatized in Elia Suleiman's work, particularly in *The Time That Remains* (2009). The figure of the impotent neighbour, huffing and puffing, all words and no action, is a recurring one in a number of scenes throughout the film.

Said's chapter on 'Interiors' is particularly useful in the context of the work of Suleiman and Aljafari insofar as it highlights key cinematic themes in the depiction of *Arab al-dakhil* (Palestinians living inside Israel), and the relation of the domestic interior to subjective interiority. The notions of the domestic interior as a space of repetition and excess, a space where repetition both reveals and conceals rupture, a cluttered assemblage of pictures, ornaments and religious iconography that Said sees in Mohr's still frames bear a striking resemblance to the framing of interiors in Aljafari's and Suleiman's work, particularly *Port of Memory* (2009) and *Chronicle of a Disappearance* (1997). The framing of the home as a space of privilege and hemming in can also be seen in the circling camera of Amos Gitai's *Ana Arabia* (2013), which engulfs its subjects as it dizzyingly spirals deeper and deeper into an enclave of Jaffa, without offering any revelation or escape from its oppressive orbit. The fact that these three films speak to an experience of the Palestinian in Israel, the interior Arab that Said elicits from Mohr's photographs, is no coincidence. I suggest that this particular kind of interiority has been critically ignored in the cinematic framing of Palestinians *in* Israel, an important point which Chapter 2 of this book examines in detail.

After the Last Sky draws a complex portrait of 'Palestinian-ness' that Said describes as 'a dense and layered reality' (1986: 47). Commenting on Mohr's photographs of a settlement near Ramot (ibid.: 70), Said reflects on the rapid multiplication of abnormal cell growth, as the biological cell-like homes cluster and expand into the distance. Here Said sees a hidden congruence between the topological 'interior' and the biological 'interior'. These 'interiors' are layered onto the linguistic interior Said opens the chapter with, when he refers to speaking *min al-dakhil* – from the interior, to speak from a paradoxical space of privilege and entrapment.[10]

Said explicitly draws on two literary references while speaking to Mohr's visual texts, namely *Bartelby the Scrivener's* passive nihilism, and Emile Habiby's *al-Mutasha'il* (pessoptimist) with its linguistic and subjective hybridity.[11] However, references to photographic theory are perhaps implicit in the text. The following passage describes Said's reflection on Jean Mohr's portrait of an old peasant man from Baqa'a camp in Amman, Jordan. The man is looking intently over his shoulder into the camera:

> The things you can be sure of have to do with what he can do – he's a worker, a peasant – and where he comes from (his village, his family, his past and present movements). But he does not simply express the poignant, mute and enduring sadness of an archetypal peasant people, without politics or historical detail or development. In such a face we can now discern something different: the reserve of a force building up out of a long, intense history, frustrated and angry about the present, desperately worried about the future. (Said 1986: 91)

With this passage, Said alludes to the work of Roland Barthes, notably his concept of *studium* and *punctum*. These relations co-exist in the still image. The first, from the Latin for *study*, describes the arrangement and surface details one can take from a picture. The *punctum*, unlike the *studium*, is not sought by the viewer in the image, but rather comes from the image out. It thus punctuates both the *studium* and the viewer. It is outside of the photographer's intentions, something that occurs in certain images, pointing out the 'accident' that 'pricks' and 'bruises' the viewer (Barthes 1993: 27). Barthes's language itself, the *punctum* as point or punctuation, invokes the spatial (a position), the temporal (a point in time) and the corporeal (that which pricks, bruises).

Perhaps the most striking link between Barthes and Said can be drawn from Barthes's reflection on Alexander Gardner's 1865 *Portrait of Lewis Payne*, who was to be hanged for an attempted assassination. The *punctum* that pricks Barthes in this case is explicitly temporal. Of the image, in which its subject, like Mohr's old man from Amman, looks directly into the camera, Barthes writes,

> The photograph is handsome, as is the boy: that is the *studium*. But the *punctum* is: *he is going to die*. I read at the same time: *This will be* and *this has been*; I observe with horror an anterior future of which death is the stake. (ibid.: 96)

This *punctum*, an anxiety about the no longer is and the yet to come, the dead and the dying, is the very same one that pricks Said's reflection on Mohr's photograph. But while Barthes was staring into the eyes of a man who is going to die, there is perhaps in Said's *After the Last Sky* a more heightened apprehension about the inability to determine and locate the whereabouts of a Palestinian-ness that lives and dies everywhere and nowhere.

Reflecting on how he chose which of Mohr's vast range of photographs were to be included in the book, Said's words reveal how he actively prioritized *punctum* over *studium*.

> I wasn't really looking for photographs that I thought were exceptionally good, as opposed to ones that were not exceptionally good. I was just looking at photographs that I felt provoked some kind of response in me. I couldn't formulate what the response was. But I chose them. (Said and Mitchell 1998: 16)

Said's inability to describe a response to these images betrays another level of resistance within the Palestinian image. *After the Last Sky* was published the year before the First Intifada (1987–93). Yet its questioning of a stable Palestinian identity, along with its questioning of the mythology of pan-Arabism and its evocation and framing of the interior as both a space of privilege and confinement resonates profoundly with contemporary concerns in Palestinian cinema. This resonance occurs in one of Said's final appearances, and one of his very few explicit engagements with cinema. In 2003, Edward Said gave the keynote speech to open the 'Dreams of a Nation' Palestinian Film Festival in New York. In this speech, he underscored the importance of a politics of visibility while calling for a resistance of image, claiming that

> Palestinian Cinema must be understood in this context. That is to say, on the one hand, Palestinians stand against invisibility, which is the fate they have resisted since the beginning; and on the other hand, they stand against the stereotype in the media: the masked Arab, the *kuffiyya*, the stone-throwing Palestinian – a visual identity associated with terrorism and violence. (Said 2006 [2003]: 3)

Said's positing of Palestinian cinema's double-consciousness – resisting both *in*visibility and *hyper*visibility – follows the atonal, contrapuntal logic of *After the Last Sky* in seeking out the resistance of the image, rather than presenting images of resistance. While Said would not live to see the majority of the cinema featured in this book, his contrapuntal movement between hypervisibility and invisibility is remarkably prescient to the emergent themes of the films featured *in*, and the structure *of* the present work.

Locating transnational Palestine

In the introduction to a special issue of the *Journal of Postcolonial Writing* (2014) – 'Palestine and the Postcolonial: Culture, Creativity, Theory' – Patrick Williams and Anna Ball examine the question 'Where is Palestine?' through a series of absences, or 'nowheres'; statelessness, loss of the 'peace process', Palestine's 'absence' from postcolonial theory and, finally, the temporal condition of hope, which is examined through the homophonic duality of utopia (good/ no place). As productive as these interrogations are, they lack a recognition of the contrapuntal dislocation of Palestine which is, I argue, both *everywhere* and nowhere. At one level, this corresponds to both the aforementioned invisibility/ hypervisibility counterpoint, but more productively speaks to an atonal Palestinian cinema which examines its own image (here) both from a position of homelessness and reflected in others' texts (elsewhere): be that with exilic detachment in Europe and the Americas, or exilic estrangement of Palestinians within the state of Israel.[12] Rather than a temporal and teleological thinking of utopia, located in the hope/hopelessness of a State yet to come, a more productive frame of thinking this everywhere/nowhere counterpoint might be Foucault's notion of *heterotopia*; that is, *other* spaces. These are real spaces which exist 'outside of all places, even though it may be possible to indicate their location in reality' (Foucault 1986: 24). That is to say, they exist simultaneously everywhere and nowhere. Rather than thinking purely temporally, heterotopia allows for a materialist spatial thinking which interrogates the political status quo of Palestine, but co-implicates Europe and the Americas in the political-aesthetic questions this cinema explores. This serves as a reminder that the 'question' of Palestine and its history haunts a West which would rather it remained in an orientalized 'elsewhere'. Such a practice examines both the lived territorial experience of Palestinian-ness and also its emergence as a mirror image in other cultures as a reflection of attempts to supress their own histories of colonialism and displacement. This situates the question of Palestine laterally and reflects a dispersed spatial consciousness which characterizes this atonal cinema.

There is a plethora of literature on transnational cinema, ranging from interstitial and accented modes of production (Naficy 2001) to intercultural cinema and embodied, 'haptic' ways of seeing (Marks 2000: 44). Ezra and Rowden's *Transnational Cinema: The Film Reader* (2006) aims to bridge narrative/aesthetic concerns and globalized production to fashion a transnational theory on its own terms, a point reinforced and developed by Higbee and Lim's opening contribution to the journal *Transnational Cinemas*, with the stated aim of 'rethinking existing paradigms by Marks (2000) and Naficy (2001) that locate diasporic/transnational filmmaking only in the interstitial and marginal spaces of national cinemas' (Higbee and Lim 2010: 10).

Regarding Palestinian cinema specifically, much is made of its being 'structurally exilic' (Naficy 2006: 91) necessitating transnational production and distribution modes. Whereas Naficy situates the transnational in Palestinian filmmaking in primarily logistical terms, Peter Limbrick takes a different approach. Highlighting the transnational aesthetics of the films of Kamal Aljafari, he argues,

> His two latter films are completely embedded in Palestinian locations and politics while remaining transnational in their finance, their personnel, and even in their aesthetic which ... deploys the kind of aesthetic beauty and 'spectacle' that Galt identifies in some European transnational cinemas. Yet, ... whatever his films' indebtedness to a European cinematic frame, his work studiously refuses Euro*centrism* in that it avoids an orientalising gaze from the position of a Europe looking out to 'its others'. (Limbrick 2012: 219)

These comments point to a somewhat problematic discursive framing in assuming 'indebtedness to a European cinematic frame'. This assumption presupposes that abstraction, narrative non-linearity, and a static frame are the property of the cinematic language of European art cinema, rather than a language of exilic atonality with which contemporary Palestinian filmmakers in Europe can address past European filmmakers in Palestine (such as Godard and Pasolini).

In this book, I use the term 'transnational Palestine' as an effect of an atonal decentredness and critical dissonance, to evoke a contrapuntal past/present here/elsewhere movement which the films in this book perform with one another. The Palestinian revolution was transnationally networked and of huge cultural significance to the international left, as Chapter 1 explores. Its archive of images, with which the films in this book engage, are both a source of critical self-questioning and a means of resistance with which to produce oneself within a global regime of 'Images of Palestine'. By including films not considered 'Palestinian' yet included dialogically through response and critique, I aim to demonstrate how an atonal cinema engages critically with an archive of images both from Palestine (its own transnationally scattered revolutionary archive) and about Palestine (an archive to which contemporary filmmakers respond) to rearticulate the transnational energy of Palestine's revolutionary past. Doing so builds a contemporary image that resists an everywhere/nowhere dichotomy contingent on its existing hyper-/invisibility framing and instead insists that this image lies both here (with the Palestinians themselves) and elsewhere (within the texts they critique).

An exterior minority: Deleuze, Palestine and the atonal

The most explicit reference to 'atonal cinema' in film theory appears, perhaps unsurprisingly, in the work of Gilles Deleuze. In the 'Thought and Cinema' chapter of *Cinema 2*, Deleuze first mentions an atonal cinema in relation to Jean-Luc Godard's 'unlinked cinema' (Deleuze 1989: 183), composed of 'irrational cuts, ... dissonant tunings, ... unlinked terms' (ibid.). Deleuze returns to Godard's atonality in the following chapter, highlighting atonality as the space between images, between sound and image: 'Instead of one image after the other, there is one image *plus* another, and each shot is deframed in relation to the following shot' (ibid.: 214). The reflection on Godard's atonality is followed by Deleuze's sustained engagement with political cinema as Third Cinema, founded on his notion that 'the people no longer exist, or not yet ... *the people are missing*' (Deleuze 1989: 216). The no longer/not yet dialectic structures Deleuze's minoritarian thinking starting from his work with Guattari in 'What Is a Minor

Literature (1983 [1975]), through his cinema books and *A Thousand Plateaus* (2004 [1987]). This notion of a people as a becoming rather than a fixed identity distinguishes minoritarian, variable power (*puissance*) from majoritarian, constant power (*pouvoir*). The former also has the potential (also *puissance*) to deterritorialize the latter. Deleuze sees the 'not yet' of a minor cinema emerging to create a people not exactly in opposition to the majoritarian power colonialism, but rather in rejection of the parameters that negate (post)colonial subjects in binary power relations privileged by majoritarian discourse. This is exemplified in the very rejection of a language of self-representation in favour of a language of self-invention which Deleuze sees in Third Cinema: 'The moment the master, or the colonizer, proclaims "There have never been people here", the missing people are a becoming, they invent themselves, in shanty towns and camps, or in ghettos, in new conditions of struggle to which a necessarily political art must contribute' (Deleuze 1989: 217).

Paul Willemen's reflection on Third Cinema, 'The Third Cinema Question', reflects Deleuze's de-essentializing viewpoint of Third Cinema as minoritarian (albeit not a term Willemen uses) when reflecting on 'the people' as a multiplicity to avoid the essentializing and hegemonic language of the colonizer; this is particularly in the work of Nelson Pereira dos Santos, Ousmane Sembene and Ritwik Ghatak, but more generally across Third Cinema:

> Each of them refused to oppose a simplistic notion of national identity or of cultural authenticity to the values of colonial or imperial predators. Instead, they started from a recognition of the many-layeredness of their own cultural-historical formations, with each layer being shaped by complex connections between intra- and inter-national forces and traditions. (Willemen 1989: 4)

The question arises then, as to how the atonal connects to the minor, and to Deleuze's thinking on Palestine. In a minoritarian use of language that means living in a language that is not one's own (Deleuze and Guattari 1983: 19), one hears an echo of Adorno's exilic atonality of remaining not at home in one's home. For Deleuze and Guattari, this was Kafka deterritorializing German as a Czech Jew in Prague. In the Palestinian case, however, a similarity can be seen in Anton Shammas's minoritarian use of Hebrew to destabilize Palestinian/Israeli Arab/Jewish identity as partitionable and hierarchically constructed in opposition, which Gil Hochberg explores at length in the third chapter of *In Spite of Partition* (2007). In cinema, a similar minoritarian use of both spoken and cinematic language can be seen in the work of Kamal Aljafari, as Chapter 2 of this book examines. Beyond Hebrew, the work of Elia Suleiman and Mohanad Yaqubi employs a minor use of the language of Palestinian nationalism (questioning and rearranging its codes), thus deterritorializing its hegemonic use by the Palestinian Authority. Each of these instances speaks not to a cinema of representation, but one of invention: when representation is overcoded and reinforces power, the atonal cinema of the films and filmmakers in this book looks between these overcoded images for the spaces in which Palestinians can produce themselves.

While Deleuze didn't write on Palestinian cinema, his work on Palestine, while neglected in his wider thought, situates Palestine itself as both minoritarian, and also atonal in a sense that recalls Edward Said. Kathryn Medien notes this in her reflections on Deleuze's writings on Palestine, recognizing that in 'Producing its ideal governable subject – Jewish, modern, European-facing – the Zionist state machine folds out of land and life that which is incompatible, figuratively and materially producing the Palestinian population as an exterior, diasporic minority' (Medien 2019: 54). Such an attempt at a majoritarian production of a people as exterior is, for Giorgio Agamben, doomed to fail. Towards the end of Agamben's 1993 essay 'Beyond Human Rights', which is both a reflection on Arendt's work on the refugee, citizenry and sovereignty and an attempt to think beyond the territorial nation-state, he references the expulsion of 425 Palestinians across the border to a 'security zone' in Southern Lebanon (Haberman 1992: 1). For Agamben, this expulsion 'has already started from this very moment to act back on onto the territory of the state of Israel by perforating and altering in such a way that the image of that snowy mountain has become more internal to it than any other region of Eretz Israel' (Agamben 2000 [1993]: 25). Folding out and acting back signifies the movement of an atonal cinema, one which remains out of place and without a centre, but in doing so embeds its image in majoritarian sites of power (Europe, the United States, Israel). When Medien writes that Deleuze's writings on Palestine 'de-exceptionalize Israeli settler colonialism, drawing attention to global matrix of colonial violence' (Medien 2019: 50), this manifests in a cinema of Palestinians elsewhere, about Palestinian elsewheres.

An atonal cinema: Composition of the present work

When Edward Said posited the lack of a centre (and central image), when describing the atonality of Palestinian *culture* in 1986, his words foreshadowed an atonal *cinema* yet to come. While this book traces the lineage of Adorno's philosophical homelessness through Said's own contrapuntal interpretation, this musical unwillingness (or inability) to return to the home key manifests in the here/elsewhere oscillations the films in this book move between when thinking about the reality and representation of the Palestinian present. Elia Suleiman's thinking of a 'decentred' image, in which both the author and authority of the image are open to dialogue, is visible in his deconstruction of the overcoded symbols of Israeli and Palestinian national identity in his early work. Such thinking echoes Said's view that being Palestinian means being unable to rely on a central image (a home key, if you will). This atonality, a decentring of place and image, extends to a decentring of the subject between place and image. Both Said and Suleiman frame narrative as an act of positioning, or perhaps more accurately, space-making; echoing Said's aforementioned thinking of narrative as 'speaking from a place', Elia Suleiman describes exile in contrapuntal terms, never quite dwelling in the here or elsewhere: 'What is important is to be able to position oneself in relation to the world, to give spatial support for your perception of the world' (Suleiman 2000: 96). It is just such a relational proximate distance which informs more recent work, notably that of Basma Alsharif, whose filmmaking departs from a point of receding hope of an end to the status quo, and increasing distance from her ancestral home (Gaza) to find, from her diasporic stance, correlative experiences to Palestine in the margins of other cultural histories (the United States, Italy, France). Kamal Aljafari, whose own work complicates nostalgia and homelessness along Arab-Jewish/Palestinian lines, explicitly references Adorno's exilic atonality in what he sees as his own cinema as a dwelling in exile, stating, 'Adorno says that for a man who no longer has a country, to write becomes a place to live. I would say for a Palestinian, the cinema is a country' (Aljafari 2010). This atonal register, in which homelessness and dissonance become a place from which to examine Palestine as a place and idea, is both a tendency in the films under study, and the organizing principle of the chapters which examine them. From Said's 'atonal culture' to Suleiman's 'decentred image' and Basma Alsharif's 'post-Palestinian' consciousness, the atonal and contrapuntal slippages between Palestine's 'here' and its 'elsewhere', its past and present, its image and reality constitute a critical practice: one in which Palestinians are producing themselves on their own terms, both between and beyond their historical images.

Tracing the cinematic lineage of the resistant images Said read contrapuntally in *After the Last Sky*, the first chapter examines the relationship between the

Palestinian revolution and its international contemporaries (primarily Jean-Luc Godard and Jean Genet), situated relationally with recent Palestinian cinema's engagement with and questioning of this archive. My argument is that elements of this archive inform a contemporary 'resistance of image', rather than the traditional 'image of resistance' frame employed to analyse contemporary Palestinian cinema. This 'image of resistance' employs a visual language that resists overcoded signifiers of resistance associated with Palestine, and actively deconstructs the commodification of such images by both the Israeli State and the Palestinian Authority as empty signifiers of oppression and resistance. The conceptual framework of this resistance of image draws on both a literary genealogy (Emile Habiby, Edward Said and Jean Genet) and a cinematic genealogy (the PLO's Palestine Film Unit (PFU) and Jean-Luc Godard's 'resistant images' of the Palestinian revolution). This framework is then employed to analyse recent works by Annemarie Jacir, Eyal Sivan and Mohanad Yaqubi, and their contrapuntal dialogue with these historical images. Godard's own engagement with Palestine starts in this atonal register with *Ici et ailleurs* (Here and Elsewhere) (1976). As I examine in detail in the first chapter, the gestation of this film inverts the trajectory of the filmmaking of the PFU, metamorphosing from an ideological and didactic *image of resistance*, to a critical and questioning *resistance of image*. Such a questioning emerges in the filmmakers featured in this book and their relationship with an archive of images with which they conduct dialogues. The relationship between what Deleuze terms Godard's atonal cinema, 'forbidden' montage and the resistance of image emergent in contemporary Palestinian cinema will be traced throughout this opening chapter.

Moving onto what Edward Said termed *al-dakhil* (the interior), the second chapter examines the contrapuntal movement between presence and absence of Palestinians in Israel. In a 2003 interview with the *Journal of Palestine Studies*, Elia Sulieman evoked the spectre of the revenant, citing Israeli anxiety over its Arabs 'becoming Palestinian' again. This is both an allusion to a historical legal condition of present absence (the Knesset's 1950 Law of Absentee Property), and a hauntology/ontology of the cinematic image of the Palestinian in Israel. This chapter argues that the cinema of Palestinians in Israel is essentially a cinema of ghosts, from the haunting of Jaffa in the work of Kamal Aljafari, where Palestinian ghosts are re-inscribed onto the work of Israeli director Menahem Golan, to the ghostly lacuna between Arab and Jew which haunts Amos Gitai's *Ana Arabia* (2013). This chapter examines how Palestinian cinematic remnants of the interior stubbornly refuse to be buried, haunting and acting back on the State which has attempted to repress them.

The third chapter moves out from the interior, to a critically neglected site of the Palestinian diaspora – Chile – to examine the complex and multidirectional currents of diaspora and exile. Miguel Littín's engagement with both Palestine and Chile is complicated by his hybridity, part of Chile's Palestinian diaspora yet exiled by the Pinochet regime for his role as head of Allende's Chile Films, his position poses challenges to how exile and diaspora are discussed in scholarship on Palestinian cinema. This chapter examines his notable engagements with Palestine, *Crónicas Palestinas* (2001) and *La Ultima Luna* (2005), arguing that these late career works read the themes of his early Chilean exilic work contrapuntally, re-awakening a resistant diasporic Palestinian consciousness after the end of his Chilean exile. The latter film focusses on the transition from Ottoman to British rule, complicating the notion of pre-1948 Palestine as a 'lost Eden' presented in both scholarship and cinema (notably, but by no means exclusively, in the work of Michel Khleifi). Further, this diasporic identification with Chileans of Palestinian descent is both largely neglected in scholarship of Palestinians outside of the Occupied Territories/Israel and counters the framing of the Palestinian filmmaker as 'exilic auteur', a label applied to Elia Suleiman, Kamal Aljafari and Annemarie Jacir, among others. This chapter analyses Littín's shifting contrapuntal movement between diaspora and exile (diasporic Palestinian in Chile/Chilean exile in Mexico) throughout his work on Palestine. The chapter argues that Littín's own Chilean exile and engagement with Third Cinema, almost concurrent with the PLO's nascent PFU and its re-politicization of diasporic communities in Latin America, informs his late career diasporic re-engagement with Palestine.

Moving from Palestine/Chile to Palestine/Italy, the fourth chapter examines the place-myth of the holy land in both Italy and Palestine. Pier Paolo Pasolini's *Sopralluoghi in Palestina* (1964) documents the filmmaker's search for the archaic: the remains of a biblical world within which to locate his telling of the Gospel According to St Matthew, *Il Vangelo secondo Matteo* (1964). Pasolini's search in Palestine-Israel was eventually abandoned – the landscape and people deemed, paradoxically, 'too modern' and 'too archaic' – and displaced to Basilicata. While Pasolini's failed search for the faces and places of his biblical imagination contains problematic issues of representation, it provokes a fascinating dialogue about the cultural borders of East and West, particularly around the Mediterranean.

Drawing on two responses in contemporary Palestinian cinema to Pasolini – *Pasolini Pa* Palestine* (Ayreen Anastas 2005) and *Ouroboros* (Basma Alsharif, 2017) – alongside Carlo Levi's (1945) memoir *Christ Stopped at Eboli*, the chapter interrogates Pasolini's and Levi's Basilicata and Anastas's and Alsharif's responses from Palestine. In examining the blindspots, limits and unrealized potentiality in Pasolini's work opened by these contrapuntal readings, the chapter argues that these four works constitute a 'dialectical' cinematic image of Palestine, between image and reality, the archaic and the contemporary.

Revisiting Said's own notion of 'Palestinianism', the book concludes by examining recent works which, following Eyal Sivan's description of Basma Alsharif, might be termed 'post-Palestinian': not as a marker of periodization, but rather a call to imagine alternative 'anterior' futures foreclosed by the contemporary political impasse. Arguing that recent works by Palestinian artists indicate a trend towards spatialized imaginings of 'heterotopian' futures which use the present as a site to reimagine both past and future, the conclusion will examine the convergence of fiction features and more experimental visual art to argue that emerging works by Larissa Sansour, Basil Khalil and Elia Suleiman continue to develop this dialectical, contrapuntal critical practice as a vital mode of political critique in the face of stasis.

1

Between here and elsewhere: Godard, Genet and the resistance of image in contemporary Palestinian cinema

> I've only to hear the phrase 'Palestinian Revolution' even now and I'm plunged into a great darkness in which luminous, highly coloured images succeed and seem to pursue one another.
>
> (Jean Genet, *Prisoner of Love*)

An image of resistance

The words of Jean Genet, as he struggles to order the images of his memory among the Palestinian fedayeen, speaks generally to a struggle to comprehend and represent images of revolution or resistance, and perhaps more specifically, a wariness as to how images of Palestinian resistance are (and have been) circulated and used. The term 'resistance' is deeply evocative to the political imagination, most seductively as what might be termed 'images' of resistance, be they historical (such as the French resistance, or Algeria's own resistance to France) or contemporary and spatial (the squares of Taksim and Tahrir or the Occupy movements).

Resistance also has a strong resonance in the history of Palestinian cinema and more broadly in Palestinian culture, particularly in the related Arabic terms *qadiyya* (which translates as cause, but also case, in the legal sense) and *sumud* (which translates as steadfastness, retaining the will, or capacity to continue struggling). The image of *sumud* or the cause as a homogenous struggle for Statehood – a singularly national struggle – is a perfectly understandable way of framing Palestinian cinema, given the asymmetrical nature of power relations between Palestine and Israel. It is just such a framing which conditions what is still the dominant text in English on theorizing Palestinian cinema, Nurith Gertz and George Khleifi's *Palestinian Cinema: Landscape, Trauma and Memory*

(2008). This work disregards the atonality of Said's analysis or the polyphonic cinema identified by Ella Shohat, in favour of an approach which orders Palestinian filmmakers as a homophony, around the central melody of national struggle – an image of resistance – as the following quote illustrates:

> To a large extent, the new directors have joined forces to protect Palestinian unity and identity in the face of the threat of extinction … Thus, the diversity of the Palestinian society, the everyday and the personal, all eventually unite in these films under a single homogenous national identity coping with collective hardships and struggles. (Gertz and Khleifi 2008: 135)

The fears of 'threat of extinction' evoked by Gertz and Khleifi are perhaps as much about the loss of Palestinian 'unity and identity' as they are about the loss of Palestinian cinema itself. Such fears were undoubtedly conditioned by historical circumstance. Namely, a book written and first published in Hebrew in 2005 – in such proximity to the Second Intifada (2000–5) – is perhaps inevitably focussed on framing contemporary Palestinian cinema as a cinema of resilience, a collective form of struggle. However, during this same period,[1] Edward Said gave the keynote speech to open the 'Dreams of a Nation' Palestinian Film Festival in New York, underscoring the importance of a politics of visibility while calling for a resistance of a certain form of image, a contrapuntal move between resisting the *in*visibility of lived experience and *hyper*visibility of globalized image articulated in the previous chapter.

Gertz and Khleifi's fears are also somewhat misplaced insofar as they stem from a certain reading or, as I will argue, a *mis*reading of cinematic consciousness emerging from Palestinian revolutionary cinema, which Nick Denes (2014) has criticized, in part for an overt focus on suffering in these films at the expense of their formal experimentation.

A further criticism of the homogenization of differing subjectivities into a collective *coping* in the face of hardships and struggles is that it accepts the neo-colonial, biopolitical parameters of the contemporary political stasis. Rather than articulating a resistant subjectivity, it engenders a *resilient* one that stoically accepts suffering as its perpetual and unchanged fate. This is what Julian Reid identifies as a troubling discourse of contemporary neoliberalism, one that evolved from the colonial project as essentially a security project. Resilient subjects are those 'that have learnt the lesson of the dangers of security, in order to live out a life of permanent exposure to dangers that are not only beyond their abilities to overcome but necessary for the prosperity of their life and wellbeing'

(Reid 2012: 145). Resilience thus defines itself in opposition to resistance, and even destroys the capacity of resistance to both resist the status quo and also imagine it otherwise. In foreclosing a possible alternative to survival of the status quo,[2] resilient subjectivity can only aim to survive the threats and dangers of contemporary (biopolitical) life.

Images of resistance can manifest in these images of mere resilience, in the reductive, empty resistance commodity images of the Palestinian Authority, or in a hypervisible global image of resistance coded as 'terror' (once radical Left, now radical Islam). Each of these manifestations reinforces existing power dynamics and perpetuates the status quo.

This chapter will counter this 'image of resistance' framing that proposes national struggle and resilience form a path traceable from the Palestinian revolution to contemporary Palestinian cinema. In contradistinction to this, it proposes a 'resistance of image' innate in the archival practice which increasingly underpins this atonal cinema. The genealogy of this 'resistance of image' draws both on Edward Said's dialogue with critically resistant images in *After the Last Sky* examined in the previous chapter, and on the criticality within the revolutionary filmmaking of the PFU (Palestine Film Unit). Such a 'resistance of image' constructs a counterpoint with early Palestinian revolutionary cinema, looking to this moment not with nostalgia but with contemporary urgency. In its formal questioning of the authority and use of images by political power, such resistance uncovers and rearticulates the lost criticality of the PFU, as the revolution gradually fossilized into a bureaucratic institution post-Oslo. This atonal cinema is one which cautiously resists 'images of resistance' as always already commodifiable cliché, but rearticulates its own archive in search of a contemporary capacity to resist the political status quo.

The locus of the 'image of resistance' in Palestinian cinema emerges alongside a revolutionary Palestinian cinema conscious of the importance of its own image-making to that revolution. However, the criticality and formal experimentation of this early cinema has been neglected in a broader focus on the internationalism of the revolution, the partial 'loss' of the PFU archive in 1982[3] and, more recently, its 'rediscovery' which has informed an archival turn in contemporary Palestinian cinema (notably, but far from exclusively, in the work of Annemarie Jacir and Mohanad Yaqubi). Nick Denes's (2014) research uncovers a genealogy within PFU from radical formal experimentation to conservatism. Citing Fateh's ideological elasticity in the early years of the Palestinian revolution, Denes notes a correspondingly elastic and free-form Film Unit invested in self-invention: 'The

Film Unit, under a political order that was defying definition while advocating the spontaneous and the unbridled, enjoyed considerable license ... Like Fateh's revolution at large then, its cinema was conceived as iterative and emergent of form' (Denes 2014: 226). The free-form early work *With Soul, With Blood* (1971) and *A Zionist Aggression* (1972) would give way to the reverent *Palestine in the Eye* (1977), in which, writes Denes (2014: 38), 'the revolutionary content being transmitted appears to be a study in discipline and order'. Such a change was marked by what Denes identifies as the post-revolutionary turn of Fateh (Ibid.: 233), noting that (as Jean Genet would recognize during his time with the fedayeen) as the revolution became institutionalized so did a cinema that was 'looking to shore up and project state-like authority' (ibid.: 236).

Denes's work on early Palestinian revolutionary cinema, highlighting its openness, experimentation and essay-like form, arguably points to a lost lineage of an alternative cinematic language of resistance, an experimental critical practice and questioning of form that informs contemporary cinematic practice in the face of an emboldened Israeli state and an ageing, bureaucratized and neoliberalized Palestinian leadership. Problematizing this historically reductive – albeit seductive – homogenous image of resistance is useful in reframing a thinking of resistance as critical practice which aims to resist co-option by political power. Just such a practice can be traced through to an emergent tendency in recent Palestinian cinema. This chapter will now explicate the lineage of this resistance of image in two stages. Firstly, it will situate the PFU's relationship with two contemporary resistants, Jean-Luc Godard and Jean Genet, whose wariness of the commodifiable image as cliché in the Palestinian revolution is reflected throughout the work of Edward Said and Mahmoud Darwish. Secondly, it will examine the reawakening of this resistance of image in the archival, contrapuntal practice of contemporary works by Annemarie Jacir, Eyal Sivan, Mohanad Yaqubi and Eric Baudelaire, all of which blast images of the past out of the continuum of history to articulate a contemporary visual politics of resistance.

Godard in Palestine: 'I feel like an occupied country. Change lies between the images' (Jean-Luc Godard, *Changer d'image*, 1982)

An engagement with Palestine occurs throughout Jean-Luc Godard's filmmaking, most notably in *Notre Musique* (2004) and *Film Socialisme* (2010).

Both of these films build upon notions of 'forbidden' montage and juxtaposition developed in Godard's first reflection on the representation of Palestine, *Ici et ailleurs* (1976). Echoing the Palestinian revolution's transnational connections in general and its appeal to the French Left in particular, *Ici et ailleurs* documents the struggles of representing resistance when those images become a commodity in themselves. The conjunction in the title is the device that both binds and separates space and time. The spatial refers to the 'here' of domestic France and the 'elsewhere' of the Jordanian fedayeen camp, the temporal to the film intended to be made and the film that would come to pass six years later. The film was originally titled *Jusqu'à la Victoire* (Until Victory) and was planned for release in 1970, a documentary in solidarity with the liberation struggle of the PLO. As a militant work in the tradition of the Dziga Vertov Group, the film was intended to be 'made politically' in the sense of 'open' production with the participation of the fedayeen as both subject and viewer of the work (Emmelhainz 2019). Due to historical events (after the recording of early footage, many of the participants of the original film were killed in the Black September attacks by the Jordanian army, followed by the PLO's expulsion from Jordan), the original project was abandoned, until a collaboration with Anne-Marie Miéville produced a meditation on the failure of the filmmaking project and a wider critique of the construct and purpose of the revolutionary film itself. In its production, the film is strongly connected to the PFU, with Mustafa Abu Ali (perhaps its most prominent filmmaker) working as cameraman for Godard's film and, in turn, borrowing Godard and Miéville's 16mm camera for his own *They Do Not Exist* (1974) (Denes 2009: 26). In an inversion of the PFU's trajectory, what started out as a document of the Palestinian revolution as a teleological image of resistance (paraphrasing the PLO slogan 'Revolution until Victory' for its original title) echoing Godard's *tiers-mondisme*[4] evolved into a reflexive, open critique on the production of those images for consumption elsewhere – a resistance of image.

The footage filmed in 1970 constitutes a series of fixed frames, frames of 'reality' assembled to produce new significations, a praxis drawing on Vertov's concept of 'factography' so as not to represent reality but actively transform, or more accurately *remake*[5] it (Emmelheniz 2019: 99).

The opening few minutes act as a prelude. The five chapters that would have made *Jusqu'à la Victoire* are introduced: The People's Will, Armed Struggle, Political Work, Prolonged War and Until Victory. These capture elements of the Palestinian revolution in 1970, such as the role of women in the Revolution, the necessity of armed struggle and global revolution. These are introduced as fixed frames, until the final section hints at the experimental work to come. This fifth movement, Until Victory, prefaces the experiments with juxtaposition, superimposition and disaggregation which will come: Golda Meir's outline is superimposed over a cartoon fedayee. This move ushers in the film's fundamental linguistic instability, 'and' and 'plus'.

One image PLUS another

The ET is that which chains together and separates at the same time. Most obviously in the film's title, the ET is the conjunction which cannot quite reconcile 1970 with 1976 and here with elsewhere. However, the use of the ET also draws on rethinking of montage in the wake of the failure of *Jusqu'à la Victoire* and its political method. The teleological, dialectic method of *Jusqu'à la Victoire*, through which contradictions produce advancement towards a political goal (victory) is abandoned for a horizontal montage (Bazin 2003 [1958]), in which 'unlinked' images can be laterally combined and, with the participation of the viewer, a third image or association is formed. Deleuze references Godard in his description of his 'intersticial method', where the plus (juxtaposition) takes the place of the after (movement): 'Instead of one image after the other, there is one image *plus* another, and each shot is deframed in relation to the framing of the following shot' (Deleuze 1989: 214). Deleuze is paraphrasing[6] Godard's own understanding of montage for what he terms a shift from 'linkage of associated images' in classical cinema to 'relinkages of independent images' in modern (ibid.). The ET in *Ici et ailleurs*, literally rendered as a three-dimensional structure (as seen below), acts as the irrational cut between two independent images which provoke in the viewer the 'unthinkable in thought' (ibid.: 169), functioning in this film (to be referenced in contemporary cinema of Palestine) as forbidden montages.

These forbidden montages are mathematical combinations which produce new images dependent on historical counterpoint. For Godard, 1917 plus 1936 'equals in the month of May, the image of a '68'. That is, the hope of revolution (Russia, Front Populaire, May 68 and the nascent Palestinian revolution). However, a change in the equation from May to September transforms the result to an image of hopelessness: the uncertainty of the Bolshevik revolution plus the eighth Nazi party conference in Nuremburg produces the image of a moribund

Figure 1.1 The conjunction which binds and separates in *Ici et ailleurs* (Anne-Marie Miéville, Jean-Luc Godard, 1976). ©Gaumont Films.

Palestinian revolution in Black September. The image of 1917 produces key questions for Godard and Miéville to work through. The year of both the Russian Revolution and the Balfour Declaration produces the question of Revolution and the question of Palestine. The question of Palestine as a fundamentally European one sets up the film's most controversial forbidden montage: that of Hitler and Golda Meir. The very act of this juxtaposition implies the unsayable – that the Jewish question and the Palestine question form the image which haunts Europe – a taboo that is reflected on in Eyal Sivan's *Montage Interdit* (2012), discussed later in this chapter.

Godard's thesis of one image plus another interpreted by the viewer at a moment in time is contrasted with the more didactic montage of political propaganda. A central section of the film deals with the exposure of this conception of montage, a presentation and deconstruction of its process, in which five figures present photographs of the five chapters of *Jusqu'à la Victoire*: *The People's Will, Armed Struggle, Political Work, Extended War* and *Until Victory*. As one image replaces another on the film stock, Godard refers to these images, being shown performatively, as cinematic montage, as space in its temporal movement. Commenting on this process, Godard's voiceover is akin to a capitalist production line in which two workers, space and time, are producing a consumable product to assume a position in a flow of commodities, that of images: 'Space has inscribed itself on film, which is

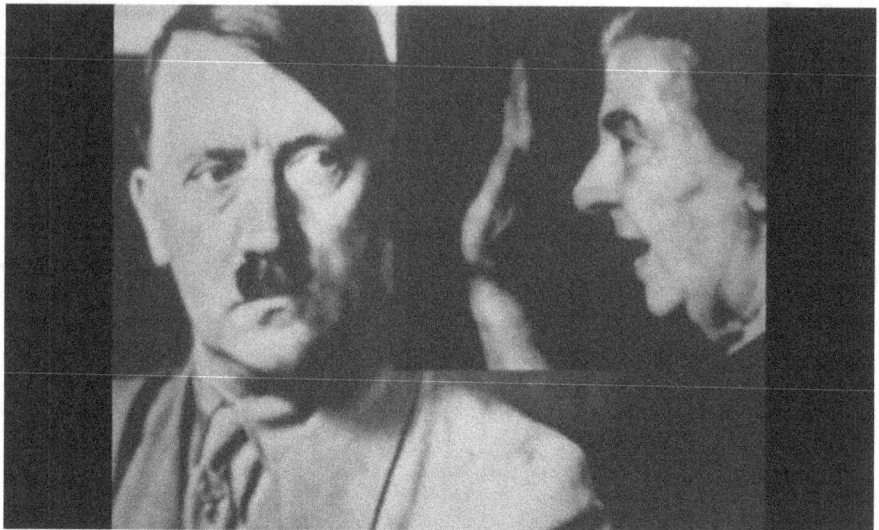

Figure 1.2 The forbidden montage par excellence in *Ici et ailleurs* (Anne-Marie Miéville, Jean-Luc Godard, 1976). ©Gaumont Films.

not a whole but a sum of translations, a sum of feelings which are forwarded … that is, time.'

The 'staging' of this production line of revolutionary images creates what Olivia Harrison terms 'a *mise en abyme* of the fictional making of the film *Jusqu'à la victoire*' (Harrison 2018: 187; emphasis in original). However, far beyond just this scene, the film uses the mise en abyme as an organizing motif. The 1970 film is presented, repeated and deconstructed throughout, in a wider reflection on the international Left, Marxism-Leninism and the role of revolutionary filmmaking. Nonetheless, this is the film's most explicit critique of the political film as consumption-image, dismantling and deconstructing the process of montage and questioning the value, authority and consumption of the revolutionary image when it becomes just a commodity in a flow of images. This becomes explicit when Godard contrasts the 'poor revolutionary fool' of 'elsewhere' with the 'millionaire in images of revolution' of 'here'. The revolutionary loses control of their own image and the European leftist is seduced by this image as 'exotic' commodity but fails to listen to it. It is breaking this flow, or chain of commodity images which *Ici et ailleurs* sees as one aspect of the work of revolutionary filmmaking, through its production of the 'shocks' of forbidden montage which provoke thought.

Figure 1.3 A production line of images in *Ici et ailleurs* (1976). ©Gaumont Films.

Learn to see here in order to hear elsewhere: An image resistant to discourse

A key critique of revolutionary filmmaking in the wake of the failure of revolution takes the register of the aural rather than visual. That is, *Ici et ailleurs*'s central thesis is a plea to 'turn down the volume', a verbal and visual citation repeated in the latter half of the film. What this means in practice is that the film marks a shift from constructing images of resistance to allowing a resistance of image to take place. This is achieved by disaggregating sound (discourse/ideology) and image. Shortly after the half-way point in the film, Godard contemplates, with the image of a Hitler speech heard hitting the red zone of a VU meter, the power of sound to 'take and keep power'. Reflecting on how one sound take can power over others at a historical juncture, Godard asks, 'How did that sound take power? It took power because at a given time it was represented by an image.' This power of sound to couple with an image and determine its signification and use becomes the central focus of the film. Capitalism's function is to reduce the world to an image, turn up the volume and build its wealth on this 'truth', the fact (*facere*) of image-making as world-making. However, in the wake of the failures of post-68 revolution both 'here' (France) and 'elsewhere' (Palestine) Godard contemplates the role of the deafening sound of ideology (in general) and *tiers-mondiste* enthusiasm in Europe for revolution elsewhere (in particular) in speaking both for and over the images of those revolutions. In this way, the voice of the filmmaker and the voice of Marxist-Leninist theory drowned out the voice of the fedayeen in Palestine. This is articulated in the closing words of Anne-Marie Miéville, who provides a counterpoint to the Dziga Vertov Group's paternalistic *tiers-mondisme* throughout:

> We're incapable of seeing or listening to these very simple images. How come? We have, like everyone, said something else about them, something else than what they were saying. That we cannot see nor hear, no doubt. Or that the sound is too loud, and covers reality. Learn to see here in order to hear elsewhere.

In the Palestinian context, a regime of consumable, overcoded and loud 'images of resistance' which can effectively erase the complex subjectivity behind them is something both Edward Said and Jean Genet warned of in the imagery of the Palestinian revolution. The former laments a reductive imagery of 'postures, guns and slogans' co-opted by the Israeli state to codify and the complexity and multiplicity of struggles for Palestinian rights as 'terrorism' (Said 1986: 107). Jean Genet similarly laments the empty signifiers through which images of the Palestinian revolution circulate in the West, claiming that 'For Westerners, he [Arafat] remains a keffiyeh with a stubble' (Genet 2003 [1986]: 141). Likewise, Serge Daney argues in *After the Image* that the empty image of Arafat 'is no doubt useful for the survival of the word "cause", but its functioning doesn't go beyond that of an advertising label' (Daney 1999: 189). Godard and Miéville's elegiac piece reflects a moment of loss which will return as nostalgia, as the optimism and energy of the late 1960s in the PLO and the *tiers-mondiste* movement transitions into the 'long 1970s', an era marked by the weakening of the international Left, the rise of political Islam in the Arab world and the neoliberalization of Oslo that sees the revolutionary spirit of the PLO fossilize into the bureaucratic image of the Palestinian Authority.

In the contrapuntal move between the 'elsewhere' of 1970 and the Palestinian revolution, and the 'here' of the 1976 deconstruction of its meaning, Godard shows a critical awareness of both his position among (rather than with) the Palestinian fedayeen and the need to allow to listen to the images beyond their original context. Godard's method of forbidden montage and contrapuntal dialogue across time and place would provide something of a toolkit for contemporary Palestinian filmmakers. A toolkit with which they could interrogate images of themselves and of their representation, with an eye on both how this self-production was co-opted by institutional power and how a contemporary language might rearticulate the iterative, spontaneous and questioning form of the early filmmaking of the Palestinian revolution.

Prisoner of love, prisoner of images: Genet in Palestine

Like Godard, Jean Genet documented his time among (ever cautious of remaining an outsider) the fedayeen of the Palestinian revolution, at a similar spatial and temporal distance. *Prisoner of Love* (2003 [1986]) is Genet's account of the Palestinian revolution and his time spent with the fedayeen in Jordan between 1970 and 1972 written over a decade later in the wake of his time in Beirut during the 1982 invasion. Like Godard's, Genet's 1970 is an 'elsewhere': a time spent among a revolution for which he struggled to find a representative vocabulary; that is, its very reality escaped any discourse which tried to contain it. Genet's 'speaking' to his own recollection of the images of revolution bears a striking resemblance to both Said's struggle to find a discursive register for Jean Mohr's images in the photo-essay *After the Last Sky* and Godard's fear of drowning out the images of the Palestinian revolution. The conjuring of Genet's memories displays at times a remarkably cinematic quality of visual memory, but also a resistance to captioning these memory images, encapsulated by the confession that 'I feel now like a little black box projecting slides without captions' (Genet 2003 [1986]: 348). The explicit unrepresentability of these images, born of a care not to speak for them, opens Genet's account of his time in Jordan. In a claim bearing parallels to Godard and Miéville's desire to turn down the volume of revolutionary discourse and listen to the reality of the Palestinian revolution, Genet posits that this reality exists beyond the register of representation, in the spaces between the words which attempt to do this:

> Was the Palestinian revolution written on the void, an artifice superimposed on nothingness, and is the white page, and every little blank space between the words, more real than the black characters themselves? ... If the reality of time spent among – not with – the Palestinians resided anywhere, it would survive between all the words that claim to give an account of it. They claim to give an account of it, but in fact it buries itself, slots itself exactly into the spaces, recorded there rather than in the words that serve only to blot it out. (ibid.: 5)

If Genet's self-confessed failure to understand the Palestinian revolution echoes Godard's, his concern for the institution it might become points to a resistance to the yet-to-come of a Palestinian Authority trading in the nostalgia of the Revolution while fossilizing in stasis: this a resistance shared by Edward Said and Mahmoud Darwish and reflected in the recent films by Annemarie Jacir and Mohanad Yaqubi. Speaking of the 'violent' resistance of the Palestinians, a category which is not to be confused with the 'brutality' of oppression, Genet claims that 'they inflict violence not only on the Israelis, but also on the Arab world, the Islamic world in general and even the Western world that refuses them' (Genet 2004: 246).Genet embraces an idea of violence while distancing himself from brutality, a distinction he insists is discrete.

Genet recognizes in the nascent Palestinian revolution a violent resistance to refusal of acknowledgement, but also a resistance to power, authority and subordination, which occurs in many forms. However, the gradual movement from a resistant violence to an institutionalized, revolutionary brutality is one Genet witnessed in the PLO, documented in both *Prisoner of Love* and *The Declared Enemy* (2004). This would seem to mirror the move from experimentation and questioning to discipline and order which Nick Denes locates in the PFU, as revolution becomes institutionalized.

What might be termed then Genet's 'poetics of resistance' rests on always maintaining a position on the outside, at a critical distance from power, to retain the capacity to resist – or in his own words, *revolt* – which, he suggests, in an interview a year after Sabra and Shatila massacre, is distinct from the institution of revolution:

> For the moment I adhere completely to Palestine in revolt. I don't know if I will adhere – I will probably, even certainly be dead by then – but if I were alive I don't know if I could adhere to a Palestine that has been made into an institution and has become territorially satisfied. (Genet 2004: 251)

Taken at face value, this appears a problematic assertion, in so much as it abstracts an idea of Palestine to one a moment of revolution to be sustained in perpetual exile, and doesn't suggest a conception of political subjectivity beyond this. However, the question of resistance to the institution of the state, and a caution as to what form that state may take, has a lineage in the writing of both Edward Said and Mahmoud Darwish and the views of filmmaker Elia Suleiman, as examined in the introduction of this book, with both expressing a position of critical distance towards state power as the telos of redeemed homeland and a duty to remain atonally dissonant with such a position. This reflects a particular scepticism towards the stasis of post-Oslo Palestinian leadership.

Suleiman's cinema in particular utilizes a language which resists both the Occupation and the liminal condition of the Palestinian in Israel on the one hand, and the overcoded images of resistance which have become the empty political capital of Arab states and the Palestinian Authority on the other. The figure of the neighbour is critiqued throughout Suleiman's *The Time That Remains* (2009), a subtle allegory for Palestine's Arab neighbours' empty support of the Palestinian cause as political capital for them to trade in, which – notes Edward Said in 1979's *The Question of Palestine* – 'does not seem to be diminished by periodic expulsions of Palestinians from one or another Arab state' (Said 1992 [1979]: 154). Suleiman's follow-up, *It Must Be Heaven*, depicts Suleiman's frustrated attempts to leave Palestine and the images of occupation and resistance behind, which he finds continually thwarted by an increasingly securitized world reflecting the 'Palestinization' of a global surveillance industrial complex (Collins 2011).

However, this contemporary movement extends beyond Suleiman. In the last decade, a critical engagement with both the colonial and anticolonial archive has increasingly informed this thinking of a resistance of image. This archival practice, I argue, marks a shift from the 'resilience' framing of Palestinian cinema post-Second Intifada, to a more questioning, essayistic mode of what Godard might term a quest to look *between* the images of here and elsewhere. Chapter 4 of this book examines Ayreen Anastas's *Pasolini Pa* Palestine* (2005) and its quest to look *beyond* the 'Image of Palestine' Pasolini creates in his 1965 documentary, 'liberating' those images by resituating them in contemporary geopolitics and among Palestinian subjects. A correlative freeing of the PFU's images from their use as commodities to sustain the fossilized power of the Palestinian Authority marks Mohanad Yaqubi's engagement with the archive, *Off Frame AKA Revolution Until Victory* (*Kharij al-Itar: Thawrah Hatta al-Nasr*) (2016). Annemarie Jacir's *When I Saw You* (2012), a narrative engagement with the Palestinian revolution, employs a different approach to embalm the lost moment of secular, globalized resistance of those early days of the revolution, in the hope that it might be revived.

This archival paradigm shift stems from a generation of filmmakers, following Elia Suleiman, who are growing up in a period of stasis, in which the political status quo in Palestine-Israel, along with an increasingly globalized understanding of Palestine has forged a new consciousness. This consciousness harnesses the spirit of the early Palestinian revolution's seizing of the means of production of Palestinian images and brings it back to haunt the present and awaken a contemporary visual language of resistance and liberation decoupled from institutional power, rearticulating Palestine's here in the margins of its elsewhere. Godard's legacy from his brief engagement with the Palestinian revolution, particularly in his use of what Eyal Sivan and Mohanad Yaqubi term 'forbidden montages' will inform an image-making practice which asks provocative contemporary questions of the proximity of the Palestine-Israel 'question' to Europe. The restoration and digitization of copies of PFU films over the last decade has informed this archival turn, in which images of the Palestinian revolution are placed contrapuntally beyond the horizons of their own moment to speak to the contemporary one. Such contrapuntal engagements in the work of Eyal Sivan, Mohanad Yaqubi, Annemarie Jacir and Eric Baudelaire will be the focus of the remainder of the chapter.

Taboo Memories, forbidden montages: *Montage Interdit* (2012, Eyal Sivan)

In Eyal Sivan's archival practice, the contemporary legacy of Godard's Palestine engagement is rearticulated in a work in which a politics of opacity is reformulated into a politics of taboo. Sivan's web-based archive, *Montage Interdit* (2012), pushes the limits of montage, its title is both a reference to Bazin's 1958 essay on the virtues and limitations of montage and an experiment in forbidden, contrapuntal juxtapositions. These are presented to the viewer almost as hypertext, whereby combinations ask taboo questions of the West, its self and its others. The title also draws on a cinematic reference of notoriety in Sivan's filmmaking career, a barber scene in the second part of his collaborative documentary *Route 181: Fragments of a Journey in Palestine-Israel* (Michel Khleifi/Eyal Sivan, 2004). The scene takes place in Lod (Lydd), as an old barber cuts Khleifi's hair while recounting the expulsion of Palestinians from the city in 1948 and ensuing massacre. The scene drew comparisons with the barber of Treblinka scene in *Shoah* (Claude Lanzmann, 1985). *Route 181* was attacked in France for this scene to the extent that Sivan left France and the film was censored by the French Ministry of Culture. This refusal to consider the Shoah and the Nakba on a continuum of time (albeit not scale) is the forbidden aspect, that 'the Palestine question and the Jewish question are both European questions at the same time' (Sivan 2013).

Figure 1.4 Screenshot from *Montage Interdit* (Eyal Sivan, 2012). ©Momento Films.

The work builds on both Bazin and Godard's notion of montage as a thinking form, particularly Bazin's concept of 'horizontal' montage in his description of Marker's *Letter to Siberia*, in which 'a given image doesn't refer to the one that preceded it or the one that will follow, but rather it refers laterally, in some way, to what is said' (Bazin 2003 [1958]: 44). This dialogue between images works on multiple levels. The structure of the project is such that essayistic assemblages combine, such as Mohanad Yaqubi discussing Godard's use of 'forbidden' montage (Hitler/Golda Meir) in *Ici et ailleurs* (Here and Elsewhere) (1976) in concurrent frames. These lateral relations are further horizontalized by the participatory nature of the technology. Being a digital archive, the viewer is invited to produce forbidden montages by juxtaposing thematic frames (such as Arab and Jew) in ways which decentre discursive norms on Israel/Palestine, Arab/Jew and East/West. This gives the project an atonal structure, a digital development of the potential of Elia Suleiman's decentred image, in which the viewer (or, more accurately, *user*) can 'complete' the work in multiple ways by making dissonant, 'forbidden' cuts. Sivan's work invites the viewer, in a manner which will be echoed in Basma Alsharif's later work, to make cuts which reveal Palestine as the hidden index within European history, bound up with its colonial legacy despite attempts to always situate it 'elsewhere'. By contrast, the film invites users to reveal Palestine as always already in the 'here' of European discourse, reading such discourse contrapuntally through Palestine.

Liberating the Palestinian image in *Off Frame AKA Revolution Until Victory (Kharij al-Itar: Thawrah Hatta al-Nasr)* (2016, Mohanad Yaqubi)

Mohanad Yaqubi's *Off Frame AKA Revolution Until Victory* (2016) follows a Godardian logic in both its reflection on the purpose and use of political filmmaking and its reflexivity in the assembling of a political film, albeit with a local focus on how Palestinians might free these images *of* themselves *for* themselves, liberating them from their co-option as mere visual capital for the fossilized bureaucracy of the Palestinian Authority.

As the present/past duality of its title suggests, Yaqubi's film follows a contrapuntal method which puts the 'elsewhere' of the revolution's historical image with the 'here' of the filmmaker's fossilized present. The film recovers and rearticulates elements of the PFU archive, alongside images of Palestine from 'elsewhere'. The film includes rushes from *Tall el Zaatar* (1977) (discovered in 2015 in Rome), scenes from early PFU works, still photographs, scenes from Godard's engagements with Palestine, *Ici et ailleurs* (Here and Elsewhere) (Godard 1976) and *Notre Musique* (Our Music) (Godard 2004), and British Mandate reportage. These sources form a reflexive essay film on both images of Palestinians and Palestinian image-making (in the case of the PFU), asking how contemporary Palestinian filmmakers might go about what Edward Said describes as Palestinians '*producing themselves*' (1986: 108; emphasis in original) with a critically resistant agency. Nadia Yaqub, in the closing pages of *Palestinian Cinema in the Days of Revolution*, reflects on Yaqubi's seizing of 'his right to make images of this period in Palestinian history that had been monopolized by the Palestinian Authority, just as the Palestinians of the late 1960s seized their right to make their own image' (Yaqub 2018: 220). With this right comes the burden of critical reflection. In a 2017 interview, Yaqubi reflects on the specular nature of the images of resistance with which the revolution would furnish the Palestinian leadership, so as to question their contemporary authority, claiming,

> For me as a Palestinian, I was looking at all of these images and thinking 'What does the revolution mean, how can we see it? Where are the shots where we can see our own struggle?' But when you're dealing with cinema, you are dealing with reflection. And once you realise that, there's a kind of freedom there; it makes you disbelieve or unsettle your image of yourself and that is the process that we need. (Yaqubi 2017)

The film opens with a series of still images of Ottoman and British Mandate Palestine, the transitions consciously made with the click of slide show projector transitioning to the whir of a film projector as we see Yaqubi in the editing suite, working on Ministry of Information footage describing the situation in Palestine in 1930 and Germany in 1933. The film then makes its most explicit reference to Godard, a scene from *Notre Musique* where Godard restages his forbidden montage technique from *Ici et ailleurs*: the shot/counter shot of Jews arriving by sea to the 'Promised Land', 'becoming the stuff of fiction' and Palestinians fleeing by sea, 'becoming the stuff of documentary'. This scene is juxtaposed with a series of what might be termed 'false starts' in the film's opening five minutes of newsreel, still image and scenes from Godard before we see Yaqubi himself contemplating the footage. A fadeout then transitions to an intertitle: 'The following film tells a story of people in search of their own image.'

This explicit thesis statement, that the film is an attempt to both demystify the images of the Palestinian revolution and decouple them from the teleology that leads to their co-option by the Palestinian Authority, structures the film's contrapuntal movement between past and present and its own forbidden montages.

Much of the film juxtaposes footage of PFU films, notably Mustafa Abu Ali's *With Soul, With Blood* (1971) and *They Do Not Exist* (1974), with interviews with fedayeen on the nature and interconnectedness of their liberation struggle. This transnational dimension is emphasized by the inclusion of Vanessa Redgrave's documentary on the PLO, alongside Godard clips. These early scenes discuss the role of armed struggle, which both Arafat and a refugee camp classroom deem a 'right and obligation'.

The question of armed struggle is one the film subtly interrogates throughout. This is most pronounced in the juxtaposition of its two classroom sequences. The first, occurring at the fourteen-minute mark, centres on students answering their teacher's questions on how to liberate Palestine ('Why do the Palestinians arm themselves?'). The students are engaged and active throughout, as negotiations are seen as incompatible with revolution, and the PLO's slogan – *tharwrah hatta al-nasr* ('revolution until victory') – is elicited. This scene is in marked contrast to the films closing five minutes, in Ramallah. The school scene is reprised, as distracted students in a classroom adorned with symbols of the Palestinian national movement (a framed portrait of Yasser Arafat and a poster of Mahmoud Darwish occupy the back wall). The students are asked 'Who wishes for the establishment of the State of Palestine?', to which they wearily raise their hands. Taken in isolation, these two sequences might be read as a nostalgia for revolutionary armed struggle. However, while the latter scene is an ironic critique of the endlessly deferred state building project and the transition from a liberation struggle into a struggle for an institutionalized State, the film makes use of its footage and its own forbidden montage to question armed struggle as a tactic and propaganda tool that could provide a path 'until victory'. The 'forbidden montage' in question makes use of a scene in Mustafa Abu Ali's *They Do Not Exist*, in which the loading and launching of Israeli war planes is accompanied by Vivaldi. Abu Ali famously used this technique to signify that the barbarism and high culture of Imperialism were one and the same. Yaqubi's 'forbidden montage' edits together Abu Ali's footage of Israeli warplanes with armed fedayeen training manoeuvres, with Vivaldi continuing into this second sequence. The implication here is twofold. Firstly, the violence of the Palestinian revolution is futile with such a disequilibrium of military force. Secondly, this resistant 'violence' in fact foreshadows the revolutionary 'brutality' that Genet was so insistent on marking as discrete. That is to say, the optimism of the late 1960s and 1970s faded into defeats, expulsions and an increasingly institutionalized PLO which, as Yaqubi's film suggests, leads teleologically to the bureaucratic stasis of the contemporary Palestinian Authority.

The film's penultimate movement echoes the elegiac tone of Godard's *Ici et ailleurs* as a series of hospital scenes in which wounded and maimed fedayeen proclaim their thanks for international solidarity and their commitment to continue fighting. These mournful scenes transition to contemporary Ramallah, signifying the dual loss of the radical, secular and international early years of the Palestinian revolution, and its archive of self-made image-making partially lost in the siege of Beirut in 1982. This loss of revolutionary potential and democratic image-making post-1982 is engaged with in a different manner in Annemarie Jacir's engagement with the archive.

The future that came to pass in *When I Saw You* (2012, Annemarie Jacir)

At first glance, Annemarie Jacir's *When I Saw You* (2012), seems to pay a more conventional homage to the Palestinian revolution than *Off Frame AKA Revolution Until Victory*. However, the film, which is set in the wake of the *naksa* – the war and exodus – of 1967,[7] in fact performs a complex relationship of nostalgia for the archive. After the Six-Day War, Israel occupied Gaza and the West Bank, resulting in refugees heading across the Eastern border into Jordan. The film takes place both in and between two camps, the fictional Harir Refugee Camp, and the fedayeen camp in the forest. The film tells the story of Tarek and his mother, Ghaydaa, who have become separated from Tarek's father while leaving. Despite being shot on digital, the film has a distinctly vintage aesthetic, with the somewhat harsh, bleached palette of white, grey and stone that comprise the camp scenes conveying both the graininess of 16mm film and the arid dryness and boredom of the camp.

Indeed, the airlessness of the camp is conveyed both formally and textually. The faded, dry colour palette dominates the mise en scène, which conveys the interminable waiting of the camp; but also Tarek's frustration is expressed narratively at points as an inability to breathe. The loss of space and the loss of his father provoke Tarek to lash out at his mother, complaining that 'you're suffocating me!' While this suffocation can be read as the protectiveness of a single parent, it can also be seen as a wider malaise in the refugee camp, an oppressively corporeal experience of occupation and displacement.

When speaking of the effects of colonization in *A Dying Colonialism*, Frantz Fanon is careful to point out that the territorial impact extends to both the corporeal, and even the respiratory.

> There is not occupation of territory, on the one hand, and independence of persons on the other. It is the country as a whole, its history, and its daily pulsation that is contested, disfigured, in the hope of a final destruction. Under these conditions, the individual's breathing is an observed, an occupied breathing. (Fanon 1965: 65)

Despite the harsh lighting of the camp, this is a film of warm, transnational nostalgia, both in its cinematic references and its framing of a historical, internationalist and secular moment of resistance. The film's use of Mahmoud Asfa, a non-professional actor, as Tarek (alongside a mix of professional and non-professional cast members) echoes certain films of the Iranian New Wave, particularly Abbas Kiarostami's *Where Is My Friend's House?* (1987) and Jafar Panahi's *The White Balloon* (1995). Another stylistic lineage the film has with those films is in its use of the freeze-frame, which Chaudhuri and Finn (2003) cite as a key constituent element of what they term 'open images' or 'closing scenes which try not to close down a narrative but rather open it out to the viewer's consideration, to live on after the film itself has finished' (Chaudhuri and Finn 2003: 52). However, perhaps the film's clearest stylistic antecedent is François Truffaut's *Les Quartre Cents Coups/The 400 Blows* (1959). Much like Antoine Doinel, Tarek spends much of the film in flight between oppressive institutions. Antoine flees both school and home, whereas Tarek runs between school, the refugee camp and the fedayeen camp. They are both articulate and rebellious characters marginalized by their teachers (Tarek is shown to be highly numerate and bright, but illiterate, and thus scorned by his teacher). Both films end in arrested movement, as flight becomes stasis. While the framing is notably discrete, the movements of both films act almost as inverse relation. In Truffaut's famous ending, Antoine escapes the juvenile centre he's been placed in (by the sea, at his mother's request) and runs to the beach and into the sea.

His face and movement are frozen in medium close-up as he turns to the camera. The scene spatially and temporally traps Antoine in a moment, the openness of the sea as restrictive as the classroom and the home. However, the scene also encapsulates Antoine's ambivalent relationship with his mother. The absence of a paternal figure dominates the film, as Antoine's biological father is absent. An English lesson in an earlier scene centres on the pronunciation of the question 'Where is the father?' His relationship with his mother is one of neglect and aloofness. However, the rush to the sea at the end, with the ambivalent steps and half turn that freezes Antoine in liminality, has maternal significance. The sea (la mére) and mother (la mer) are homophones in French, which leaves Antoine frozen both physically in isolation and psychologically in an ambivalent embrace.

In the freeze-frame ending of *When I Saw You*, Tarek runs from his mother and the fedayeen camp with a handful of fighters and his mother, Ghaydaa, in pursuit. However, as he heads for the wire fence separating Jordan from the West Bank, his mother catches up with him. Having been, in Tarek's eyes, the figure pulling him from his father and home, here she takes his hand and they quicken their pace towards the border. The film ends on a long shot of them in flight, the hills of the West Bank rising in the distance.

In addition to its formal nostalgia, the film enacts a textual nostalgia: that is, nostalgia for both the ethics and aesthetics of radical leftist resistance. This can be seen in the shift in colour palette that marks the transition from the harsh bleached tones of the refugee camp, to the warm, softer greens of the fedayeen camp. This camp is located in Dibeen Forest, which brings a verdant hue to the mise en scène. Nonetheless, the fedayeen camp is lit in softer, warmer tones than the film's opening segment. The contrast between these two palettes can be seen in the images here:

Figure 1.5 Between emergence and the yet-to-come. The freeze-frame ending of *When I Saw You* (Annemarie Jacir, 2012). ©Philistine Films.

Figure 1.6 The bleached palette of the refugee camp in *When I Saw You* (Annemarie Jacir, 2012). ©Philistine Films.

This textual and formal nostalgia can also be seen in *When I Saw You*'s homage to both the secular radical left, and the guerrilla and internationalist filmmaking of the PFU. Cinematic nostalgia for the radical left in the Arabic-speaking world is the focus of Chapter 5 of Laura U. Marks's *Hanan al-Cinema* (2015). In reflecting on the chapter's title – *Communism, Dream Deferred* – Marks

Figure 1.7 The soft warm greens of the *fedayeen* camp in *When I Saw You* (Annemarie Jacir, 2012). ©Philistine Films.

acknowledges that terming Communism a 'dream' may seem provocative, but less so in the Arab world.

> In many parts of the Arabic-speaking world, Communism – or, to begin to be more precise, the secular, radical left – was a dream cut short by deals with global superpowers, the rise of religious fundamentalism, and historical bad luck. (Marks 2015: 97)

In its textual nostalgia, the film seemingly romanticizes the moment between the defeat of pan-Arabism and the rise of the PLO alongside international anti-colonial movements. This brief temporal moment was also an extraordinarily complex spatial network, a 'global network' (Marks 2015) of fedayeen extending through Latin America, China, Algeria, Vietnam and farther afield. This is referenced at points on the film where the fighters open supplies of rifles and boots, checking their provenance.

The reflexive scenes in the fedayeen camp are acutely aware of both the image-making potential of armed resistance – the *keffiyeh* having long since become a commodity of resistance aesthetics, or what Marks (ibid.: 99) refers to as 'radical chic' – and of the role of image-making in growing the nascent Palestinian resistance of 1967. A shot/reverse shot sequence in the film during military exercises demonstrates the tension between armed struggle and the iconography of armed struggle, as a couple of young fedayeen stare purposefully down the lens of a photojournalist's camera, while their older commanding officer disapproves.

While the film's romanticizing of the 'image of resistance' may appear formally conventional, its reflexive embrace of, and references to Third Cinema in general, and the PFU in particular make *When I Saw You* a more layered work than is initially apparent. In addition to being a filmmaker, Annemarie Jacir also curated the *Dreams of a Nation* film festival, with iterations held in both New York and Jerusalem. At the latter, she screened *They Do Not Exist* (1974) and hosted its director Mustafa Abu Ali at the screening. Abu Ali is perhaps the most prominent of the filmmakers from the PFU, and also worked more widely within the context of global radical militant cinema (both Nick Denes (2009) and Laura Marks (2015) reference the relationship between Abu Ali and Jean-Luc Godard). The work of the PFU is subtly referenced throughout the film, from the importance of image creation in messaging, through photography and poster art. Nick Denes highlights the use of mixed media in compiling the bricolage-like experimental form of the early works of the PFU, particularly 1972's *With Soul, With Blood*, which constructs a 'visual mosaic of archive photographs, newspaper headlines, caricatures, poster art and original footage' (Denes 2014: 227).

However, perhaps the most striking homage to the PFU comes in the mise en scène of the fedayeen camp itself. The structure and framing of the camp, along with the scenes of distributing of mail and singing of revolutionary songs are remarkably similar to the fedayeen camp that features in the middle sections of Abu Ali's *They Do Not Exist*, as can be seen in the images here.

Jacir has acknowledged the influence of her research into the PFU on the 'look' of *When I Saw You*. In its dual homage to both a political and aesthetic moment and movement in Palestinian history, the film appears to perform a romanticized nostalgia. However, in arresting the moment between a series of emergences and disappearances – of the secular radical left after the defeat of 67, of the PLO in Jordan and of the Palestine Film Archive before its 1982 disappearance – the film's nostalgia can be read differently. That is, as an unconscious resistance to the future that came to pass, a painful (yet hopeful) attempt to open reawakens radical secular futures. A similar arresting of the moment of traumatic political loss occurs in post-coup Chilean filmmaking, as examined in Chapter 3, an exiling of revolutionary politics familiar to both the Chilean and Palestinian within Miguel Littín, the focus of that chapter.

Figures 1.8 and 1.9 The similarities in mise en scène between *They Do Not Exist* (Mustafa Abu Ali, 1974) and *When I Saw You* (Annemarie Jacir, 2012). ©Philistine Films.

Figure 1.9

To return briefly to Jean Genet and his time with the fedayeen, of all the images that flashed up in his attempts to recall and represent the Palestinian revolution, the one that haunted him most was a prescient contemporary sense of the transition from a form of secular martyrdom to a fundamentalist one, which he evokes in a reflection on the French term for dusk, *entre chien et loup*,[8] signifying the liminal condition of the fedayee. With uncanny prescience, Genet confesses:

> What I feared most were logical conclusions: For example, an invisible transformation of the fedayeen into Shiites or members of the Muslim Brotherhood. None of the people around me thought such a thing possible, perhaps rightly if it were a matter of a simple, external, visible change. (Genet 2003 [1986]: 254)

When I Saw You's freeze-frame ending evokes a moment of nostalgia for the political moment of the waning of pan-Arabism after the defeat of 1967, and the waxing of the nascent PLO as a secular armed resistance. While the fate of Ghaydaa and Tarek is left open, the technique also arrests the yet-to-come. That is, its temporality dwells in the lacuna between Godard's *Jusqu'à la Victoire* (1970) and *Ici et ailleurs* (1976), the film that would be assembled from the spectral remains of the former. *When I Saw You* ends on a crystallized image of stasis, an index of the lost yet-to-come. In ending in a photographic image, the film performs an 'embalming' (Bazin 1967) of the moment between life and death, emergence and disappearance. In freezing the Palestinian revolution, *When I Saw You* ends in an attempt to suspend the future which came to pass: the emergent 'counter-revolutionary Arab order' Bashir Abu-Maneh highlights in the wake of the PLO's expulsion from Jordan, which became 'soaked in oil money and bureaucratized' (Abu-Maneh 2016: 145). Doing so arrests the defeats, failures and compromises of the yet-to-come and leaves the Palestinian revolution, as it is for Mohanad Yaqubi, a historical monad of potentiality, not a static object of loss but something which, when read contrapuntally, offers a Foucauldian 'history of the present' with which to rearticulate a contemporary politics.[9]

Both here and elsewhere: *The Anabasis of May and Fusako Shigenobu, Masao Adachi, and 27 Years without Images* (Eric Baudelaire, 2011)

Nostalgia for the loss of both the archive and its revolutionary conjuncture and a contemporary articulation of a resistance of image are the past/present contrapuntal currents which structure Eric Baudelaire's (2011) documentary on the politics of revolutionary filmmaking, *The Anabasis of May and Fusako Shigenobu, Masao Adachi, and 27 Years without Images*.

The film takes as its 'subject' the legacy of the Japanese Red Army (JRA), a radical, armed Marxist group in the late 1960s that declared war on the Japanese state. In the early 1970s, they aligned themselves with the Popular Front for the Liberation of Palestine (PFLP) in Lebanon, becoming embedded in the Palestinian revolution. Fusako Shigenobu is the film's central absence. The founder of the JRA, she spent thirty years in Lebanon until her arrest in 2001 after entering Japan, after which she was sentenced to twenty years in prison from 2006 for her involvement in the attack on the French Embassy in The Hague in 1974. The film oscillates between two voices and two locations. The locations are Beirut and Tokyo. The voices are that of May Shigenobu, the daughter of Fusako and an unnamed PFLP leader, and Masao Adachi, a radical filmmaker who gave up filmmaking to participate in the JRA's strategy of global revolution. This struggle over the efficacy of making films politically permeates the film, with Adachi asking rhetorically 'where is the frontier between a film "about" struggle and a film "in" struggle?' The question of the relationship contemporary political filmmaking has to its radical past is one Baudelaire's film examines.

The elsewhere of here: A history of the present

Baudelaire's film interrogates two concepts which give it its formal structure. These are the *anabasis* and *fukeiron*. The first of these draws on the *Anabasis* of Xenophon, an account of homeward circuitous wandering which signifies both departure and return. The second concept, *fukeiron*, was a filmmaking approach pioneered by Adachi. Loosely translating as 'landscape film', the technique eschews human subjects for the landscapes which produce subjectivity. The most famous example, referenced throughout *The Anabasis*, is *AKA Serial Killer* (Adachi 1969). In a work which prefaces both the landscape/violence relation in the landscape films of James Benning, and the later thought of Felix Guattari (2000 [1989]) regarding the multiple ecologies capitalism inhabits (socio-political, environmental and subjective), *AKA Serial Killer* elides its subject (serial killer Norio Nagayama). Instead, the film examines the politics of landscape: the extent to which the built environment both reflects dominant power relations and produces pathological subjectivities. In testing Adachi's thesis, Baudelaire's film also eschews its human subjects (heard only offscreen) for landscapes, or more accurately cityscapes. Aesthetically, the film makes a point of blurring its 'here' and its 'elsewhere' to the point of indistinction. Tokyo and Beirut are both shot on Super 8mm, giving the film both an untimely nostalgia and tactile fragility in its texture. The absence of landmarks or distinguishing features and use of shots which frame the infrastructure and commodities of capital mean the cities are sometimes only rendered discrete by graffiti on walls in Arabic/French or Japanese. Just such a scene of indistinction occurs at around eight minutes into the film. As a camera tracks right along the Tokyo subway, Adachi describes the *fukeiron* process of his *AKA Serial Killer*, explaining that during the location scouting process, they began to notice the capitalist homogeneity of late 1960s Japan, with the countryside increasingly dominated by high-rises and motorways. This urban sprawl, laments Adachi, meant 'small towns everywhere are being transformed into reproductions of Tokyo'. A bleach out acts as a Deleuzian irrational cut and the camera tracks left along a train track in urban Beirut. These shots, accompanied by a series of followed-up shots of workers in Beirut and Tokyo loading and unloading clothes and electronics respectively, suggest that the capitalist homogenization of Adachi's Japan is now a world system of identikit sprawl from Tokyo to Beirut. This comparative device, however, gives the film its contrapuntal structure, allowing it to transpose the spirit of Japan's radical student politics and the images of the PFLP in Lebanon onto contemporary Beirut. Just such a scene of contrapuntal sound/image occurs at the fourteen-minute mark, as footage of Arab Spring protesters in Beirut is accompanied by Adachi's voiceover describing his role in the 1960s Anpo protests in Japan against the US-Japan Security Treaty of 1960, a treaty which led to an increased military presence of the United States in Japan and further aligned Japan with the United States in the Cold War. The repression of the protest movement and its ultimate defeat leads Adachi to reflect on armed struggle when faced with the military might of an armed State, while images of 2011 Lebanon protests (an ultimately failed peaceful uprising) circulate. This contrapuntal movement between past/present and voice/image constitutes an essential element of Baudelaire's work – notable more broadly in the archival turn in contemporary Palestinian cinema – which conducts a history of the present, in the sense that the revolutionary historical archive is resituated to question the politics of the present. The past here is not an object of nostalgia but a condition of possibility.

The revolution will not be photographed: Twenty-seven years without images

The film's primary concern is for both the exile of images and images of exile. The twenty-seven years of the title signifies a loss of the image on a number of levels: Adachi's own near thirty-year break from filmmaking; his loss of footage alongside the wider loss of the archive in 1982 Beirut; the loss of revolutionary struggle through cinema; and the loss of control over the images of these period. The latter is a similar concern to that expressed in Mohanad Yaqubi's engagement with images of revolution in *Off Frame AKA Revolution Until Victory*. This polysemic loss is referenced throughout the film. Baudelaire's images of Beirut, an elsewhere for the exiled Adachi, are referenced in an epistolary sequence where Adachi's email to Baudelaire requests images of Lebanon in exchange for his participation in the film. This is both a lament for a loss of place and also a loss of image, as Adachi explicates when reflecting on the 200 hours of footage destroyed in the bombing of his apartment building. This constitutes a grief so great that he claims 'I can only think that the lost footage never existed.' May Shigenobu's own lost images are articulated in the scene preceding Adachi's lament, as she refers to the photos being burned as the family moved around in ever clandestine manner, fearful of comrades and locations being identified, meaning that only the most opaque, unreadable images remained. These losses punctuate the film both textually and formally, the bleach outs and colour distortions of the Super-8 stock acting almost as ellipses in themselves.

One of the very few shots of faces takes place a third of the way through the film, as Baudelaire's camera zooms into a poster of wanted Japanese Red Army members. May reflects on the strangeness of seeing these images in Japan, barely recognizable masks in this designation as enemies of the state, when she knew them all as fully human, expressive faces. The opacity of these images builds on the opacity of the few images the Shigenobus carried with them, signifying the wider non-representability of these images of the Palestinian revolution, a struggle Godard and Genet both had capturing their time among the fedayeen in Jordan.

The Anabasis's indeterminacy of place and time, along with its absence of diegetic sound, imbues it with a novel radicalism. On the one hand, in making contemporary Tokyo and Beirut indeterminate from a journey in which radical politics led from Japan to the Palestinian revolution, it folds 1968 into 2011, suggesting the spirit of a Global Palestine can be co-present in both times. On the other, in turning 'down the volume' of its images it invites the viewer to contemplate and listen to them. In doing so, it employs a resistance to speaking for, and thus overcoding these images, heeding the warnings of Godard and Said.

The contrapuntal turn in transnational Palestine

The films examined in this opening chapter trace a resistance of image from the early experimentation of the PFU in the Palestinian revolution and its international contemporaries in Jean-Luc Godard and Jean Genet, with which a contemporary dialogue can be constructed. Godard's praxis in particular employs a contrapuntal method which puts the 'here' of the Western consumer of Palestinian images in dialogue with the 'elsewhere' of that image of the Palestinian Revolution, and in doing so develops a (self)critical practice which will inform contemporary Palestinian filmmakers' relationship with the archive and their own image-making.

In differing ways, as we have seen, Jacir, Yaqubi and Baudelaire's works treat the Palestinian revolution as a past which must be read contrapuntally so as to provide a history of the present. This contrapuntal dialogue with an archive globally dispersed and rediscovered, but also with European filmmakers who engaged with revolutionary movements and moments across the non-aligned world, characterizes the atonal cinema examined throughout the rest of the book. Thus the practice of forbidden montage which Sivan and Yaqubi borrow from Godard will appear in the later work of Kamal Aljafari, Elia Suleiman and Basma Alsharif. These are filmmakers for whom the proper noun 'Palestine' haunts the frame of Israeli and European visual culture, a noun which refuses its stubbornly persistent discursive positioning as an orientalized other. The Palestinians elsewhere and Palestinian elsewheres discussed throughout the rest of the book articulate – from a position of critical (and often physical) distance – an atonal cinema, in which dissonance and a remaining out-of-place collapse a discursive East/West binary which aims to keep the Palestinian image a perpetual invisible/hypervisible other.

2

Between presence and absence: Remnants and revenants in the cinema of the interior

Building on the archival turn identified in Chapter 1, this chapter explores the archival practice of Palestinian filmmaking in Israel. Drawing on the notion of the 'forbidden montage' examined in the previous chapter, this chapter argues that the archival practice of the filmmakers follows a logic of taboo haunting. That is, the spectre of Palestinian-ness in the Israeli state is itself aesthetically and culturally forbidden, and even the legal proper noun 'Israeli-Arab' is haunted by two figures it represses, the Palestinian and the Arab-Jew. Haunting the centre of the Israeli State from the periphery, the figure of the Palestinian in the films in this chapter enacts a contrapuntal movement between absence and presence, problematizing the ongoing political partitioning of Palestine/Israel and Arab/Jew.

In a 2003 interview with the *Journal of Palestine Studies* about his film *Divine Intervention*, the Nazarene director Elia Suleiman describes the oppressive pressure of his home city, Nazareth. As the largest Arab Palestinian city within Palestine-Israel, the city essentially exists as an enormous Palestinian enclave within the Israeli State. This enclave-like status is reinforced both architecturally and economically – with the city overlooked by its Jewish neighbour, Nof HaGalil (formerly Nazareth Illit), and both watched and neglected by the state.[1] The need for observation, claims Suleiman, stems from the perpetual haunting that the figure of the present-absentee[2] represents in the Israeli psyche. Unlike the Occupied Territories, where the dynamics of oppression and resistance are overt and hypervisible, Suleiman (2003: 70) refers to the 'psychological and economic' occupation that is internalized by Palestinians in Israel, creating a condition of cultural and discursive invisibility. The intolerable pressure of this condition leads Suleiman to conjure the revenant of the former Palestinian within the proper noun 'Israeli-Arab', when he claims, 'Israel knows this. They are haunted by the fear that their "Arabs" are going to become "Palestinians" again' (ibid.: 71). This notion of revenance, a coming into being that begins by coming back,[3] is,

I argue, crucial to understanding how the cinema of Palestinians inside Israel articulates a spectral politics, one which destabilizes its Israeli counterpart by bringing back the ghost of Arab and Jew as that which, to paraphrase Mahmoud Darwish (2012: 52), dwells within the other and, as such, is unpartitionable. The politics of haunting at work in the liminal cinematic space of Palestine-Israel, which is characteristic of what I term the 'Cinema of the Interior', is the focus of this chapter.

As described in the introduction, the two major filmmakers featured in this chapter – Elia Suleiman and Kamal Aljafari – have an atonal relationship with notions of home, exile and image making. Suleiman, echoing Said's own exilic identification as the last Jewish intellectual, describes his humour as 'conceptually Jewish' and cites Primo Levi, Maurice Blanchot and Walter Benjamin as influences on his formal and aesthetic approach to an atonal decentring of self and image (Suleiman 2003: 26). Further, rejecting exile and home as binary constructs, he cites both Nazareth and New York as 'both simultaneously exiles and homelands' (Suleiman 2000: 96), retaining an atonal right to remain out of place.

Similarly, Kamal Aljafari, in addition to citing Adorno in his thinking of cinema as a home, examines in his work both the burden of returning to the ghosts of his youth and archiving the disappearance of his city. The duty of not being at home in one's home Said sees in following Adorno's thinking of exile carries a painful ambiguity for Aljafari when regarding both the cinematic and political erasure of Jaffa, a further manifestation of the privileged affliction of returning to the interior. When contrasting the Jaffa that he returns to film with the Jaffa of his childhood, he states, 'Gentrification, and in this case there is a political meaning to it, makes you feel not at home in your home' (Aljafari 2016).

Aljafari's own thinking of exile is complicated, as will be seen, by his thinking of Beirut as a spatialized memory of Palestinian exile and also by his citing of the influence of Federico Garcia Lorca's poem *Romance Sonámbulo* (1928) on his short film *Balconies* (2007):

> In 'Romance Sonámbulo', he wrote, 'But now I am not I, nor is my house now my house. Let me climb up, at least, up to the high balconies.' His high balconies reminded me of where I come from, a place with unfinished balconies. Lorca's emotions and metaphors spoke to me. I felt Lorca came from where I come from. (Aljafari 2016)

Lorca and Andalusia – more accurately *al-Andalus* – were a thematic concern of Mahmoud Darwish's poetry, notably '11 planets at the end of the Andalusian scene' (1992). In this poem, Lorca and the loss of Granada are put in contrapuntal relation in the final stanza: 'The violins cry with gypsies going to the Andalus. The violins cry over Arabs leaving the Andalus' (Darwish 2009 [1992]: 67). In the third stanza, the loss of Palestine as the loss of *al-Andalus* is evoked: 'I am the Adam of two Edens, I lost them twice' (ibid.). For the exilic Arab poet, Darwish explicates: 'Andalusia was the lost place. Later, Palestine became Andalusia. The popular poetry written about Palestine in the 1950s and 1960s formulated the comparison: We lost Palestine just as we lost Andalusia' (Darwish 2012: 51). Beyond just a notion of a lost Eden though, it is a lost memory of Muslim and Jewish co-presence in Europe. This 'taboo' memory is one Ella Shohat (2006) cites as sustaining the East/West binaries founding Zionism, binaries which erase the hyphen in Arab-Jew and can thus negate and partition the Palestinian as mere Arab. This is a move central to the continued project of partition and, this chapter argues, a move which the Cinema of the Interior resists.

Spectres of partition, spectres of binationalism: Situating the Cinema of the Interior

The question of partition, which Gil Hochberg (2007) engages with in cultural terms, refers most explicitly to a historical event, or rather its failure. That is, UN Resolution 181, the 1947 partition plan which failed to establish two states from Mandate Palestine. The ghost of this partition line informs Michel Khleifi and Eyal Sivan's (2004) documentary *Route 181*, which traces the pathology of partition, the continued legacy of political and cultural attempts to partition Palestine-Israel. It is precisely this continued legacy that I argue haunts the cinematic space of Palestinians in Israel.

This issue of haunting in the *Israeli* visual field (Hochberg 2015) is, I argue, neglected in the *Palestinian* one by either the omission of a sustained discussion of the specificity of place in Palestinian filmmaking in Israel (Gertz and Khleifi 2008; Tawil-Souri 2014) or an explicit focus on production contexts on Palestinian filmmaking in Israel (Friedman 2010). This chapter addresses this by examining the double nature of this haunting; that is, the spectre of a partition which haunts from the past and a binationalism which haunts from the future.

Binationalism as a progressive, culturalist approach to moving beyond the cul-de-sac of the two-state solution is a unifying thread which runs through the postcolonial theory of Edward Said, Ella Shohat and Bart Moore-Gilbert and the filmmaking of Juliano Mer-Khamis, Amos Gitai, Udi Aloni and Elia Suleiman. The defeats and concessions of Oslo, along with the intransigence of Israel's government under Likud and Netanyahu and the rise of political Islam in Gaza have contributed to an emergent one-state thinking to challenge the de facto one-state reality. Between the pessimism of the status quo, and the idealism that Suleiman (2016) acknowledges as being both utopian and necessary lies the 'pessoptimism' of Emile Habiby[4] that Moore-Gilbert (2018) endorses in his culturalist thinking of a binational, democratic State. Such thinking is not limited to a tendency in theory and contemporary cinema, however, with activists from Yoav Hafawi (2018) in Tel Aviv to Ahmed Abu Artema (2018) in Gaza endorsing the idea of a single, radically democratic state. While the political stasis of Palestine/Israel remains, its cinema, and increasingly activism at a grassroots level, points to a critical approach to the continued political project of partition.

The haunted cultural imagination of Palestine-Israel

The trope of a repression of the ghosts of the past – that which the politics of the present tries to exorcize (or at least keep hidden) – extends beyond cinema, recurring throughout the broader cultural imagination of Palestine-Israel. As such, it requires some brief explication.

It is precisely this logic of haunting, repressed memory which opens Gil Hochberg's *In Spite of Partition*, where she highlights a short story by Orly Castel Bloom, in which an elderly Arabic-speaking woman appears under the bench of a young Israeli woman, insisting on their kinship, which the young woman denies, doubting the reality of the encounter (Hochberg 2007: 1). The slippage between Hebrew and Arabic which defines the encounter, along with the haunting figure that dwells beneath the surface as a repressed traumatic memory, hints at the resistance of the interior to partition, be that spatial or psychic. A key spatial marker of this haunting beneath the surface is the figure of the cave or the ruin from which the Palestinian literally or psychologically emerges. The cave *within* the ruin is a key feature of Emile Habiby's landmark ironic novel of Palestinian life in Israel, *The Secret Life of Saeed the Pessoptimist* (1974), in which the cave beneath the ruined village of Tanturah is the site of a family treasure. The treasure itself is something of a Macguffin, more figuratively engaging Saeed with a quest to locate the remnant of historic Palestine within Israel. Lital Levy has traced the history of the allegorical cave in both Israeli and

Palestinian tradition, noting that 'Avot Yeshurun's 1952 poem "Pesah 'al kukhim" (Passover on Caves) … ties the cave to the suppressed Palestinian presence within Israel' (Levy 2012: 12). He also recognizes the figure of the cave in the work of Habiby, Shammas and Khoury as constituting 'a multidimensional spatiality that is at once psychological, political, and historical in nature' (ibid.).

Absent Presence (2010), one of the final works by Palestinian poet Mahmood Darwish, is haunted throughout by a series of ghosts coming back in various forms. The title itself evokes the aforementioned juridical condition of Palestinians within the Israeli State, and the interplay of absence and presence and visibility and invisibility of a Palestinian past that is rendered invisible in the cultural logic of Zionism, yet precisely because of this very negation, cannot be buried. In a long passage which evokes the history of Deir Yassin[5] as a metaphorical ghost which haunts the contemporary political project of Zionism, Darwish writes of this ghostly memory which dwells in the lacuna between sleep and wakefulness, refusing to be exorcized:

> We became the ghost of a murdered man who pursues his killer asleep or awake or on the borderline between the two, so that he is depressed and complains of sleeplessness, and cries out, 'Are they not dead yet?' … Aeroplanes chase the ghost in the air; tanks chase the ghost on the ground; submarines chase the ghost in the sea, but the ghost expands, occupies the consciousness of the killer till it drives him mad. (Darwish 2010: 47)

The despairing use of the interrogative in this passage evokes a point of view towards those outside the parameters of 'grievability' in Western media discourse which, Judith Butler (2004: 33) argues, occasions 'the violence of derealization'. In *Precarious Life* (2004), Butler argues that such violence renders lives deemed ungrievable as always already spectral. That is, while these lives are *discursively* unacknowledged, *corporeally* they remain animated and as such, states Butler, 'must be negated again (and again)' (ibid.). Yet also, by evoking the ghosts of Deir Yassin, Darwish articulates the inability to lay to rest the ghosts of the past which haunt the Israeli imagination. Indeed, a fictionalized version of the psychiatric hospital on the grounds of Deir Yassin is the setting of Udi Aloni's *Forgiveness* (2006), which tells of the disquiet stemming from repressing the ghosts of the past, rather than reconciling with them. This cultural amnesia of the Palestinian Nakba of 1948 in the Israeli visual field, according to Gil Hochberg (2015), puts the ghost at the threshold of visibility/invisibility: a haunting presence through its conspicuous absence. The effect of the Nakba of 1948, therefore, 'is seemingly erased or hidden from Israeli eyes, and yet nevertheless finds its way into the Israeli visual field as a haunting presence of *visible invisibility*' (Hochberg 2015: 38; emphasis in original). This haunting absent presence is particularly prevalent in the liminality of Palestinians within Israel. Therefore, some analysis of the specificity of the subjectivity of Palestinians within Israel – what Edward Said (1986: 51) terms *al-dakhil* (the interior) – is required.

Edward Said, absent presence and the haunted Palestinian 'Interior'

In the second chapter of his collaborative photo-essay, *After the Last Sky*, Edward Said speaks of Palestinian experience *min al-dakhil*, which translates as 'from the interior'. This interior manifests itself in different ways. Firstly, in a tangible geographical sense, it refers to Palestinians in Israel – whose status as viewed from those in exile such as Said changed from 'different in a pejorative sense' to 'still, different, but privileged' (Said 1986: 51) – as the tide of Arab nationalism ebbed and the status of those *fil-kharij*[6] ('in the exterior') diminished. A second meaning is spatial in a more psychological sense, that is, a psychological and linguistic interiority that is collective, an experience of being on the outside while dwelling in the interior, which is a space 'always to some extent occupied and interrupted by others – Israelis and Arabs' (ibid.: 53). Said dedicates an entire chapter of *After the Last Sky* – 'Interiors' – to exploring this condition of being rendered an outsider within the inside.

For Said, maintaining any distinction between outside and inside within the interior leads to a perpetual state of insecurity, leading him to conclude that 'the structure of your situation is such that being inside is a privilege that is an affliction, like feeling hemmed in by the house you own' (ibid.: 53).

The contrapuntal tension of being hemmed in but excluded was particularly pronounced for Said, since he was unable to enter Israel at the time of writing *After the Last Sky*, and thus witnessed the interior vicariously through Jean Mohr's photographs. Said's thinking of the 'privileged affliction' that is the experience of *al-dakhil* – the interior – will inform my reading of what I term the *al-dakhil* films (the Cinema of the Interior) in this chapter, particularly the ghostly structures that dwell within this cinema and articulate its politics.

The essence of the *al-dakhil* Palestinian finds its ontological roots in the historical-legal condition of the 'present-absentee'. This seemingly paradoxical historical-legal condition emerged in the years after 1948, with the 1950 Law of Absentee Property. This determined Palestinians who left their villages during the 1948 war but found themselves within the new state, as corporeally present within the State but legally absent from their place of origin, as Hillel Cohen (2002) has identified, particularly – but by no means exclusively – in the case of Galilee. This historical-legal status occasions a contemporary trace of ontological displacement visible in the cinematic language of the *al-dakhil* directors, both caught within the state apparatus and held outside it.

The ghosts which haunt both the project of partition, and the respective nationalisms of Israel *and* Palestine, will be examined in a close reading of Elia Suleiman's 'Nazareth' trilogy, Kamal Aljafari's 'Jaffa' trilogy and Amos Gitai's *Ana Arabia* (2013). These films in particular (but not exclusively), I argue, examine the political 'spectre' of partition, as both a political and cultural project, through the ghostly figure of the *Arab al-dakhil* – a figure who haunts the lacuna between both Palestine-Israel and Arab-Jew.

Spectrality and stasis in Elia Suleiman's Nazareth

Elia Suleiman's 'Nazareth Trilogy' – *Chronicle of a Disappearance* (1996), *Divine Intervention* (2002) and *The Time That Remains* (2009) – occupies the threshold of visibility/invisibility, the spectral visual plane of being a Palestinian in Israel. Each film, either in its making or its setting, is associated with a Palestinian historical moment. The earliest film comes in the wake of the Oslo Accords, the second shortly after the Second Intifada and the third is the most explicitly historical – in part, telling the story of Suleiman's father and the experience of 1948 in a Nazarene context. Nazareth itself, despite the shifting political contexts of the films, remains something of a ghost town. As Gil Hochberg (2015: 62) has recognized, the Oslo Accords left the issue of Palestinians in Israel completely unresolved, increasing their spectral liminality within both Palestinian and Israeli nationalisms. Suleiman's eponymous alter ego, E.S., is himself a ghostly figure throughout the trilogy, particularly in *Chronicle of a Disappearance*. The alter ego, a silent, tragicomic observer of events, has been likened to Handala, the child with his back turned famously depicted in the political cartoons of Naji al-Ali (Dabashi 2012).[7]

Chronicle of a Disappearance (1996) is structured as a series of vignettes, ostensibly split into halves: 'Nazareth Personal Diary' and 'Jerusalem Political

Diary'. While the Nazareth half is more quotidian, its politics erupts through scenes of inter-neighbour aggression and the exaggerated invisibility of the Palestinian within Israel. The latter is illustrated in an early scene which shows E.S. in his apartment as it is searched by Israeli police. The radio conversations back to base reveal this ghostly Palestinian (who is missed in the search despite standing in the middle of the room) as a mere extension of the inanimate objects in the flat: 'nylon curtains, a guy in pajamas, over'. This invisible ghostliness in plain sight echoes an anecdote Suleiman tells, during the filming of *Chronicle of a Disappearance*, of the repressed memory of Arab Palestinians in the Israeli imagination. Reflecting on a conversation with a young assistant director, Suleiman (2003: 27) recalls, 'When we were denied permission to shoot in West Jerusalem, I realized that he didn't know what the term "Arab houses" meant. He just thought the Hebrew words referred to an architectural style.'

Unlike the ghostly Palestinian which haunts the Israeli imagination, or literally 'ghosts' its cinema in the case of Kamal Aljafari's work (as will be seen), the absence of the State in Nazareth (other than its panoptic presence around the city) creates a haunting among neighbours in the absence of a political 'other' to haunt.[8] The sense of being abandoned but watched pervades Suleiman's Nazareth, in a particularly heightened sense in his second film, *Divine Intervention* (2002). Like the previous film, this film is spatially divided, with Suleiman's Nazareth juxtaposed with a car park near Qalandia checkpoint (between Jerusalem and Ramallah), where E.S. and a love interest meet. While the State is no more present Nazareth in this film, the historical context of the Second Intifada means the absent presence of the Palestinian in Israel is given heightened visibility through its association with another spectre of the Israeli (and Western) imagination – the 'Palestinian terrorist' (Hochberg 2015: 68), a spectre whose overcoded image further obscures the Palestinian in Israel. This spectre is quite literally conjured in the *Divine Intervention* as pure signifier in the closing Jerusalem sequence of *Divine Intervention* as an invincible, computer game-like character who is an assemblage of reductive resistance clichés which, as Edward Said lamented, could easily be weaponized by the Israeli state to flatten the complexity of Palestinian identity and struggle for Palestinian rights to the signifier of mere terror.

The dialectic of surveillance and neglect structures the Nazareth sequences of *Divine Intervention* with its tension between civility, docility and hostility. In an interview given to the *Journal for Palestine Studies* at the time of *Divine Intervention*'s release, Suleiman expands upon the play of forces that produce the stasis of contemporary Nazareth which is 'a very claustrophobic space, no land, no possibility of expanding in the city, no cultural venues, unemployment is rife, frustration, stasis, a sense of despair and hopelessness' (Suleiman 2003a: 71).

Unpacking the term 'stasis' is crucial to understanding the spatial politics of Nazareth. While stasis conveys a sense of political stagnation and forces cancelling one another out, the etymology from ancient Greek conveys the sense of taking a stand in a dispute against others. Specifically, in both Plato's *Republic* and Aristotle's *Politics*, the term *stasis* named the conditions for domestic conflict in the *polis*, to be contrasted with the ideal of *homonoia*, civic harmony or consensus. In *Stasis: Civil War as a Political Paradigm* (2015), Giorgio Agamben draws on the work of both Nicole Loraux and Thomas Hobbes to take his interpretation of the Greek notion of *stasis* to its logical extreme; that is, civil war rather than just mere factional strife.[9] For Agamben, *stasis* is something that dwells in and erupts from the interior. It is a 'war within the family and comes from the *oikos* and not from the outside' (Agamben 2015: 8). The stasis of contemporary Nazareth conveys this duality of meaning, both of time on hold and civic stagnation, and also a taking of stands, the compartmentalization of the neighbourhood into warring factions. This is a tension Janet Harbord describes as 'an endless dialectic of aggression and response' (Harbord 2007: 157).

Divine Intervention opens with an extraordinary series of vignettes lasting around thirty minutes. The film begins with a scene of surreal physical and aesthetic violence of Father Christmas figure being pursued and violently attacked by children, which prefaces several episodes of violent speech and gesture indicating the political *stasis* of Nazareth. Watching/being watched is a key dynamic of these opening sequences. The frequent use of the long take, along with the high-angle long shot gives these scenes the quality of surveillance imagery. Doorways, houses and yards are framed at an impersonal distance, blurring the line between neighbourhood voyeurism and surveillance footage. The claustrophobic political and personal space of Nazareth is bookended by the presence and absence of Suleiman's father. One early scene is of Suleiman's father driving down a Nazareth Street and waving at neighbours while simultaneously cursing each one under his breath. The film ends after Suleiman's father has been hospitalized by a heart attack, with E.S. and his mother sitting in the kitchen, impassively watching a pressure cooker build until his mother announces 'That's enough'.

A Different Land: *The Time That Remains* (2009)

Nazareth (alongside Suleiman's father, Fuad) is more fully the biographic character, of *The Time That Remains* (2009). The film charts a personal history of Nazareth, from the 1948 battle for the city during the Nakba, through the death of Nasser in 1970 and the Land Day Protests of 1976, to the present day. The film opens in the present, with E.S. being taken to his home in Nazareth by an Israeli-Jewish taxi driver. The film opens in darkness, punctuated by the opening of the car boot. Shot from a low angle, looking out from the boot, the *mise en scène* is claustrophobic. The opening shot is also laced with irony, as on the solid grey wall looming above the space behind the almost silhouetted form of the driver are posters of rolling, pastoral landscapes with Jaffa oranges in the corner. The slogan 'Eretz Acheret', meaning 'Different Land' in Hebrew, is written at the bottom.

This concept of difference is played with throughout the film, as the estrangement experienced by the present/absent citizenship of a Palestinian in Israel but also by a State itself haunted by the project of partition and its psychological impact, hinted at in the taxi ride itself. Shot in shallow focus with a rainstorm disorienting both the driver and the viewer, this continues the scene's sense of enclosure and confinement, with the driver losing his way in the rain and beginning a monologue lamenting the loss of the collective *kibbutzim* but also his disorientation in the Galilee in this more Palestinian corner of the state. 'We lost our way. How do I get home?' he asks. A sense of loss (expressed as abandonment) in Suleiman's Nazareth milieu similarly pervades the film.

The ghost of pan-Arabism means the figure of the neighbour in Nazareth is presented somewhat differently in *The Time That Remains* to the preceding *Divine Intervention*. The nature of this difference is primarily due to historical circumstance. The film's critique of the neighbour focuses, historically, on the neighbour *without*, in contrast to contemporary Nazareth's neighbour *within*. The former's historical political critique uses irony and wordplay to frame domestic, seemingly quotidian scenes as forums to critique the contemporary geopolitical climate. The first of these scenes comes in the middle of the film, in the '1970' section in which Fuad's (E.S.'s father) alcoholic neighbour pivots between desperation and defiance. In his more lucid moments, he interrupts Fuad's fishing trips to offer his 'solutions' to the question of Palestine, often hinging on an absurd logic – a logic that he nonetheless proudly defends. These scenes are juxtaposed with Fuad wearily exiting his house and confiscating the neighbour's matches as he attempts, repeatedly, to immolate himself in despair. These scenes, full of pathos and the absurd, convey the 'weepy sorrows of Arab nationalism' (Said 1986: 51) following the defeat of 1967 and the death of Nasser, the figurehead of pan-Arabist ideology.

A modification of this critique – as sorrow moves to cynicism – occurs around an hour into the film. E.S. and his two friends are sitting around a table outside a Nazareth gift shop when a newspaper boy walks by, announcing the prices of his papers in shekels.[10] The newspaper vendor's cry of '*Kul al-Arab balash!*' combines the newspaper title *Kul al-Arab* (a weekly Israeli Arabic language newspaper, based in Nazareth) and the colloquialism 'balash', which can mean both 'free' and 'nothing' – literally *balaa* (without) and *shi* (thing). One of E.S.'s friends requests the paper *al-Watan* (the Nation/Homeland), only to be told, 'No more "Nation" (*al-Watan*). Only "All the Arabs" (*Kul al-Arab*) left'. The man nonchalantly takes the paper and discards it on the table. The wordplay rests on duality of meaning. On the one hand, the boy is merely stating that this is a newspaper that costs nothing. However, the phrase 'as a whole' contains an implicit political critique. 'All the Arabs for nothing', with the play on *Kul-al-Arab* seen as a critique of Palestine's Arab neighbours – albeit in a slightly more hardened manner than previous scenes – for their empty talk of an endlessly deferred promise of a 'liberated' Palestine which has increasingly become an empty signifier.

Stasis and intertextuality in Nazareth: *Wajib* (Annemarie Jacir, 2017)

Suleiman's fossilized Nazareth is evoked in images which construct a contrapuntal, intertextual dialogue on Nazareth's enduring stasis in Annemarie Jacir's *Wajib* (2017). The film tells the story of a single day in Nazareth, through a road trip around the city taken by a father and son, Abu Shadi and Shadi. Shadi is returning to Nazareth for the first time in many years for his sister Amal's wedding. The purpose of the trip is to hand-deliver the wedding invitations to friends and family. Edward Said's concept of *al-ghurba* (estrangement) is examined through a family portrait of a father who saw it as his duty to remain in Nazareth, and a son who had to leave by necessity but has grown up *in* and grown accustomed *to* the diaspora, having met a Palestinian woman in

Rome, where he lives. The film depicts a series of polite, sometimes awkward encounters with friends and extended family amid the tensions of a strained father/son relationship and an estranged mother with a sick husband who may miss the wedding. These familial and generational tensions underpin the broader tensions of ways of looking at and imagining Palestine *min al-dakhil* (from the interior) and *fil-kharij* (from the exterior/outside).

The film's title, *Wajib*, ostensibly refers to the ceremonial 'duty' of delivering invitations by hand to the guests, a Palestinian, but particularly Nazarene tradition the director observed her husband perform for her sister-in-law's wedding (Jacir 2017a). The film examines the concept of *wajib* (duty). However, throughout the film, *wajib* (which also translates as necessity) corresponds to a whole complex and networked structure of *nomos* that runs throughout the film, a series of intersecting personal and societal necessities.

The film exhibits a contrapuntal tension of place, in that it brings together the 'elsewhere' of exile/diaspora, and the 'here' of Palestine-Israel. The former is embodied by Shadi, the Palestinian who left, settled in Rome and is seduced by stories of the Palestinian revolution told by his girlfriend's father (an exiled intellectual). The latter is embodied by Abu Shadi, his father, who remained in Nazareth and is seen by his son as almost pitifully compromised by a State that actively suppresses the Palestinian in him. In this sense, he is almost a ghostly figure: the Israeli-Arab revenant Elia Suleiman evokes in this chapter's opening. The Palestinian in him is buried so deep it can barely be conjured, despite his son's efforts (which themselves demand an idealized Palestinian-ness nurtured in the diaspora 'uncorrupted' by living in a State which has abandoned him).

Formally, the film also evokes Suleiman's Nazareth with several scenes which can be read contrapuntally: both as nostalgic homage to Suleiman and also a critical commentary on stasis. The double sense of *stasis* in Nazareth examined in Elia Suleiman's *Divine Intervention* (2002) in the previous section is reflected in *Wajib*'s Nazareth, despite the decade and a half between them. While Gertz and Khleifi argue that Suleiman's first two feature films, *Chronicle of a Disappearance* (1996) and *Divine Intervention* (2002), reflect what 'had transpired in Palestinian society in general and its cinema in particular between the signing of the Oslo peace accords and the Second *Intifada*' (Gertz and Khleifi 2008: 171; emphasis in the original), a close reading of Nazareth on screen in both of Suleiman's films and *Wajib*, on the contrary, reveals a resistance to such discrete periodization – in Nazareth in particular and *al-dakhil* more generally. Rather, there is a continuum of quotidian tedium, punctuated by episodic aggression.

A recurring vignette in *Chronicle of a Disappearance* is one where a car screeches to a halt outside a Nazareth café, before two men leap out bickering, before breaking into a physical struggle. While car and relation change, the pattern remains the same. In the first vignette, two friends have to be separated beside their white saloon car, as each attempts to attack the other with a jack. In the second, a small red car stops suddenly, and a father and son get out and start fighting, again separated by the café owner.

The Nazareth that exists outside the car in *Wajib* has some strikingly intertextual referents to those in Suleiman's Nazareth in *Divine Intervention*, despite the fifteen years that separate the two films. The escalating violence in Jacir's Nazareth is first mentioned in passing at an early 'invitation stop' in the context of intra-family violence, with a case of fratricide in a Nazarene family lamented almost casually. The first visual eruptions of aggression mirror the neighbourhood tensions that simmer in Suleiman's Nazareth of *Divine Intervention*. On a visit to a family friend, Abu Shadi is making small talk when suddenly a bag of rubbish drops past the living room window. Enraged, the friend leaps up and curses the neighbour for using his garden as a rubbish dump. The scene mirrors one in *Divine Intervention*, when we see the culprit this time, casually leaving his house with a black bag, before tossing it over his neighbour's wall. When the bags come back and a confrontation ensues, the man calmly highlights how shameful and unneighbourly he views simply throwing the rubbish back without 'discussing the matter'. Such mannered enmity simmers below the surface of both Suleiman's and Jacir's on-screen Nazareth.

On the same visit, when Shadi and his father return to the car they find the tyre of their Volvo slashed, having parked it in an unsigned part of the neighbourhood. This dialectic of aggression and response in which Shadi and Abu Shadi get caught up is evocative of a similar act of petty revenge in Suleiman's Nazareth. A repeated sequence centres on the repair of a road and its retaining wall, which are consistently sabotaged to thwart the approach by car of the neighbour seen dumping rubbish earlier. In a previous scene, he manages to avoid the missing asphalt, but in a later repetition the car becomes stuck.

While the intertextuality of the two films' portrayal of Nazareth suggests on the surface an homage-like quality to *Wajib*'s mise en scène, there is also a commentary on the continual economic and political stasis of Nazareth, despite the decade and a half between the two films. In an interview with Stephen Elphick, Jacir (2017) states that contemporary 'Nazareth is a violent, tense city'. These sentiments echo Suleiman's description of his hometown fourteen years previously in an interview, as a 'claustrophobic space' of explosive tension (Suleiman 2003a: 71).

Kamal Aljafari's 'Jaffa' trilogy: From the architectural uncanny to spectral politics

Haunting enacts a political critique of a different kind through the possibilities of digital format in Kamal Aljafari's 'cinematically occupied' Jaffa, as Aljafari's texts contrapuntally decentre the Zionist cinematic history of Jaffa, and expose some of the blind spots within the constructed enmity of Arab-Jewish history.

Kamal Aljafari's trilogy, *The Roof* (2006), *Port of Memory* (2009) and *Recollection* (2015), make up a haunted triptych of his paternal city, Jaffa. Aljafari is based in Germany, but – as his surname indicates – has paternal ties to Jaffa and maternal ties to Ramle. The three films chart a shifting relationship with haunting throughout his work, from a ghostly architecture which haunts its inhabitants in *The Roof*, to a spectral politics which 'ghosts' the political and aesthetic consciousness of Zionism in *Port of Memory* and *Recollection* by bringing back the Palestinian revenants captured in the margins of the frames of Israeli cinema.

The idea that cinema is a technology of ghosts – an inherently spectral technical apparatus – is developed extensively within Jacques Derrida's later hauntology (2002, 2015). Derrida contends that the spectral can appear in the cinema 'almost head-on, to be sure, as in a tradition of fantasy film, vampire or ghost films' (Derrida 2015: 26), or lie in the structure of the image itself. This content and form, however, 'must be distinguished' (ibid.). Cinema as a medium is both a haunted and also *haunting* technology, in its capacity to arrest time and 'embalm' the moving image, in a Bazinian sense. Drawing on the experience of watching Pascale Ogier in *Ghostdance*, Derrida (2002: 120) refers to the 'dissymmetrical gaze' of the cinematic revenant, watching, observing and surveying the viewer who is conscious of being unable to return the gaze. In *Specters of Marx* (1994), Derrida will evoke the cinematic in a definition of the spectre as that 'which one projects – on an imaginary screen where there is nothing to see' (Derrida 1994: 125). In its ability to preserve an index of death through a projection of light, cinema itself is a spectral apparatus, an apparatus whose digital possibilities Aljafari will – in *Port of Memory* and *Recollection* – exploit to haunt the political present.

Architectural Haunting in *The Roof* (2006)

Aljafari's first feature, *The Roof* (2006), unpacks some of the subjective complexities of 'home' for a Palestinian from Israel living overseas, particularly in a scene towards the middle of the film. Structurally, the film is an essayistic blend of documentary, historiography and memoir that employs a reflexive and ironic register in the tradition of Emile Habiby. Its focus is the Aljafari family homes in both Jaffa and Ramle, the latter providing the missing titular roof. During a telephone conversation with Aljafari, Nabieh – an old friend living in Beirut – suggests that Aljafari visit him in Lebanon. 'I can't enter the Arab countries' comes Aljafari's reply. This is due to Aljafari's complex legal status as a Palestinian filmmaker based in Germany with Israeli and German citizenship. In fact, the filmmaker himself, following Adorno's comments on literature and exile, has referred to cinema as a 'homeland' (Aljafari 2010), a place where alternative histories and futures can be imagined. In the same conversation, Aljafari evokes his longing to hear Beirut's sea, a sight/sound he is unable to access, denoting a fluidity of place that articulates just some of the subjective and territorial complexity of the contemporary Palestinian subject: one who is legally a citizen of Israel, educated and living in Germany and homesick for the sea in Lebanon, a place which – through force of law – he can only visit in his imagination.

Shortly after an establishing opening scene, in which Aljafari and his sister discuss his experience of incarceration during the First Intifada, the film fades to black and a quote by Anton Shammas (2002) appears on screen, articulating the ghostly weight of home for those it haunts in exile: 'And you know perfectly well that we don't ever leave home we simply drag it behind us wherever we go, walls, roof and all. Home – it is probably the one single thing we don't leave home without; and that would explain the rumbling in our wake.' It is clear from this quote and what follows that *The Roof* is a film about the pressing weight of home and the ghosts that dwell within (or more accurately, *above* it).

The scene which follows the Shammas quote is one that employs a spatial logic of inversion. A camera pans steadily and slowly to the left, scanning the earth as stones and rubble give way to foundations and remains of houses. Aljafari narrates over this scene, a tale of dispossession of 1948 that took place in Jaffa (his father's origin) and Ramle (his mother's). It is a familiar tale. Forced to leave their homes, they became present-absentees. The shot foregrounds the archaeological evidence. The foundations and origins were right here in the ground. This archaeological (and architectural) connection to the earth grounds contested claims of national belonging. In the national narrative of Zionism, Palestinian ruins have to be subsumed into a wider taxonomy of 'archaeological particulars' (Said 2003: 47), which, Said argues in his 2003 lecture *Freud and the Non-European*, have made archaeology '*the* privileged Israeli science *par excellence*' (ibid.: 46). Without such an absorption, these ruins remain a haunting presence that awakens the Palestinian remnant within the State. For Said, therefore, a Palestinian archaeology must open up the land to heterogeneity: its multiple pasts and multiple peoples.

The above scene in *The Roof* quite literally turns a nationalist logic of archaeological foundations – the connection to the land providing the collective grounding and historical claim – on its head. The past is not buried, in the land or the earth itself, but is something rather that *buries*: 'My parents live on the first floor,' states Aljafari, 'and the past lives above them.' In this inversion, archaeology becomes architecture as the unfinished roof looms over its inhabitants who are, quite literally, buried alive beneath it.

We are introduced to the eponymous roof by way of a slow, one-minute tracking shot, as the camera tracks left with tight framing as the unfinished roof is slowly revealed, along with a number of discarded objects. Accompanying this languid tracking shot is the song *Ya Habibi Taala* by Asmahan, a song of love, absence and ghosts. The song seems appropriate, as the spectral absent presence of the unfinished roof haunts the Aljafaris: an uncanny or rather *unheimlich* haunting that permeates the film throughout.

The Arabic title of the film – *al Sateh* – gives an ambiguity lost in its English translation. While meaning 'roof', it can also convey flatness and surface, marking a slippage and instability at work in a number of other scenes. The linguistic slide from roof to surface gives a sense of something concealed.

A similar semantic instability underpins the Freudian uncanny. Freud locates *Heimlich* and its antonym *unheimlich* (uncanny or literally 'unhomely) as interchangeable. This comes from a dual sense of *Heimlich* (which translates as 'homely') meaning both that which is familiar and comfortable and that which is concealed and hidden. *Unheimlich* then, Freud notes, 'applies to everything that was intended to remain secret, hidden away, and has come into the open' (Freud 2003: 132). Thus, Freud locates the *unheimlich* within the logic of the familiar. The homely is always already unhomely in that the familiar is repressed in the form of a secret and the unhomely is 'what was once familiar [homely, "homey"]. The negative prefix *un-* is the indicator of repression' (ibid.: 151).

Figure 2.1 The spectral roof in *The Roof* (Kamal Aljafari, 2006). ©Filmstiftung Nordrhein-Westfalen.

Through the use of German *Heimlich/unheimlich* and the blurring of separation between the two terms, Freud explicitly frames a discussion of the uncanny in terms of domestic architecture. The semantic shift in *al Sateh* from roof to surface allows for a thinking of 'home' as the unhomely repressed coming to the surface of the image. Such a movement from architecture to image manifests in an aesthetic experience of the *unheimlich*, occurring in the first ten minutes of *The Roof* in a scene of domestic 'normality' in the Ramle house. After a scene in which the family dine together in virtual silence, there is a cut in extreme close-up to a hand on the edge of the sofa. The extreme closeness and shallow-focus photography that (de)frames the twitching, hairy hand evokes an aesthetic sense of the uncanny.[11] The framing of the disembodied hand, until a zoom-out reveals Aljafari's uncle, gives the viewer an uncanny shock, particularly given static framing of many of the human subjects in *The Roof*'s mise en scène.

The film's closing scene appears to echo the anxiety triggered by the foundations and the burden of the home seen in the opening shots of Ramle and the weight of the past on top of the Aljafaris. The scene begins with a shot of Kamal and his mother sitting opposite one another in silence. The shot then cuts to the mother, who asks, 'Do you want to finish the house?' to which Kamal replies: 'I don't know – it's strange finishing something that doesn't belong to us.'[12] This brings the rueful response from his mother that 'everyone has left. Not just them – left their homes.' Belonging and home have a heavy weight for Aljafari, seemingly (recalling Shamas's words) rumbling in his wake as he returns. Returning from Berlin, where he is based, the exilic spectrality of the roof weighs heavily. The privileged affliction that Said cites as the exile of *al-dakhil* manifests here as a weight that grows heavier as one draws nearer. The unfinished, abandoned home, with its paradoxical weight of presence and ghostly absence, seems to bury the family beneath the surface of the spectral roof. Aljafari's focus on the spatial dimension of haunting in this film, with the architecture itself having an uncanny effect, continues seamlessly with the opening scene of his second feature, *Port of Memory*.

Let the ghosts come back: *Port of Memory* (2009)

Aljafari's *Port of Memory* (2009) opens with a slow, quiet tracking shot, the only audible sound that of birdsong. Tight framing and a low-angle close-up slowly reveal the wall of a ruined house. The fading twilight casts a blue, cold hue over the shot, which slowly tracks left along the wall, revealing scars of neglect; a broken balcony here, the jagged struts of a staircase jutting out like spikes there, giving the house a somewhat menacing air. The looming wall fills the frame, introducing a language of looming architectural ruin which permeates the film, hemming its characters in.

Similarly to *The Roof* before it, Aljafari's *Port of Memory* (2009) employs a non-anthropocentric camera-eye, as walls and the fabric of Jaffa are foregrounded, with human figures often wandering into and out of frame. The corporeality of the city itself is as 'alive' as the humans who dwell within it. The film's narrative, such that it is, tells the story of Salim and the lost deeds to his house. The threat of eviction, and the wider sense of erasure of Jaffa permeates the film, as the perpetual sound of construction and the presence of gentrification documents a city increasingly being swallowed by neighbouring Tel Aviv. However, the film's most telling scene, which utilizes digital editing to enact a form of spectral politics, occasions a Palestinian haunting of Israeli's cinema's past.

This scene and Aljafari's method have been hinted at throughout the film, with a character repeatedly and impassively watching sped-up clips from *The Delta Force* (1986), in which Chuck Norris and his team of US operatives pursue 'terrorists' across a non-localizable and orientalized Middle East, with Jaffa standing in for Beirut. The film is a Menahem Golan production, and the scenes appear as a mise en abyme of Hollywood destruction within the wider cultural destruction and decay of Jaffa on screen in *Port of Memory*. In the key contrapuntal scene in *Port of Memory*, through digital manipulation, Salim, the film's main character, is inserted into the cinematic space of Zionism, here a musical performance from an Israeli film. The scene begins with a graphic match, as Salim (played by Aljafari's uncle) wanders Ajami (his neighbourhood), before being inserted into shots from which the scenes were taken, an Israeli film *Kazablan* (1973). This film manages to layer a fictional cinematic occupation on top of the factual occupation of Jaffa during this period, as the film tells a narrative of oppressed Mizrahi Jews living in Jaffa, and the scene in question is the sung lamentation of Ashkenazi oppression, a narrative which, as Aljafari states, 'completely elides not only Jaffa's Palestinian history, but also its remaining Palestinians, enacting a virtual, cinematic emptying of the city' (Aljafari 2010). As the character wanders the crumbling architecture of an abandoned Jaffa, he sings the lyrics to *Yesh Makom*, his lament to his former life in Morocco:

> There is a place beyond the sea,
> Where the sun shines over the market, the street and the port,
> Home beyond the sea.

Salim's spectral appearance troubles this scene, briefly haunting the frame from the edges and fracturing and undermining the fictional narrative of the

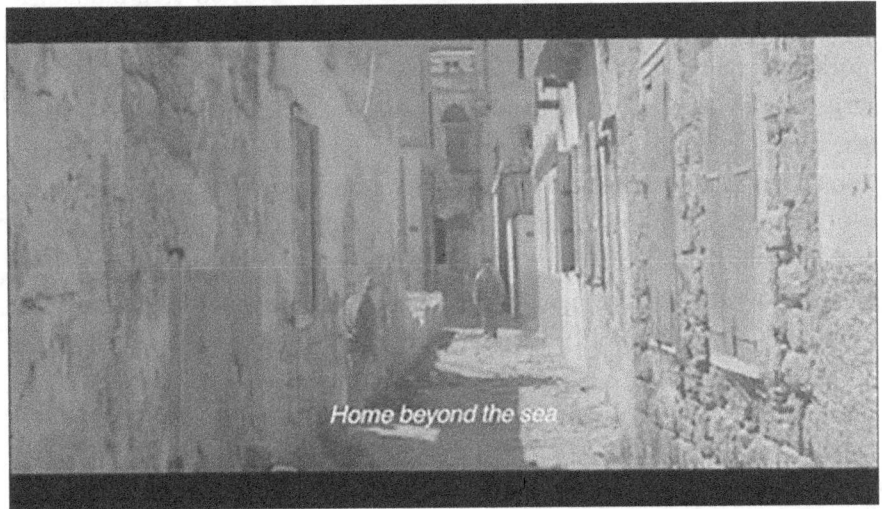

Figure 2.2 Digital haunting as cinematic occupation in *Port of Memory* (Kamal Aljafari, 2009). ©Novel Media.

scene's Mizrahi lamentation. By re-appropriating a Hebrew song of loss and longing the scene counters a hegemonic national space, by interrupting its fictional unity. The complete elision of the Palestinian, or *Arab al-dakhil*, is countered by the staking of the claim that there have always been *peoples* in Palestine-Israel, never simply *a people*.

A remarkably similar 'ghosting' of the cinematic space of Zionism can be seen in Annemarie Jacir's *Salt of This Sea* (2008). In the scene in question, Soraya, the film's Palestinian-American protagonist, visits the remains of Dawayima with Emad – a Palestinian from Ramallah – while looking for Soraya's ancestral home in Jaffa. The village (in which Emad's family lived before 1948) is in Israel, through which the two are passing disguised as settlers. They are awoken by a school tour, led by a teacher who – startled by a figure emerging from the cave-like ruin – assumes Soraya is a Jewish-American tourist and explains (switching from Hebrew to English) that camping is forbidden in these 'ancient archaeological remains'. The traumatic memory of this figure/place being a hidden remnant of historic Palestine within Israel is unlocalizable to the teacher, and thus must be transferred to that of a lost tourist in 'biblical' space.

While Aljafari's use of digital enacts a 'ghosting' of Jaffa by its present-absentees, the unnamed presence of the Arab-Jew also constructs a complex double haunting in which the figure of Arab-Jewishness haunts *Port of Memory* by way of its own repression. Menahem Golan's *Kazablan* (1973) is one of the most successful 'Boureka' films, a musical genre which often used humour to depict the class politics of Israeli society, with Mizrahi Jews outwitting uncaring bureaucratic authorities, depicted as cold, managerial Ashkenazi Jews. The third act usually involves a resolution under the banner of unified Jewishness. *Kazablan* tells the tale of a Moroccan-Jewish gang leader in love with a young Ashkenazi woman in the context of a Mizrahi neighbourhood which is being threatened with demolition. *Port of Memory* both *consciously* engages in the spatial politics of Jaffa's 'cinematic occupation' (Aljafari 2016) but *unconsciously* highlights the marginalized, liminal figure of the Mizrahi[13] as analogous to the erasure of Palestinian presence in Jaffa. In doing so, the film highlights a double negation by the hegemonic State: the marginalization of the orientalized Arab-Jew to the always already spectral space of the Palestinian. The figure of the Mizrahi is thus a detotalizing figure for both Israeli and Palestinian nationalisms, forming an 'in-between figure, at once inside and outside, "in" in terms of privileged citizenship within the Jewish state, in contrast to the Palestinian citizens of Israel, but hardly "of" the hegemonic national culture' (Shohat 2010: 266). It is this very

'Eastern-ness' that must be paradoxically both orientalized and assimilated by the State in a paternalistic double movement to suppress the ghost of 'Eastern-ness' used to other Ashkenazi Jewish communities in Europe – thus repressing the 'Arab-ness' that bonds Jewish identity to Palestinian identity.[14]

Aljafari's primary concern in *Port of Memory* (2009), which he fully realizes in *Recollection* (2015), is to 'ghost' cinematic Jaffa to issue a demand, much like Derrida's revenant: that the destruction of the city witnessed in *The Delta Force* and the story of eviction and dispossession in *Kazablan* were always already the hidden history of Palestinian Jaffa.

Remnants of Palestine: *Recollection* (2015)

The spectral politics of *Port of Memory*, inserted into a wider narrative of loss, are fully realized in Recollection (2015), a film which abandons narrative altogether to construct an archive of the city of Jaffa, along with an excavation of the cinematic remnants (and revenants) of that city. The film is composed entirely of found footage, with Aljafari composing a portrait of Jaffa sourced from a huge number of Israeli and American films made in the city from the 1960s to the 1990s.[15] The film opens with a cinematic preface, as its methodology is revealed. The characters of Israeli films shot in Jaffa are frozen, before being digitally removed, to clear space for the city and its inhabitants – whose spectral presence is revealed by this foregrounding of the margins of the cinematic frame. In a striking opening an entire ensemble scene from *Kazablan* (1973) is digitally spirited away. The film's structure, following this methodological preface, adds to the spectral reconstruction of the space of the city in a way that makes topographic sense. In an interview with Nathalie Handal, Aljafari (2016) stresses the importance of this noting that the archive of films he is working from cared only for an orientalist aesthetic quality they imposed on Jaffa: 'For someone who knows and comes from this place, these films do not make sense. It was important for me to have the character in my film walk and make sense of all of it, and project the place as it is, streets that lead to other streets as they are.'

Indeed, when Aljafari mentions the character of his film, it is important to stress that this character itself is more a phantom, wordless witness documenting a historical cinematic record of a city. The fabric of the city of Jaffa, which features so prominently in *Port of Memory*, is quite literally the protagonist of this film. The camera-eye constructs a tour of the city – arriving from the Mediterranean in a subversion of colonial Europeans' view of the city, before silently taking in the walls, steps and squares of a cinematic Jaffa. The digital removal of the original films' protagonists creates an eerily silent – albeit not entirely *empty* – city. What this digital rendering of Jaffa does do, rather, is make space for what previously went unseen. This is brought into stark relief with the first entrance of human figures into the frame, around twelve minutes into the film. A series of freeze-frames and zooms foreground these unwitting extras, the most striking being a zoom of the child caught in the top left of the frame in the scene below, taken from *Kazablan*.

The close-up here highlights a dual spectrality in both its production and reception. For the latter, the boy is the ghostly temporal 'punctum' which Roland Barthes (1993: 96) highlights in his analysis of the 'anterior future' (ibid.) at stake in a still image's capturing of a life preserved before death. This sense of 'loss to come' extends into the images of city lost to demolition and development. Regarding reception, the scene's technical use of digital foregrounding of the margin highlights cinema's own possibility to bring forth the ghosts of the past – a possibility which simply didn't exist on analogue film at twenty-four frames a second, as Laura Mulvey highlights in her analysis of Douglas Sirk's

Figures 2.3 and 2.4 Excavating the hidden Palestinian in *Recollection* (Kamal Aljafari, 2015). ©Novel Media.

Between Presence and Absence 81

Figure 2.4

Imitation of Life (1958). In an analysis of the opening 'boardwalk' scene in which black extras at the edges of the frame appear so fleetingly, 'it is only when the film is halted and the frame can be scanned these significant details becomes visible' (Mulvey 2006: 156). In Mulvey's analysis, the becoming-visible of the spectral extras is made possible digitally by a delayed mode of viewing. In Aljafari's film, the possibilities of digital technology to give the stage to ghosts lie in post-production. In inverting the politics of visibility/invisibility which elides Palestinians in Israel by digitally removing that which has concealed them and allowing them to gaze at us, *Recollection* gives amplified presence to Jaffa's 'present-absentees' and also, in a Derridean sense 'the right of absolute inspection' (Derrida 2002: 121). This amplification is further intensified by the film's sound design. The sound design gives corporeal weight to the fabric of the city in a remarkable manner, bringing the walls of the city to life, and bringing back the ghosts of its demolished neighbourhoods.[16] Aljafari describes the pioneering and spectral use of sound design in the film, worth quoting here at length:

> While recording we used special microphones that could record the sound inside the wall. … It was important for me to listen to the sound of the walls, life

buried beneath, inside the sea. The Israeli government and the municipality of Tel Aviv destroyed Jaffa. They threw the homes they destroyed into the sea. But every year, in the winter, when the sea rises, it throws part of these homes back on to the shore. (Aljafari 2016)

There is both a poignancy and political force to Aljafari's words here; the former as in his first feature *The Roof*, a conversation with his grandmother reveals that the family stayed in Jaffa in 1948 as the waves were too strong and forced them back into the port. The notion of the sound-image of these ruins acting as a remnant in the Agambian sense (Agamben 2005: 52) – an irrepressible, irreducible figure which resists the act of division (as partition) and renders it inoperable – both resonates personally and reinforces the spectral politics of the film; crucially, it reiterates the ethical demand of the ghost, or in Aljafari's (2016) words, for 'cinematic justice'.

Cinematic Jaffa: A contrapuntal reading and the spectral demand

This ethical demand of the ghost is a question Derrida returns to in both *Specters of Marx* (1994) and 'Spectographies' (2002). The idea of the ghost keeps open the space of the 'yet-to-come' (how Derrida frames the deferred promise of justice). The revenant must always be permitted to come back, warns Derrida in 'Spectographies', as it keeps open the promise of a future which disrupts the status quo: 'As soon as one calls for the disappearance of ghosts, one deprives oneself of the very thing that constitutes the revolutionary movement itself, that is to say, the appeal to justice, what I call "messianicity"' (Derrida 2002: 128). It is this bringing forth of the remnants and revenants of Palestinian Jaffa, I argue, which constitutes the shift in the function of haunting in Aljafari's trilogy; from documenting a haunted architectural uncanny in *The Roof*, to harnessing digital technology's spectral potential to open up the present to the possibility of imagining the political otherwise. In his contrapuntal reading of cinematic Jaffa, Aljafari constructs a history of a disappearing city in the margins of the Israeli and American cinematic frame. In bringing those margins to the centre and reclaiming the cinematic city for its ghosts, Aljafari's work writes back against a history of displacement, finding ironic similitude in a Mizrahi song lamenting Arab-Jewish loss in Palestinian Jaffa and reclaiming a cinematic archive in the margins of a cinema blind to – yet nonetheless haunted by – its presence.

The haunting hyphen: Between Arab and Jew in Amos Gitai's *Ana Arabia* (2013)

Amos Gitai is an Israeli filmmaker, but his critical relationship with the Israeli State saw him spend the 1980s and early 1990s in self-imposed exile in France. This was in particular prompted by his Occupied Territories-based documentary *Field Diary (Yoman Sadeh)* (1982), the reaction to which was one of great hostility in an Israel embarking on the invasion of Lebanon. An architect by training, his first documentary – *House (Beit)* (1980) – was banned by Israeli television and tells the story of Palestinian exile through a house in West Jerusalem. This explicit concern for Palestinian memory in Israeli cinema along with the subconscious spectre of Arab-Jewishness conditions his 2013 French/Israeli co-production, *Ana Arabia*. *Ana Arabia* is ostensibly an 'Israeli' film about *al-dakhil*, yet shares a number of striking similarities with Kamal Aljafari's *Port of Memory*, a 'Palestinian' one, alongside both directors' 'architectural' framing of mise en scène. In this sense, the films could be argued to 'take place' in a liminal space both threatened and abandoned by the State. Both films dwell within the shadow of Tel Aviv, with Gitai's film taking place entirely in an enclave between Jaffa and Bat Yam. They also share a spatial urban politics, as in both films, the main characters, Yusuf in *Ana Arabia* and Salim in *Port of Memory*, are being threatened with eviction by the municipality. Linguistically, both move between Arabic and Hebrew and are occupied by the hauntings of Israel's repressed others; that is, both its present-absentee Palestinians and its marginalized Arab-Jews.

Ana Arabia is primarily a film about the haunted/haunting spaces between Arab/Jew and Palestinian/Israeli. The film unfolds in real time, as the main character Yael, a journalist, explores the story of a Jewish holocaust survivor, who converted to Islam and married a Palestinian. Technically, the film is almost without precedent, consisting of a single shot lasting eighty-one minutes.[17] The location is an important element of the film's mise en scène, it essentially being a threshold space. It is an enclave that exists as a liminal space in a number of ways; geographically, it sits between but outside cities (on the edges of both Bat Yam and Jaffa). The significance of this liminality is that this enclave constitutes a community of outcasts. That is, the figures dwelling in this space have all been expelled from a community. The absence structures the film, the figure of Hannah Kiblanov, who became Siam Hassan (known by her Arabic nickname

Ana Arabia) was born Jewish, converted to Islam and declared herself an Arab. However, it was the transgressive act of marrying Yussuf which brings her into the space, with the marriage causing problems among friends and family. Sara the Jewish woman who was married to Jihad (one of Yussuf and Siam's sons) was also subject to ostracism from the sons of his previous marriage, who gave Jihad an ultimatum. Her own marriage became violent, and the violence and madness that ended in Jihad's death in Nablus suggests a complex religious fault line beneath Gitai's professed message of secular co-existence. In Arabic the term *al-kharij* contains within it a semantic ambiguity. It is both 'the exterior', that which is outside of *al-dakhil* but also carries, in a religious sense, the meaning of leaving or being cast out from an order. This space of *Ana Arabia* thus plays out this tension of *al-kharij* both outside of, and caught within *al-dakhil*; its inhabitants cast out of a religious and political order, yet still contained (or perhaps abandoned) within the interior, a forgotten enclave in the shadow of Tel Aviv.

Arguably, the spectral structure of the film is actually what haunts its form. In a number of interviews given at the release of the film, Amos Gitai has spoken of his desire for both a different way of consuming images of Israel/Palestine and also for the use of the single take so as not to 'interrupt' the relation between Arab and Jew.[18] The film's grammar then is interesting in that it constructs and dissolves a separation between Arab and Jew, which Gil Anidjar (2003: xxv) recognizes as a constructed relation of enmity between ostensibly ethnic (Arab) and religious (Jew) markers – a constructed enemy opposed (in the European imagination) to both Europe and each other. This distinction is of relevance to *Ana Arabia*, as the proper nouns 'Arab' and 'Islam' are often collapsed into indistinction; the film tells of the conversion of a European Jewish woman (Hannah/Ana/Siam, the dead woman at the 'centre' of the narrative) to Islam in order to marry Yusuf. Ella Shohat's work on postcolonial studies (2006: 208) has critiqued this Eurocentric approach of constructing Arab and Jew in opposition, and also the binary that has evolved aligning Jewish and Christian identity as Western, and Muslim as Eastern.

In its construction and erasure of the Arab/Jew binary, *Ana Arabia* is haunted throughout by the figure of Arab-Jewishness, a haunting evoked by the title; literally, 'I am an Arab.' In the film this is intended to show the movement in identity from Hannah (Jew) to Ana (Arab) but betrays the always already dwelling of Arab within Jew and vice versa: a dwelling repressed by the political erasure of the hyphen which falsely 'rendered the concept of "Arab-Jew" oxymoronic' (Shohat 2010: 266).

A complex, contrapuntal movement between presence and absence haunts the Cinema of the Interior of Palestine-Israel. This is an interior characterized by a logic of haunted surfaces and repressed depths. This haunting, a tension between visibility and invisibility, characterizes both the being of the 'present-absentee' Palestinian and haunts the peripheral vision of the Israeli cinematic frame (witnessed in both Aljafari's spectral politics, and the spectral hyphen in Gitai's film).

The cave and the ruin are, I argue – as intimated in the first section of the chapter – the haunted site of the interior *par excellence*. They mark a key site of haunted encounter where the ghost of the Palestinian can no longer be repressed and emerges into presence; witnessed not only by Salim's 'ghosting' of the ruined port of Jaffa in *Port of Memory* but by David's descent into the caves beneath Deir Yassin in Udi Alon's *Forgiveness* (2006) and Soraya's emergence from the cave-like ruined building in the village Dawayima in Annemarie Jacir's *Salt of this Sea* (2008).

The Cinema of the Interior, then, is essentially a cinema of ghosts; the ghost of the unfinished roof of the house in Ramle, in Aljafari's *The Roof* (2006), which traps its occupants beneath the weight of the memory of the Nakba and creates a contemporary excess of home/sickness; the Palestinian of Jaffa who ghosts the edges of the frame of Israeli cinema's Jaffa productions in *Port of Memory* (2009) and *acts back* on the space of that cinema and *speaks back* against a cultural history of erasure. There is also the double haunting at work in *Port of Memory*, which consciously resists the elision of the Palestinian from the Israeli cinematic frame, but unconsciously re-inscribes the ties that bind Arab and Jew (the erased hyphen) and folds them into a Palestinian narrative of loss and nostalgia. *Recollection* conjures a lost Jaffa as a new digital archive (echoing the 1982 loss of the Palestinian Film Archive), its Palestinian revenants digitally brought back to resist an Israeli cultural hegemony which has erased them from the frame.

The hyphenated identity of the Arab-Jew enacts a haunting of its own, one which might be termed the spectre of the impossibility of partition. It is the ghostly lacuna *between* the Arab and Jew, the erased hyphen that Ella Shohat (2006) speaks of, which haunts Amos Gitai's *Ana Arabia* (2013) and its attempts to bridge the space between these two figures, a space in which the Arab-Jew already dwells.

The 'ghost' of nostalgia Is a topic Ella Shohat explores in her essay 'Taboo Memories, Diasporic Visions: Columbus, Palestine and Arab-Jews', when examining the taboo of nostalgia for the Arab world within Euro-Israeli culture in Israel. Reflecting on the East/West partition that Zionism reinforces to also partition Palestine-Israel and Arab-Jew, she writes, 'The pervasive notion of "one people" reunited in their ancient homeland actively disauthorizes any affectionate memory of life before the State of Israel' (Shohat 2006: 222–3). This taboo, repressed nostalgia is expressed in the final scenes of *Route 181*, Michel Khleifi and Eyal Sivan's sprawling documentary that travels the ghost of the partition line of UN Resolution 181 – the 1949 partition which never came to pass. Towards the end of the documentary, the film travels to Shefer, on the northern border with Lebanon. Here, the filmmakers encounter a group of older Jewish friends who immigrated from Morocco and Tunisia in the 1950s, one of whom expresses his desire to retire to Morocco and displays an intense longing for it; at the filmmakers' prompting, he recalls some long-forgotten Arabic.

A theme common to the Cinema of the Interior is how haunting problematizes nostalgia for place grounded in nationalism. That is, nostalgia is for a *home* rather than a home*land*. An early scene in *The Roof*, in which Kamal Aljafari asks his friend via telephone to hold the receiver close to the ocean so that he can hear the sea in Beirut, does not dramatize a nostalgia for the lost home of pre-1948 Palestine, but rather a yearning for Beirut, both a Palestine in exile and an Arabness exiled from him by virtue of his passport. These complex and subversive intersections of nostalgia – the Arab-Jewish nostalgia for a time before and a place beyond Israel, the Palestinian nostalgia for a Palestinian place-time in exile as much as the land lost in the Nakba – haunt their respective nationalisms, and complicate a totalizing notion of a homeland, pointing to a 'stubborn historical intimacy' (Hochberg 2007: 8) between the proper nouns Palestine/Israel and Arab/Jew which renders the political and cultural project of partition inoperable. To end with a return to where the chapter began, to Suleiman's ghostly figure of the Israeli-Arab as becoming Palestinian, one notes that the partition project is one beset by ghosts of the past. To the future then, in the spirit of Derrida, one might paraphrase Marx's own ghostly invocation: a spectre is haunting Palestine-Israel – the spectre of binationalism.

3

Between diaspora and exile: Palestine, Chile and the cinema of Miguel Littín

The previous chapter explored the contrapuntal rhythms of exile through a logic of haunting. The internal exile of the 'present-absentee' draws on an archive of spectral images and sounds which construct a Janus-faced remnant that refuses to stay buried: that of Palestinian memory within Israel and that of Arab memory within Jewishness. These two taboo memories which refuse to be forgotten haunt the frames of the cinema of the interior.

This chapter examines the complex contrapuntal movement of exile and diaspora in relation to Palestine through a focus on a largely neglected pre-Nakba memory of Transnational Palestine more than 8,000 miles away: Chile. The complex intersection of notions of diaspora and exile in the experience of Chileans of Palestinian descent will be explored through a close reading of the exilic and diasporic works of Miguel Littín. Littín is more often positioned as a prominent filmmaker of the Latin American New Wave and widely known, in no small part thanks to the work of Gabriel Garcia Márquez, as a prominent Chilean exile. Littín's fame as a Latin American Leftist and a Chilean exilic filmmaker somewhat obscures his identification as a diasporic Palestinian. While there has been some scholarly focus on Chilean exilic post-dictatorship cinema (Waldman 2009; Traverso 2010; Blaine 2013; Palacios 2015), and some limited engagement with the cultural output of Chile's Palestinian diaspora (El Attar 2019), Littín's position as both an exilic Chilean and a pre-Nakba diasporic Palestinian complicates a thinking of the ruptures of 1973 (Chile) and 1948 (Palestine) as formative to those identities. This chapter aims to analyse Littín's shifting and multidirectional diasporic and exilic subject positions (diasporic Palestinian in Chile/Chilean exile in Mexico) throughout his work on Palestine and his responses to the Pinochet regime, arguing that this multidirectional 'double vision' presents a significant challenge to the somewhat schematic distinctions of exilic and diasporic experience laid out in Naficy's *An Accented Cinema* (2001) which, I argue, has led to a paradoxical distinction and slippage between these terms in cinematic scholarship on diaspora and exile since.[1]

Littín's engagement with both Palestine and Chile is complicated by his hybridity. Part of Chile's Palestinian diaspora yet exiled by the Pinochet regime for his role as head of Allende's Chile Films, his case poses a number of challenges to how 'Palestinian' filmmaking is situated in scholarship. His two cinematic engagements with Palestine, *Crónicas Palestinas* (2001) and *La Ultima Luna* (2005), coincide with the Second Intifada. The latter film focusses on the transition from Ottoman to British rule, complicating the notion of pre-1948 Palestine as a 'lost Eden' presented in both scholarship (Gertz and Khleifi 2008; Souri 2014) and cinema (notably, but by no means exclusively, in the work of Michel Khleifi). This diasporic identification with Chileans of Palestinian descent is largely neglected in scholarship on Palestinians outside of the Territories/Israel.[2] It also counters the persistent framing of the Palestinian filmmaker as 'exilic auteur' – a label applied to Elia Suleiman, Kamal Aljafari and Annemarie Jacir, among others.

The chapter utilizes a topological analysis of place to connect these discrete experiences of diaspora and exile to the unstable loci of trauma (the events of 1948 and 1973) to examine how Littín's work constructs a field of diasporic and exilic historical experience, whereby the moment of exile awakens a latent diasporic consciousness. *El Chacal de Nahueltoro* (1969), *Acta General de Chile* (1986) and *Los Naufragos* (1994) – made in anticipation *of*, in response *to* and in reflection *on* his exile from Chile – will be read contrapuntally alongside his two works on Palestine. This will demonstrate how Littín's own Chilean exile and engagement with Third cinema – almost concurrent with the transnational growth of the PLO's PFU and its re-politicization of diasporic communities in Latin America – informs his late-career diasporic re-engagement with Palestine. By situating Littín as a filmmaker of Transnational Palestine, I argue that his way of seeing, as both an exilic Chilean and a diasporic Palestinian, is rooted in a politics of global struggle borne in the non-aligned world, in which the unrealized potential of the Palestinian revolution and the Allende government construct a painful nostalgia (as articulated in Chapter 1) from which a memory of secular, anti-colonial resistance is transposed to question the contemporary political status quo. However, before focussing on Littín and his work, it is first necessary to contextualize the contested notions of exile and diaspora and their discursive use in the Palestinian experience.

Diaspora, exile, estrangement: Locating the Palestinian elsewhere

The notion of a Palestinian 'diaspora' is deeply complex in Palestinian culture, which by extension causes challenges in naming a 'diasporic' or 'exilic' cinema. In Arabic, problems of definition stem from the co-existence of three terms used in different contexts. Three terms are used, and their meanings convey the interconnectedness and interrelation of displacement. The first of these is *al-shatat*, which is closest in meaning to an English language understanding of diaspora and occurs with some regularity in the social sciences (Schulz 2005; Hilal 2007). The other terms, *al-ghurba* (estrangement) and *manfa* (exile), have more complex shades of meaning and are found more commonly in Palestinian literature. While Said uses both terms *manfa* for exile and *ghurba* for estrangement, the latter term has a more nuanced, existential meaning as to the foreignness and strangeness of exile.

Hans Wehr's Arabic English dictionary translates *al-ghurba* as follows: 'absence from the homeland; separation from one's native country, banishment, exile; life, or place, away from home' (Wehr 1994: 783). *Ghurba* draws its root from the Qur'an from the verb *gharaba*, which, since its opposite *sharaqa* is connected to the sun and East, thus orientation, can be taken as disorientation, being cast from the light. Julianne Hammer, when tracing the philological complexity of describing the Palestinian experience, notes this dual use:

> Edward Said translates *ghurba* as estrangement, and uses the term *manfa* for exile. Indeed, *manfa* is exile in a more literal sense, as the verb *nafa* means [to negate], to banish or expel. In Palestinian literature and poetry it is *ghurba*, where the Palestinian is a stranger that carries all the notions of suffering, cold, winter, estrangement and dislocation. (Hammer 2005: 60)

Said describes this strange chill of displacement, disorientation and abandonment – following Wallace Stevens – as a 'mind of winter', 'in which the pathos of summer and autumn as much as the potential of spring are nearby but unobtainable' (Said 2000: 186).

By contrast, *shatat* is a literal translation of 'diaspora' in the English usage, whose etymology comes from Ancient Greek: a combination of the verb *speiro* (to sow) and preposition *dia* (over). The word connotes a notion of productive scattering; seeds from a parent body in order to reproduce. Thus, the words hold in relation notions of both traumatic separation and successful reformation. It is the latter half of this relation, in the context of both the colonial reality of the Occupied Territories and the struggle for rights in *al-dakhil* (the interior), which is a source of anxiety over the potentially depoliticizing elements of *shatat*.

In her 2007 article 'Problematizing a Palestinian Diaspora', Julie Peteet follows Edward Said in choosing the term *al-ghurba* as a translation of exile/diaspora, and consciously leaving aside the term *al-shatat* or *manfa*. Further, Peteet highlights the problem of framing Palestinian subjectivity through a lens of postcolonial discourse, claiming that 'Palestinians do not always fit easily into contemporary theoretical frameworks. In an era of post-colonial studies, they remain firmly in the grip of modern colonialism' (Peteet 2007: 631). This claim follows the work of Jospeh Massad (2000), whose essay '"The Post-Colonial" Colony: Time, Space and Bodies in Palestine/Israel' recognizes the complex multiplicity of claims within the space of Palestine-Israel to both projects of a colonial/and postcolonial nature, and statuses of both colonizer and colonized, particularly complicated in the figure of the Mizrahi Jew. This was seen in the previous chapter in Kamal Aljafari's 'resistant co opting' of a Mizrahi song of oppression in the Israeli film *Kazablan* (1973) in his *Port of Memory* (2009), keeping the Hebrew lyrics to present a song of displacement and oppression of the Palestinian in Israel. Further, the figure of the 'returning outsider' complicates a thinking of exile/diaspora/estrangement. For example, while Elia Suleiman's autobiographical figure 'E.S.' in *The Time That Remains* (2009) is a returning figure to his parents in Nazareth, his juridical status as an Israeli citizen combined with his life in Europe and the United States gives him an 'internal' outsiders' perspective of being a Palestinian in Israel.

In her 2010 article 'Displacement and Memory: Visual Narratives of al-Shatat in Michel Khleifi's films', May Telmissany engages with the problematic terminology around the notion of diasporic Palestinians, specifically engaging with the term *shatat* in a more critical manner. Telmissany traces the evolution of *shatat*, 'which has come to replace *tashteet* (displacement)' (Telmissany 2010: 72). It is this latter term which signifies the element of force behind the 'milestones' of both the Nakba and *naksa*, and needs to be thought of as a constitutive (but not totalizing) element in any thinking of *shatat* (ibid.: 73).

In *The Politics of Dispossession* (1994), Edward Said is wary of the term diaspora so as to avoid parallels with the biblical Jewish experience; this is in order to retain a sense of scale, avoid a notion of a 'redemptive homeland' and maintain a contemporary focus on rights (Said 1994b: 114). A tension in the language of rights – between the right of return and the right to remain 'out of place' – is, for May Telmissany (2010: 83), constitutive of a contemporary thinking of *shatat*. While a productive re-articulation of *shatat*, it is nonetheless one restricted to 'Palestinian artists of the diaspora' (ibid.).

This complexity in terminology and the Saidian notion of 'remaining out of place' expressed in the ontological condition of *al-ghurba* with the retention of a right of return tied to the historical traumas of the Nakba and *naksa* is yet further complicated in the case of the focus of the diasporic identity formation that is the focus of this chapter: the Palestinian diaspora in Chile. This is a diaspora largely dislocated from the rupture of the *Nakba* and perhaps more properly indicative of *shatat* in its biological sense, yet whose relationship with Palestinian and Chilean history and, in Miguel Littín's case, exile gives it a complex relationship with memory and forgetting.

The diaspora before the Nakba: Locating Palestine in Chile

With a diasporic third-generation population of Chileans of Palestinian descent who can largely be traced back to two villages around Bethlehem, Bayt Jala (Beit Jala) and Bayt Sahur (Beit Sahour), Chile has the largest Palestinian diaspora – around 350,000 (Baeza 2014) – outside of the Middle East. This diaspora is notable for both its spatial distance from Palestine-Israel and also its temporal disconnection from the Nakba of 1948 and the *naksa* of 1967. Between 1860 and 1914, 1.2 million Ottoman subjects migrated to the Americas (Karpat 1985: 185), with the pejorative term *turcos* being applied to Ottoman subjects regardless of religious or national identification. In the case of Ottoman Palestine, this migration was accelerated by the Young Turk Revolution of 1908 and the outbreak of war in 1914, with a conscription law passed in the wake of the former driving migration of Christian families with little appetite to fight for the Empire (Baeza 2014: 60). It is primarily through these identifications – religious minority under Empire and regionally, rather than nationally anchored – that this diasporic formation complicates the dominant framing of Palestinian consciousness outside the West Bank, Gaza and Israel as a dispersal radiating outward from the founding rupture of the *Nakba* of 1948. Baeza notes,

> Until the 1920s, immigrants from Palestine had four major loci of identity: their home-towns (Bethlehem, Bayt Jala, Bayt Sahur, etc.); their region (*Bilad al-Sham*); their religion (Christianity), including, more broadly, their consciousness of

coming from what was broadly referred to as the Holy Land; and lastly, their 'Arab-ness'. (Baeza 2014: 63)

Legal status as Ottoman subjects has little bearing on identity formation, and Palestinian-ness as an identification begins to emerge with the founding of *Club Sportivo Palestina* in 1916 (Schwabe 2018: 654) (which would become known from 1920 as *Club Deportivo Palestino*), the first of a number of social and members' clubs in Chile. These events coincided with the dissolution of the Ottoman Empire and emergence of the British Mandate signifying both a continuum of Imperial control and, given some of the promises made during the First World War (in particular the 1915 McMahon-Hussein Correspondence), the possibility of (and agitation for) an independent Arab State in Palestine. This pre-1948 Palestinian diasporic consciousness necessarily problematizes the situating of the *Nakba* as a singular, foundational catastrophic event, but rather sees Palestine and its history as a continuum of occupying forces, from Ottoman to British to Israeli. This is a diaspora for whom the Palestinian cause and the Nakba are not bound together as they are in the popular imagination and in existing literature on Palestinian cinema. Rather, writes Siri Schwabe, this diaspora 'is only to a very limited extent directly marked by the trauma of Israeli violence' (Schwabe 2018: 654). Nonetheless, the experience of the First World War and its aftermath meant that 'the Palestinian cause and the struggle for a free Palestine became an early and lasting concern' which would condition cultural life in Chile (ibid.).

There is an obvious irony that Ottoman Palestinians emigrating to Chile to escape conscription to fight for an Empire to which they felt no affiliation found themselves pejoratively designated *turcos* on account of the passports they held, this being a pejorative familiar in its use against Ottoman rulers (*al'atrak* in Arabic) in the nascent Political Arabism of the time in Ottoman Palestine. As this diaspora begins to establish itself in Chilean society from the 1920s onwards, however, its politics and identification with Palestine as a place and a cause are complex, with this complexity compounded by Chile's dictatorship years (1973–90).

Diaspora and Dictatorship: Two Palestines in Santiago

In her ethnographic study of Chilean-Palestinian communities in Santiago, Siri Schwabe finds both a generalized depoliticized remembrance of Palestine and a suppression of traumatic Chilean memory politics. Yet within this seemingly cohesive sense of Palestinian historical memory, there also lies a political fragmentation along class lines. Wealthier Chilean Palestinians, established in Chile's business communities and with the societal locus of Club Palestino (a members' club in the wealthy, suburban Las Condes district North-East of central Santiago), found themselves at odds with Salvador Allende. Instead they aligned with the neoliberal economic policies of the Dictatorship, and continue to be on the political Right in Chile (Schwabe 2018: 658). By contrast, political sentiments in Patronato – a working-class neighbourhood and the other major site of diasporic life in Santiago – are, as we will see shortly, markedly different.

It is worthy of note when considering the transnational links between the Palestinian and Chilean Left (and Chilean-Palestinian Left) that Chile and Palestine's 'revolutionary moments' are both short lived and overlap historically. Allende's democratic Marxist government comes to power in 1970 and is violently deposed by the coup of 11 September 1973. The Palestinian revolution emerges out of the loss of pan-Arabism in the 1967 war and by September 1970 is mortally wounded,[3] after many fedayeen are killed and driven out of Jordan by King Hussein's Army. These overlapping narratives of ephemeral revolutionary socialist liberation movements were lost to the future anterior; a 'what might have been' is fossilized in those two Septembers in Chile and Jordan. However, the Palestinian revolution becomes a focal point for the international Left (as examined in Chapter 1), and the PLO uses this momentum to build transnational links with Third World countries, established both through PLO offices and chapters of the General Union of Palestinian Students (GUPS). Juan Abugattas cites 1974 as a key year in the awakening of the 'Palestinian Question' more broadly across Latin America, driven in no small part by Yasser Arafat's visit to the UN (Abugattas 1982: 125). Within the Chilean context, Jessica Stites Mor notes that 'Chile was home to a small local chapter of Arafat's General Union of Palestinian Students, which tended to view the cause of Palestine as part of a broader resistance to military rule and imperialism' (Stites Mor 2022: 27). After 1973, the Chilean-Palestinian Left in the working-class neighbourhood of Patronato connected the Palestinian struggle with the struggle against military dictatorship in Chile and broader revolutionary struggle (Schwabe 2018: 656). This sentiment is exemplified in an interview, conducted in Patronato, in Schwabe's (2018) ethnographic study of third-generation Chilean-Palestinian communities in Santiago. Andrea, who was a member of the Chilean GUPS, saw the Palestinian and Chilean struggle as an intersection of a national and international Left, and notes that a politics openly symbolizing Palestinian and

Leftist resistance was fraught with risk: '"Back then," she explains, "we were harassed, called communists, *turcos* and terrorists for wearing our *keffiyehs* in the street"' (Schwalbe 2018: 657). This memory is striking on two counts. Firstly, how the symbol of Palestinian resistance here becomes overcoded to convey terror in the manner that Edward Said recognizes in the hypervisibility of Palestinians across the world. Secondly, *turco* returns in its original orientalizing usage, but with a new political signification which connects the Chilean and Palestinian Left as a transnational threat to (military) order.

The fragmented politics of the Chilean-Palestinian diaspora somewhat challenges Schwabe's forgetting Chile/remembering Palestine binary that suppresses the fragmentary trauma of the Dictatorship and foregrounds remembrance of a cohesive Palestinian identity. Rather, there is on the one hand a depoliticized focus on Palestine from those with conservative politics and who benefitted from the neoliberal economic policies of the Dictatorship, who don't connect the Palestinian cause to a wider anti-colonial struggle on the Left; on the other there are those whose politics 'did in fact spill over from the Palestinian cause to the Chilean Left wing, as many saw the struggles of ordinary Chileans as symbolically connected to the struggle of the Palestinian people' (ibid.). This brings us to perhaps the Chilean-Palestinian Leftist par excellence, Miguel Littín.

Miguel Littín: From exilic to diasporic resistance

Miguel Littín was born to a Palestinian father and a Greek mother in 1942 and came to prominence on the political Left for his radical critique of Chilean society, his debut film *El Chacal de Nahueltoro* (Miguel Littín 1969), a formative work of the New Chilean Cinema. The film tells the story of José del Carmen Valenzuela Torres, an alcoholic with a childhood of exploitation and abuse, and his drunken murder of a widow and her five children. The film blends documentary aesthetic with non-linear narrative jumps to move, in stark black and white verité, between the murders, José's bleak and impoverished youth, and his redemption as he learns to read and construct guitars in prison. The film's denouement, and its wider indictment of Chilean society, is the execution of José by firing squad. Having been rehabilitated in prison, the execution starkly focusses on the resources allocated to death (rifles, protocols around the firing squad) in contrast to the lack of resources allocated to life. A State that cared nothing for him until his notorious crime now ostentatiously executes a man whose life had begun to take on a structure. The film's penultimate scene, initially incongruous, of José reading a soft pornographic magazine in his cell prior to the execution is revealing. This is a man without a childhood, entering into adulthood on the eve of his execution by the State. Littín's thesis is essentially that José's violence is a product of a violent rural poverty, abandoned by an uncaring, corrupt State that fetishizes discipline and punishment but allows poverty to fester.

El Chacal de Nahueltoro is one of just three films Littín made before his exile in 1973. The social critique of his debut film was characteristic of the New Chilean Cinema which emerged in the late 1960s and was distributed socially, rather than commercially, as Littín elaborates:

> We discovered that it was absolutely impossible to try and distribute these films through the commercial cinemas, so we created a highly efficient parallel distribution network, through the unions, clubs, schools etc. The functioning of this network reached its maximum efficiency during Allende's electoral campaign: films were projected to the masses before his speeches. (Littín 1976: 55)

With the election of Allende in 1970 Littín became head of Chile Films, which became the filmmaking wing of Allende's democratic socialist revolution. This revolutionary spirit is captured in the Popular Unity Filmmakers' Manifesto, (*Manifesto de los cineastas de la unidad popular*), written in 1970. This stated within its twelve declarations that 'the Chilean cinema, because of a historical imperative, must be a revolutionary art' (Littín 2014 [1976]: 250). In words anticipating Deleuze's notion of political cinema as that which must summon a people as a becoming (Deleuze 1989: 217), the manifesto declares 'that there exists no such thing as a film that is revolutionary in itself. That it becomes such through the contact that it establishes with its public and principally through its influence as a mobilising agent for revolutionary action' (ibid.: 252).

This manifesto comes in the wake of Otavio Getino and Fernando Solanas's manifesto *Toward a Third Cinema* (1969), which crystallized a *tiers-mondiste* cinema as anti-imperialist and revolutionary in form, content, production and distribution. That text had been an influence on emerging Third World militant cinemas, notably the PFU (the filmmaking arm of the PLO). As filmmaking in the Palestinian resistance grew across factions and the PLO's support for the PFU remained lukewarm (Yakub 2018), the Palestinian Cinema Group emerged in 1972 and issued its own six-point manifesto, drawing on the Palestinian revolution's transnational appeal, a Marxist critique of Arab commercial cinema and the radical formalism of the early days of the Palestinian revolution (Denes 2014). While the two revolutionary third cinemas of the Popular Unity Filmmakers and the PFU have very obvious structural differences (revolution *within* a State and revolution *without* a State), it is the loss of their nascent political projects in the 1970s, and exile from both a place and political idea that gives them commonality.

In the case of Miguel Littín, his position as a prominent Leftist and cultural figure in Allende's political project enforces his exile in 1973, first to Mexico and then to Spain. While Hebar El Attar argues that the 'inherited displacement [from his paternal grandfather] silently nurtured his diasporic subjectivity' (El Attar 2019: 187), it is my contention that it is the painful nostalgic exile from both his country and from the idea of a secular liberation project that nurtures his exile but also awakens a post-exile 'late style' diasporic re-engagement with Palestine. This is prompted by the political uprising of the First Intifada and a revisiting of his popular memory structures of his early 'resistance in exile' works. As explored in Chapter 1, the shared loss of Palestine and Chile is a secular revolutionary politics lost to those Septembers of 1970 and 1973. Namely, an archival nostalgia *for* and questioning *of* a revolutionary politics lost to institutionalization, defeat and the 'long night of counterrevolution' that is neoliberalism's hegemony (Wayne 2001: 130). Littín discussed what might be termed his 'becoming-Palestinian' as a Chilean youth in a panel discussion with PFU filmmaker Khadijeh Habashneh in 2020, 'Filming Revolution, Building Solidarities'. The focus of the discussion is the transnational connections of the Third World in general and Third cinemas in particular. Littín notes that he was educated as a child as a Chilean citizen, but as a student and Leftist in the late 1960s, his Palestinian consciousness was awakened in part by racialized insults at school and university (Littín 2020), such as *turco* and *turco comunista* (recalling the anecdote of Andrea earlier in this chapter). Such pejoratives 'led us to radicalize in university and understand the struggles of the Palestinian people and the fedayeen' (ibid.). This personal awakening is in conjunction with Littín's growing political awareness of Tricontinental revolutionary struggle tying Latin America to Palestine and other liberation movements. The struggle of the fedayeen is one Littín frames as somewhat analogous to the Chilean one, in that as much as it is a national liberation movement, it is fundamentally also a class struggle, focussed on the impoverished conditions and marginalization of the rural peasant class (in Chile, the focus of Littín's first film). The opening pages of Edward Said's 'Emergence' chapter of *After the Last Sky* (1986) discusses the class aspect of the Palestinian struggle at length, focussing on rural and migrant labour. It is the class struggle of 'alienated labor' that Said recognizes as obliterating any orientalist 'exotic romance' attaching itself to Jean Mohr's images of rural Palestinian labourers. Despite a sometimes problematic representation of Palestinians, a similar class consciousness sustains Pier Paolo Pasolini's notion of a pan-South (examined in detail in the next chapter), a topos which includes Palestinian rural workers at the margins of Israel, and South Italian rural workers at the margins of Italy. Littín's political-aesthetic concerns for emancipatory politics, popular memory and class struggle – forged as a young Chilean-Palestinian Leftist engaged in *tiers-mondisme* and sustained among the Chilean-Palestinian Left in 'an inherent opposition to miliary rule' (Schwabe 2018: 657) – would inform his diasporic return to Palestine more than thirty years later.

Littín's exile from Chile would interrupt his third film, *La Tierra Prometida* (The Promised Land, 1973), which was shot in Chile and edited and released in Mexico, where Littín spent his first decade of exile. The two films bridging his exile, *La Tierra Prometida* and *Actas de Marusia* (Letters from Marusia, 1976), very much correspond to a 'popular memory'[4] structure which Littín proclaims as a maxim of the Popular Unity Filmmakers' Manifesto and Teshome H. Gabriel cites as the 'cultural front' of militancy in Third Cinema (Gabriel 1989: 55),[5] a front in which he places Miguel Littín. Littín himself states that it is a duty of Chilean revolutionary cinema to 'recover the traces of those great popular struggles falsified by official history, and give back to the people the true version of these struggles as a legitimate and necessary heritage for confronting the present and envisaging the future' (Littín 2014: 251). Gabriel's spatial distinction within Third Cinema of a militant struggle and a cultural struggle in regions within and without the Third World is an interesting one (Gabriel 1989: 55), particularly as he focusses on Chile and Littín's work before and after his exile. The question of semantics over 'a cinema of resistance' and a 'cinema of exile' in post-1973 Chile caused contention among Littín and his contemporaries. José Miguel Palacios charts the trajectory of post-coup Chilean cinema with a focus on Miguel Littín and Raul Ruiz, charting in particular the former's resistance to terming a cinema *in* exile, 'of exile'. In part, this is due to what Palacios, drawing on Littín's own thought, refers to as a shifting of temporalities, from acceleration, to arrest and suspension (Palacios 2016). Palacios expands on these temporalities in the following passage:

In Allende's last months in power, the historical experience of the Chilean people was defined by velocity: important events would succeed each other in a matter of hours, not even days. But once in exile, their experience became defined by waiting: nothing happens because the only event that *could* happen would be the fall of the dictatorship, which would allow the exiles to return. So if the popular unity meant historical acceleration, resistance meant arrest. (ibid.: para. 52)

The semantic tension between a 'cinema of resistance' and 'a cinema of exile' is somewhat complicated by the notion of return. Exile as nothing more than waiting for a return somewhat underplays the role of, to borrow from Said, remaining philosophically out of place: that is, in an untimely position in relation to one's contemporary moment. Littín's multiple returns during exile, after exile and from the diaspora to Palestine, all retain a critical untimeliness, in which he is never at home when home, in the spirit of what Said saw as Adorno's ethical demand of exile. The films which chart these journeys will be the focus of the rest of this chapter.

Clandestine in Chile: *Actas de Chile* (Miguel Littín, 1986)

Miguel Littín's exile from Chile was temporarily interrupted in 1985, in circumstances made famous by Gabriel Garcia Marquez in his mimetic memoir,[6] *Clandestine in Chile* (1987). Littín entered Chile disguised as a Uruguayan businessman, accompanied by three film crews who entered Chile legally with permits to work (putatively) on different documentaries (Marquez 1987: 3). Littín and his crews shot over 100,000 feet of film (ibid.: xxix), with the resulting documentary, *Acta General de Chile* (General Report on Chile, 1986), running for 4 hours. Littín edited a 105-minute version, *Actas de Chile* (Reports on Chile, 1986), for international theatrical release. The film, as the title implies, is constructed of the testimonies of those subject to Pinochet's regime, who give 'reports' on the state of the nation. It is constructed of both Littín's reflections on his clandestine return and the toll of the dictatorship and its capacity for resistance.

The clandestine sensibilities of the film go beyond Littín's own covert operation, to the very functioning of the dictatorship itself. The film opens on a stark image of Littín in the snow-capped Andes, before transitioning to a somewhat anonymous looking Santiago to which Littín has clandestinely returned after twelve years, a city that looks 'strange, faded and absent'. The theme of a dull, superficially innocuous veneer concealing terror runs through Littín's experience of the city on his return: a disquieting calm evaporates like the Santiago fog as one ventures deeper into Pinochet's capital, of which Littín states: 'Soon, with terrifying clarity, the true face of the hidden city begins to appear. Santiago de Chile, the country of oppression, the country of the absent smile … the country of the underground war.' These disquietingly quotidian scenes of Santiago punctuate interviews with those mostly resisting but sometimes complicit with the dictatorship. A similar scene occurs around twenty minutes in, as a seemingly innocuous night scene of traffic and a shopping centre is juxtaposed with Littín's voiceover as he states that 'behind an apparent calm, the nights of Santiago hide the dangers of a closely policed society. Plainclothes police, informers, the hours where everything is possible: arbitrary arrest, surveillance, murder, torture. Terror, in short, communicates the *raison d'etre* of the state.' This scene segues into an interview with a former agent of the regime, detailing how he would surveil, arrest and torture dissidents.

The tone and structure of the film move between mourning and defiance, particularly as it leaves Santiago, travelling to Norte Grande, Chile's most northerly region and site of the Atacama Desert and La Pampa, a mining region. This scene opens with the lyrics of *Arriba quemando el Sol*, a folk song by Violeta Parra, which tells of the harsh and unjust conditions of miners in the region. This section of the film traces the birth of the Chilean proletariat and the influence of Antofagasta-based socialist Luis Emilio Recabarren, and creates a continuum of the violence of the Chilean military towards workers, referencing the 1907 massacre of striking workers in Iqique as analogous to the assaults, detentions and disappearances the workers' movement is subjected to in Pinochet's Chile. Mourning and resistance carry the film through its next sequences, a journey to Neruda's house in Isla Negra, followed by an interview with two representatives of the Manuel Rodríguez Patriotic Front (FPMR), a Marxist-Leninist guerrilla organization which fought against Pinochet's military throughout the 1980s. In discussion with Littín they invoke the spectre of Allende in animating their struggle, claiming: 'For the Chilean people, Allende is still alive. He is still alive and he endures through the struggle of the Manuel Rodriguez Patriotic Front.' This scene, in a manner echoing Mohanad Yaqubi's *Off Frame AKA Revolution Until Victory* (2016) and its reflection on armed struggle in the wake of the lost Palestinian revolution, also reflects on the efficacy of non-violent and violent revolutionary struggle after Allende, with the FPMR seeing armed struggle as the continuation of Allende's democratic revolutionary project.

The revenants of both Allende and Pablo Neruda haunt the film's long final sequence, which begins in the rebuilt Moneda Palace. Littín's camera tours the presidential palace, while the soundtrack simultaneously plays Allende's final radio broadcast (in which he refers to the enduring 'seed' of socialism), overlaid by Littín reading a statement by Neruda in the aftermath of the coup. These two voices haunt the building and suggest the revolutionary movement arrested by the coup remains a force that can be actualized in a new form, its arrest in fact a deferral. This scene transitions into Littín's reconstruction, in an editing room, of the sounds and images of Allende's downfall. This sequence uses a combination of interviews, archival footage and freeze-frame still images of the coup. This use of still imagery recalls the arresting of the moment of loss among characteristic of earlier Chilean revolutionary cinema,[7] notably the still image in the Atacama that closes the final part of *La Battalla de Chile* (The Battle of Chile) (Patricio Guzman 1975), embalming Chile's revolutionary politics from being lost to the coup. Similarly, this freezing of painful images of a lost revolutionary moment, in the hope that doing so may realize an alternative future yet to come, recalls Annemarie Jacir's freezing of the Palestinian revolution in *When I Saw You* (Annemarie Jacir, 2012).

Remaining out of place: *Los Naufragos* (The Shipwrecked, 1995)

Littín's first film after his seventeen-year exile from Chile, *Los Naufragos* (The Shipwrecked, 1995), tells the story of Arón, a surrogate of Littín, as an exile returning from Chile after 20 years in Europe. The plot follows Arón's search for his disappeared brother, Ur. Unlike Littín's previous return from exile to an uncanny dictatorship-era Chile, this film takes place in the transition years of post-dictatorship democracy. However, both Santiagos are rendered unfamiliar, the city Littín found 'strange, faded and absent' in *Actas de Chile*, Arón describes as 'a strange and far away city'. The immediacy of the terror of the dictatorship may be gone, but, like Hamlet's Elsinore, the time is still out of joint. This is a Chile haunted by both the trauma of the dictatorship and also its economic legacy as the cradle of neoliberalism. The dictatorship may have gone, but so too, suggests the film, has the socialist dream arrested by the coup. Exile here is as much from a moment as a place, and remaining out of place in modern Chile is both Arón's burden and duty. Arón is a figure in whom traumatic loss and present criticality dwell in tension: a sense that mere restoration of the pre-1973 world is impossible but homogenous national acceptance of this democratic new Chile must also be resisted and is likewise possible since it is so haunted by past violence. This past violence creates a fragmentary structure throughout, composed of flashbacks and hauntings by Arón's brother and father, and a disorientation with the seeming societal amnesia he finds in post-dictatorship Chile.

The film's somewhat ambiguous final scene, which seems to offer closure but also explicitly opens up Chile's present to its violent past, takes place in the Atacama Desert, where Arón finds his brother's remains, who is then depicted running freely in the desert. Within this seemingly cathartic closure, however, is an ironic choice of location. The scene takes place in one of the Atacama's most iconic (and touristic) locations, *el Valle de la Luna* (the Valley of the Moon), a rock formation and popular destination. This is framed in a long shot, leaving no ambiguity over the location.

This seemingly cathartic scene, in its particular choice of shot, places state violence at the heart of this marketable, 'new' Chile however, leaving an

Figure 3.1 A monument to forgetting in *The Shipwrecked* (Miguel Littín, 1994). ©ACI Comunicaciones.

ambiguous tension between reconciliation and a violence embedded in the State that remains beyond the duration of the dictatorship.

Between the images: Diasporic return in *Cronicas Palestinas* (2001)

Miguel Littín's first cinematic engagement with Palestine comes six years after his reflection on exilic return in *Los Naufragos* (The Shipwrecked, 1995). This diasporic return to Palestine was inspired by the First Intifada of 1987–93 (El Attar 2019), whose global reach re-engaged Littín's dual diasporic and exilic subjectivities. His return from exile to Chile in the 1990s in turn reawakened a resistant Chilean-Palestinian diasporic politics cultivated by the First Intifada, prompting a late-career return to his ancestral home of Bayt Sahur, in the environs of Bethlehem. More so than *Los Naufragos*, Littín's return to Palestine recalls his earlier post-dictatorship work in its anti-colonial sensibilities. Its documentary focus on both resistance and State violence recalls *Actas de Chile*, while its use of popular memory through the works of Edward Said and Mahmoud Darwish recalls his immediate post-dictatorship 'resistance' cinema of *La Tierra Prometida* and *Actas de Marusia*. Littín's film takes place primarily in the Occupied Territories after the outbreak of the Second Intifada. The Second Intifada was marked by more violence than the First,[8] with the use of suicide bombings and massive and indiscriminate Israeli military assaults in the Occupied Territories reflected in Palestinian cinema of the period, notably *Paradise Now* (Hany Abu Assad, 2005) and *Jenin, Jenin* (Mohamad Bakri, 2002). This heightened aggression is reflected in the subtitle of Littín's documentary: *Cronicas Palestinas: Los Caminos de la Ira*. This translates as 'Palestinian Chronicles: Paths of Anger'. However, in spite of the provocative sounding title which seemingly accepts a logic of enmity, the documentary sets out, expressly, to both challenge this notion of intractable enmity and look behind the mediated images of hypervisibility that rendered Palestinians reductive, overcoded symbols of 'terror' in global media during this period.

In its polyphonic structure and self-conscious subjectivity, the film is somewhat essayistic in its approach to Palestine. This is demonstrated in its opening scene, in which Littín's shadow is cast on the ground with the outline of his camera, acting as a statement of reflexivity of the authored nature of the work. Other than this literal foreshadowing, Littín's presence and voice are absent. The voice of the work is that of the Chilean writer Dauno Tótoro, who narrates the journey through the West Bank, Jerusalem and Gaza. The essayistic approach is further emphasized in the film's use of literary quotation on screen, the words of Isaac Asimov and Edward Said and the poetry of Mahmoud Darwish punctuating its use of interviews. Perhaps most explicitly the film opens (and closes) in the register of attempting to tackle a problem, the representation of Palestine and Palestinians in global media. Indeed, the question of attempting, of trying to debate a problem through film is at the root of the very meaning of essay, as Edgar Morin recognizes, when he states that 'talking of essay film, I would rather refer to the attitude of he who attempts (*essai*-essay, but also attempt) to debate a problem by using all the means that cinema affords, all the registers and all the expedients' (Morin [1996] in Rascaroli, 2008: 39).

Littín's film essays/attempts a search of a Palestinian-ness between hypervisibility and invisibility. His position as a diasporic Chilean-Palestinian drives an interrogation of how Palestine is coded in global media discourse. In the film's opening sequence, after shots of protestors and tanks, Tótoro's voiceover states that 'we have become accustomed to the fact that Palestine is nothing more than permanent bad news. The images we see are disturbing: of stones thrown by children at tanks. Of blood. But what is there between the tanks and the protestors that is hidden in this dark space ignored by all, silenced?' This image, of uncoded 'gaps' between the images of a hegemonic discourse that reduces Palestinians to mere signifiers of endless conflict, recalls Edward Said's resistance to the orientalized prose he can almost see forming on the surface of Mohr's images in *After the Last Sky*. That is to say, a dense overcoding of myth and cliché (hypervisibility) has a history of obscuring the actual lived experience of Palestinians (invisibility) from the frame, as Said notes warily when contemplating Mohr's photographs of peasant workers:

> The unadorned fact that they show working people of the peasant class is constantly compromised by bits of prose floating across their surfaces. 'Shepherds in the field', says one such tag, and you could add, 'tending their flocks, much as the Bible says they did'. Or, the two photographs of women evoke phrases like 'the timeless East', and 'the miserable lot of women in Islam'. (Said 1986: 92–3)

The hypervisibility of Islam and putative invisibility of Christianity within Palestinian communities is another orientalizing discourse in global media which Littín's film attempts to address. While in its nascence in the Second Intifada, the visibility of Islamic fundamentalism within Palestinian resistance movements and the concurrent militarized securitization of the West Bank by the IDF throughout the Intifada would foreshadow a global securitization that would 'Palenstianize' (Collins 2011) those surveilled by the 'Global War on Terror'. That is to say, while Palestinian resistance, whether secular or religious, had long been codified by its opponents as 'terror',[9] the increasing prominence of Hamas and its military wing, the Al-Qassam Brigades,[10] during and after the Second Intifada, almost contemporaneous with the post-9/11 world of Western foreign policy, created a new signifier for Palestinian resistance, one which is still employed in Israeli policy. In the post-9/11 world, 'Hamas' has become a discursive synecdoche for 'Palestine', a potent linguistic weapon in particular for Likud to code Palestinian subjectivity as nothing more than a signifier of the absolute enmity of 'Radical Islam' to the West and its allies.[11] Littín's film – as its opening words suggest – looks behind these discursive figures of 'security' and 'terror', which were hegemonic during the Second Intifada, to examine Palestinian-ness fully, while also considering Israeli voices in a 'history of the present' of the political status quo (Foucault 1977). In a manner similar to his 1986 *Acta General de Chile* (General Report on Chile), the film almost presents a General Report on Palestine. It presents a range of community viewpoints, from prominent religious figures in Palestine's Christian Community, to the Israeli film director Amos Gitai, Peace Now activist Michal Shohat and Palestinian rights campaigner Hanan Ashwari. Viewpoints include binationalism and the two-State solution, and the interviews open with reflections on the colonial roots of the current situation and Muslim–Christian relations within Palestinian communities. In the opening interview, Michel Sabbah (Latin Patriarch of Jerusalem) reflects on Sykes Picot and Balfour, and the irreconcilable promises made by Imperial powers during the First World War leaving an impossible situation which, at the end of the British Mandate, the British Empire simply abandoned.[12]

The follow-up interview is with Dr Theodosius Hanna (Greek Orthodox Archimandrite of Jerusalem), in which he rejects any idea of religious conflict in a site at the epicentre of the three major monotheistic religions. Rejecting an Israeli Jewish/Palestinian Muslim dichotomous enmity, he cites Zionism, rather than Judaism, as a project that (ironically) sees Christians and Muslims as indivisible. Hanna argues, 'Christians are an indivisible part of the Arab Palestinian people. Christians and Muslims have the same roots, the same nationality, the same identity, they speak the same language … therefore, the aggressor does not distinguish between Christians and Muslims.' The distinction

Zionism makes between Jewishness and Arabness has a problematic history (as explored in the previous chapter). Nonetheless, this logic is at the core of early Zionism's settler colonialism, encapsulated in Golda Meir's oft-quoted assertion that 'they [Palestinians] did not exist'. As Littín's follow-up film *La Ultima Luna* (2005) examines, patriotism of place and Palestinian identification existed in Ottoman Palestine and denying any specificity of place to Arab peoples would be crucial to a logic of continuing displacement in the Zionist imagination. This specificity of place is insisted upon by Hanna: that Palestinian Christians and Palestinian Muslims make up the Palestinian Arab people, which for Zionism is negated merely to 'Arab', a presence defined by negation foreshadowing the words of Edward Said. Said is paraphrased in text in the subsequent scene, reflecting that, rather than being exterminated, exploited or assimilated 'we've never existed for them'. This inexistence was something Said came back to throughout his writing and reflections on his own identity, in the United States more often 'Arab intellectual' than 'exiled Palestinian'. The question of non-belonging and identity in negation is one which opens Said's *The Question of Palestine* (1979) and occurs throughout *After the Last Sky* (1986), as the following rhetorical question demonstrates: 'Who are the Palestinians? "The inhabitants of Judea and Samaria." Non-Jews. Terrorists. Troublemakers. DPs. Refugees. Names on a card. Numbers on a list' (Said 1986: 26). It is *against* this identity as negation (non-Jew), or in Littín and Tótoro's own words, *in favour* of the 'acknowledgement of the other' (recalling – or perhaps challenging – Levinas),[13] that the documentary proceeds. In spite of the Second Intifada and its dynamics of military resistance and force being the dominant context, the film makes a case for what 'Palestinian-Jewish'[14] artist and activist Juliano Mer Khamis would term 'cultural intifada'.[15] This notion that the act of making and producing art under occupation is itself a resistant (and discursively violent) act was crucial to Mer Khamis's politics of liberation, and Littín's film makes a similar statement on the Music Conservatory of Ramallah, in a sequence in the middle of his film. Tótoro's voiceover introduces the students practicing in the conservatory, noting that mere meters away from the room lies the barricade and the clash point between protestors and soldiers, and that bullets and music soundtrack the day. This juxtaposition leads Tótoro to reflect that 'perhaps, in a way both the music and the stones are part of the Al-Aqsa Intifada. Both are resistance, only the setting of the war changes.' This segment is a wider reflection on the role of art in both resistance and dialogue: Haji Ibrahim (director of the El Funoun Cultural Centre) speaks of the importance of 'politicizing' Palestinian art in a context where it is always already a weapon, before Amos Gitai stresses the importance of Palestinian and Israeli artists acting as a 'bridge' between the two porous cultures at a time of political impasse. It is striking that at a time of seeming hopelessness, in which the Western orthodoxy of the two-State solution prevailed despite the increasing archipelago-like nature of the occupied West Bank rendering it an absurdity (acknowledged by the film), *Cronicas Palestinas* seems to find hope in the very unpartitionable nature of the land and culture. Nevertheless, it is a hope founded on a mutual recognition that, as the journey progresses, Littín finds it increasingly difficult to locate. After briefly examining the politics of water access and arable land in the West Bank, the final segment takes place in Gaza. Here, Tótoro reflects that the journey 'between the images' in which they thought they might be beginning to understand 'the magnitude and difficulty of the situation' was about to descend into incomprehension. Gaza at this point was still a formally Occupied Territory, with disengagement still four years away.[16] The film's penultimate scene takes place in Rafah, on Gaza's border with Egypt. The precariousness of this border is noted by Tótoro, who notes that 'we were on the edge, and it wasn't just a geographical border: On the other side of the sandbag barricade was the border with Egypt. On this side was the border with death.' The 'border with death' refers to what at that time was known as the 'Philadelphia Corridor', a military buffer zone patrolled by Israel to prevent Palestinian movement and people (and weapons) between Egypt and Gaza (as part of the 1979 Egypt–Israel peace treaty). During the Second Intifada, the buffer zone was the site of Israeli military assaults on the Rafah refugee camp under the rubric of 'Securitization'. The camera settles on a group of children chatting and playing behind a barricade, before approaching a rifle embrasure, through which can be seen an Israeli flag, an artillery casemate with machine gun and a camera. Tótoro notes that the machine gun, hundreds of meters away, is operated remotely. This very literal asymmetric warfare, between human and non-human actors, prompts a final reflection on recognition of the other: 'We knew, at last, looking out to the other side, the one we had been looking for since the beginning of this journey descending into the hells of irrationality: there was no one on the other side.'

With a graphic match of the embrasure and the rising sun, the film ends with the words of poet Mahmoud Darwish and a lament for Kafr Qāsim.[17] This cry for justice and appeal to popular memory to politically challenge the present recalls Littín's own *Actas de Marusia* (Letters from Marusia, 1976) and his commitment to challenging the State and the status quo through popular memory's revolutionary 'look back to the future' (Gabriel 1989: 54). Closing on the words of Darwish and a poem of popular memory both recalls Littín's cinema of resistance in exile, tying his early work to his late work, and also cites a Palestinian poet whose own notion of Palestinian-ness was a composite of all the cultures that had passed through the land. It is in such a space that the figures of Arab and Jew are composites of one another. This notion Darwish expanded on in conversation with the Israeli poet Helit Yeshurun, writing,

> The Jew won't be ashamed to find the Arab element within him, and the Arab won't be ashamed to acknowledge that he is also composed of Jewish elements. Especially when speaking about 'Eretz Israel' in Hebrew and 'Palestine' in Arabic. I am the son of all the cultures that have passed through the land – the Greek, the Roman, the Persian, the Jewish, the Ottoman. (Darwish 2012: 52)

This final acoustic image of Darwish's cry of popular memory as an unpartionable Palestinian-ness allows a future anterior radical thinking of the political, opening it out beyond its horizon of the Second Intifada to contrapuntally critique the contemporary status quo: a political deadlock which is both preserved and strengthened by a false dichotomy viewing the figures of Arab and Jew and Palestine and Israel as partitionable and oppositional figures in a historically constructed relation of enmity.

'I've heard Chile is a new Palestine!': *La Ultima Luna* (2005)

Littín returns to Bayt Jala and Bayt Sahur, and to the questions of Empire raised in his earlier documentary for his second engagement with Palestine, *La Ultima Luna* (Miguel Littín, 2005). Littín's personal reflection on his diasporic Palestinian-ness tells a fictionalized account of his father and grandfather's experience of migration from Ottoman Palestine to Chile at the outbreak of the First World War. The film opens with a preface which somewhat defamiliarizes accounts of occupation and resistance in Palestine. *Sumud* here is framed not in the context of the *Nakba* and *naksa*, but rather what the film refers to as the '400-year occupation of Palestine by the Ottoman Empire' and its corresponding 'long resistance struggle'. The film treats Palestine as a resistant entity in a continuum of occupation, as the Ottoman Empire comes to an end and Jewish settlers and British soldiers occupy the periphery.

The plot tells a semi-fictionalized story of Littín's grandfather, Soliman, and his friendship with Jacob, a Jewish immigrant from Latin America. Beyond this friendship, the shifting political alliances with the Ottomans and the British divide Soliman's family, with his cousin Gorchaba expressing Ottoman loyalty while his brother Butros is in alliance with the British.

Opening credits show historical footage of Ottoman soldiers in the First World War, before the film transitions to Ottoman Palestine in 1914. The opening long shot frames a good-natured dispute over the sale of land between Soliman (the vendor) and Jacob (the buyer), with a playful disagreement over the number of steps constituting the dimensions of the plot. This opening scene frames the concept of territory in a more open sense than what Stuart Elden terms the 'political technologies' of territory (Elden 2013: 16), which function almost as a discursive formation through which State power operates and delimits borders, a heightened reality in the contemporary Occupied Territories. The term 'territory' in Arabic usage can signify unclaimed space or land ('*ard*) or, in the more political sense, property within an administrative district (*mintaqah*). Related to the former term is farmland (*al'ard alziraeia*), the cultivation and subsequent expropriation of which has been a flashpoint of protest and political awakening among Palestinians in Israel (the Land Day protests starting in the Galilee in 1976) and the Occupied Territories. The latter is perhaps most recognizable in the building of the Security Barrier around Bil'in (the subject of Emad Burnat and Guy Davidi's 2011 film, *5 Broken Cameras*). The opening scenes of *La Ultima Luna*, however, set this relation of '*ard* as a site of (initial) benevolent transaction, as Soliman sells Jacob the land, on which the two of them will build a house with stones from neighbouring Bayt Jala.

The tension between camaraderie and suspicion towards Jewish immigrants runs through the film, a tension largely framed as exacerbated by and useful for the present (Ottoman) and future (British) occupying forces. This is seen in the dynamics of power relations throughout, as the primary political event is the passing of the 1914 conscription law requiring Ottoman subjects to join the war effort. Ottoman soldiers menace the film's early scenes, as children are heard fighting offscreen while Soliman and Jacob take tea. In the subsequent scene, Soliman's cousin, Gorchaba, bemoans his lack of seriousness in 'serious times, times of war', to which the reply comes: 'It's not *my* war. It's a war between Europe and the Turks!' This sets up the film's initial fault lines as along place and faith, rather than nation. Bayt Sahur is a primarily Christian village, which has no interest in a faraway war fighting for an Islamic Imperial power. This reflects both Baeza's (2014) and Schwabe's (2018) work on identity formation in the Chilean diaspora from Ottoman Palestine, namely that hometown, region and religion

Figure 3.2 The practice of territory in *La Ultima Luna* (Miguel Littín, 2005). ©Latido Films.

were primary identifications for this diaspora, rather than a sense of belonging to a strong Palestinian national identity. The tension between patriotism of place and patriotism of nation is a complex one, as Muhammad Muslih (1987) articulates in his analysis of Palestinian identity formation in early twentieth-century Ottoman Palestine. While scholars of the Chilean diaspora note weaker ties to Palestine as both nation and territory among pre-1920 immigration from Ottoman Palestine, Muslih paints a more complex picture in an article tracing the rise of Palestinian national consciousness. Muslih (1987) notes that Arab nationalism was by 1918 still a nascent and developing ideology building upon the political Arabism (1908–14) originating as a counterpoint to the Young Turk Revolution and leading up to the First World War (ibid.). Within this evolving consciousness, the focus on the contemporaneous growth of political Zionism in the late nineteenth and early twentieth centuries meant that Palestine became a political question and identification before the emergence of the Mandate in 1920. Muslih recognizes a consensus among scholars of Palestinian Arab politics that Palestinian opposition to Zionism in the run-up to the First World War had three strands, Ottoman loyalism, Palestinian patriotism and Arab nationalism. Expanding on these strands, he writes,

> Ottoman loyalism dictated the rejection of Zionism because it was bent upon separating Palestine from the Ottoman state; Palestinian patriotism objected on

the grounds that it was a deadly threat to Palestinians; and Arab nationalism called for opposition to Zionism because it sought to wrest Palestine away from Arab hands and thwart the cherished goal of Arab unity. (Muslih 1987: 85)

This complex interaction of Ottoman, Arab and Palestinian sentiment, particularly mixed with Christian identity in Bayt Sahur and Bayt Jala, is reflected in how *La Ultima Luna* represents Palestine as both a place and idea. Early on in the film, when discussing his family's future in South America, Gorchaba claims that from the stories he's heard that 'Chile is a new Palestine'. This notion of a new Palestine free of Empire elsewhere marks Gorchaba's viewpoint as antithetical to a pre-1948 Palestine as an Eden in itself, and marks the character as something of a prototype to Emile Habiby's titular 'pessoptimist', Saeed: a figure who finds himself somewhere between hope and despair and is caught in events and power relations beyond his control. For Gorchaba, Palestine is a continuum of occupying forces from which the escape is a 'new' Palestine in South America. This is articulated in Gorchaba's despair at being a pariah for his closeness to the Ottoman regime. 'They hate me because I'm with the Turks, but your brother is with the English' he laments to Soliman. 'It's not the same' comes the reply, to which he snaps 'it's *exactly* the same!' He later tells Soliman that in turn, 'we'll do business with the Jews'. This transactional necessity, which Gorchaba sees as constituent of life under a series of occupations, marks him as a distinct character of dramatic irony beyond his time. With his contemporaries welcoming the British in the context of the promise of an independent Arab State after the First World War, Gorchaba is wearily untimely, pessimistically seeing a perpetual future of transactions with occupying forces and imagining a free Palestine only elsewhere, far from the overcoded space of the Holy Land.

Gorchaba ultimately becomes a tragic figure, after his brother Butros returns with English support to rebel against the Ottoman forces, and Gorchaba is stoned to death in an attack for his Ottoman complicity. The euphoria of the British arrival is laced with historical irony, as a voiceover laments, 'After the departure of the Turks, life changed in Palestine. Our promised land became a divided land.' This notion of the British Mandate as a time of increasing tension of the irreconcilable promises made by the British counters the Mandate's self-image (still perpetuated) as a benevolent force. This tension is realized in the film's penultimate scenes, as it dawns on both Soliman and Jacob that the tractors they thought were being used to build the kibbutz in Bayt Jalar are actually carrying canons to fortify the kibbutz's territory from attack and secure land

Figure 3.3 Chile as a new Palestine in *La Ultima Luna* (Miguel Littín, 2005). ©Latido Films.

in neighbouring Bayt Sahur. This leads to accusations of betrayal, and a closing scene laced with a contemporary critique of Israel's West Bank 'security barrier' (under construction at the time of filming): A shot/reverse shot sequence begins in close-up and slowly zooms in to Soliman and Jacob's faces, as they look mournfully into each other's eyes, the frame and their faces now striated by the barbwire fence separating the kibutz (and Jacob's house) from Soliman and his family. This scene both foreshadows and laments the occupation and partition of contemporary Bayt Sahur as not a historical inevitability but a legacy of the Empire.

Coda: A transversal consciousness

In his discussion on revolutionary solidarity in third cinemas, Littín describes Chilean revolutionary cinema's purpose as an attempt 'to create a transversal consciousness' (Littín 2020). This notion of a consciousness which intersects strata sees, at a national level, the spectator and filmmaker become 'participant comrades' in the revolutionary struggle (Getino and Solinas 1969: 130). However, at a transnational level it creates intersections between revolutionary struggles across the Third World. Both Littín and Khadijeh Habashneh (a filmmaker in her own right but also married to Mustafa Abu Ali) reflect on discussions they had with militant filmmakers in Algeria in 1973 (at the fourth Summit of the Non-Aligned Movement in Algiers). Both discuss the influence of and admiration for Cuban filmmaker Santiago Alvarez, with Habashneh recalling an anecdote in which Alvarez met Abu Ali and proclaimed him a 'new Alvarez' (Habashneh 2020). These meetings in Algeria, for Littín, would embed his Palestinian politics into his Chilean, a revolutionary consciousness which would give his late Palestinian works a diasporic and exilic positioning: a diasporic 'homecoming' infused with an exilic, critical homelessness forged in the anti-colonial Third World.

The archival turn examined in Chapter 1 is not just limited to the contrapuntal engagement with the images of the Palestinian revolution but also a wider engagement with its transnational reach and its transnational consciousness. This is demonstrated in Eric Baudelaire's focus on the legacy of Japanese and Palestinian radical politics in contemporary Beirut and Tokyo in *The Anabasis of May and Fusako Shigenobu, Masao Adachi, and 27 Years without Images* (2011) and Mohanad Yaqubi's and Eyal Sivan's engagement with Godard's forbidden montages. It is also reinforced by the bringing together of Littín and Habashneh to discuss transcontinental revolution and transversal South–South solidarity. This discussion itself builds on a 2017 documentary charting Latin American and Palestinian revolutionary networks, *Palestina: Imágenes Robadas (Palestine's Stolen Images)* (Rodrigo Vázquez, 2017). The film's point of departure is the discovery in Cuba of an Argentine militant solidarity film with the Palestinian revolution. From this, Vázquez moves between this past archive and the present, putting the Palestinian present in conversation with other liberation struggles both armed and unarmed: from the Bolivian indigenous land rights movement, to Colombia's armed Marxist-Leninist National Liberation Army (ELN). A reflection on violent and non-violent struggle and its imagery puts *Palestina: Imágenes Robadas* in conversation with Mohanad Yaqubi's work and extends it to a reflection on contemporary legacies of Palestinian and Latin American revolutionary movements in a historical moment 'without a revolutionary subject' (Malm and the Zetkin Collective 2021: 320).

A thinking of transversal consciousness operating on both a spatial and temporal plane allows the atonal cinema under study in this book to intersect vertically with a historical revolutionary archive and horizontally with other marginalized struggles, as the contrapuntal responses of a transnational Palestine to Pier Paolo Pasolini's *tiers-mondisme* examined in the next chapter will demonstrate.

4

Between Basilicata and Bethlehem: Pasolini, Palestine and the non-European

The previous chapter explored the contrapuntal currents of the *archē*,[1] between diasporic arisings and exilic becomings in Palestine and Chile and how the transnational links between those countries' lost revolutions sustain a Palestinian image that resists being partitioned from other histories of struggle. This chapter explores the virtues and limits of *tiers-mondisme* in Pier Paolo Pasolini's *Sopralluoghi in Palestina* (*Location Hunting in Palestine*) (Pasolini 1965), examining these '*archē-ic*' currents between past and present and the south of Italy and Palestine through two Palestinian works which invert the European gaze towards Palestine and in the process uncovered hidden traces of Palestine in the remnants of Euro-American visual culture.

Reading Pasolini contrapuntally

Sopralluoghi in Palestina (*Location Hunting in Palestine*) (Pasolini 1965) documents the filmmaker's search for the archaic remains of a biblical world within which to locate his telling of *Il Vangelo secondo Matteo* (*The Gospel According to St. Matthew*) (Pasolini 1964). Pier Paolo Pasolini's search in Israel and Jordan was eventually (and intentionally) abandoned, the places and faces deemed – seemingly paradoxically – both 'too modern' and 'too archaic'. Pasolini would displace biblical Palestine to Southern Italy, with *The Gospel According to St. Matthew* being filmed in and around Basilicata.

Both the failure *of* and issues of representation *in* Pasolini's search make the film a fertile object with which Palestinian artists have conducted dialogues. This chapter will read Pasolini's documentary contrapuntally through two such responses, *Pasolini Pa* Palestine* (Ayreen Anastas 2005) and *Ouroboros* (Basma Alsharif 2017a). Such a reading and focus addresses a gap in research.

Existing scholarship on Pasolini's engagement with Palestine either reads his work alongside Godard and Agamben as constructing a topology of place and language at the exclusion of responses from Palestinian filmmakers (Gustafsson 2015), or situates *Sopralluoghi in Palestina* within his *Appunti* ('Notes') essay films[2] of the late 1960s (Trento 2012; Caminati 2016, 2019). However, as Noa Steimatsky (2008: 121) has recognized, the production and funding context of *Sopralluoghi in Palestina* mark it somewhat apart from the *Appunti* films, and – as I will argue in this chapter – this context means the film lacks the openness of those works, too often flattening Palestinian subjects as mere signifiers of an archaic, biblical world. This contribution to a reductive 'Image of Palestine' has provoked responses from Anastas and Alsharif which, I argue, both critique and revitalize Pasolini's original work. While these contemporary Palestinian artists construct new works in which Pasolini's blind spots are critically examined, this very process of examination revitalizes the original text through new insights and possibilities discovered within it.

Ouroboros's engagement with Carlo Levi in its Basilicata sections means that this chapter more accurately resembles a quartet across time and place, from Levi and Pasolini's Basilicata of the 1930s and 1960s to Ayreen Anastas's and Basma Alsharif's contemporary responses from the West Bank and Gaza. This structure awakens contemporary political questions which – drawing on Pasolini's own thinking of a *Panmeridione* (pan-South) and the notion of 'Palestinian-ness' as a global *topos* of subalternity reflected in Europe and North America – challenge the reductive yet persistent East/West binaries through which Palestine-Israel is framed. With this in mind, the chapter concludes by proposing that the intersection of these artworks forms a dialectical image of Palestine, which exists as a *topos* in the currents that flow between Levi's and Pasolini's Basilicata and Anastas's and Alsharif's Palestine.

Said's contrapuntal notion of reading a cinematic text beyond both its author's critical limits and its historical boundaries will be crucial to my reading of Pasolini in this chapter. Pasolini was a figure whose Gramscian view of the revolutionary conjuncture compelled him to displace Palestine to Basilicata, but whose failure to fully realize the subjects of his documentary necessitated contemporary responses. While Pasolini's documentary is both the focus of this chapter and of Anastas's and Alsharif's films, an engagement with an archive of images both from and about Palestine, as we have seen in preceding chapters, characterizes this atonal cinema.

'Yes the biblical world appears, but it resurfaces like wreckage': Location scouting in Palestine with Pasolini

In preparation for what would become his telling of *The Gospel According to St. Matthew*, Pasolini spent the summer of 1963 conducting a location-scouting exercise, hoping to uncover authentically biblical sites for his retelling of the Gospel. Pasolini explored potential locations, accompanied by Don Andrea Carraro and Dr Lucio Settimo Caruso of the Pro Civitate Christiana, Walter Cantatore and his producer Alfredo Bini of Arco Film, and the cinematographer Aldo Pennelli. The documentary, which lasts fifty-two minutes, follows (somewhat erratically) the events of Matthew's Gospel. The film travels from the environs of Mount Tabor and Lake Tiberias, along the Jordan River and on to Nazareth. Detours take the film crew to a Druze village, a Kibbutz and Beersheba, in the Negev Desert. They then travel on to the Dead Sea and Jerusalem (then divided between Israel and Jordan), before crossing the border into Jordan and completing the trip in Bethlehem. Accompanied by his religious advisor, Don Andrea, *Sopralluoghi in Palestina* records Pasolini's quest to uncover the faces and places of his biblical imagination. What emerges through Pasolini's location-scouting exercise is a dense, overcoded and archaic 'Image of Palestine' which is always already lost to Israeli modernity. The production context of the film itself is important to understanding both the mise en scène and Pasolini's somewhat unguarded and unself-critical engagement with the subjects of his documentary. The journey to Israel and Jordan (as it then was) was funded by the Pro Civitate Christiana, with whom Pasolini had stayed in 1962, reading the Gospel and discovering the genesis for his retelling of it (Steimatsky 2008: 120). The resulting documentary is often contextualized among his *tiers-mondiste* documentaries of the 1960s, and particularly as an early 'note' towards the unrealized screenplay *Appunti per poema sul Terzo Mondo* (*Notes for a Poem on the Third World*) (Pasolini 1968) (Caminati 2016, 2019). However, the film stands as somewhat of a curiosity – particularly in its creative genesis as a work in and of itself – as Pasolini elaborates:

> When we went to the Middle East there was a cameraman with us who was sent along by the production company. I never suggested a thing to him, because I wasn't thinking of using the material to make a film, I just wanted some documentation which would help me set *The Gospel*. (Stack 1969: 73)

Pasolini is something of an unreliable narrator when retelling the genesis of the film, claiming in the same interview on *Sopralluoghi in Palestina* both that 'I realized it [the footage] was all no use – that was after a few hours of driving' (ibid.: 76), and on the relocation to South Italy that 'I had decided to do this even before I went to Palestine, which I only did to set my conscience at ease' (ibid.: 82). Perhaps this seemingly contradictory account of intentions should not come as a surprise from an artist who, by his own admission, embraced self-contradiction. Nevertheless, given what we assume is a preconceived sense of failure, Pasolini's journey is inevitably conditioned by a separation of 'modernity' and 'archaic' into orientalist dichotomies of an industrialized, Euro-Israeli culture and an ancient pre-modern Arab culture encompassing Palestinian and Druze populations. In this way, Pasolini's pilgrimage to scout face and places takes its place within a long tradition of both colonial exploration and biblical tourism in the Holy Land, particularly in the nineteenth and early twentieth centuries. Kay Dickinson (2016), following Edward Said, Mahmoud Darwish and W. J. T. Mitchell, identifies a 'place-myth' of Palestine-Israel. This refers to the historical intersection of crusades, colonialism and tourism to the region, and corresponding claims of ownership and practices of occupation which 'do not just describe the land, they have created it' (Dickinson 2016: 82). Such practices create an image so dense as to obscure the actual lived landscape, which in turn reduces Palestinians to extras in a tableau vivant of biblical imagery and elides them from the frame of 'modernity'.

Sopralluoghi in Palestina opens around 50 km from Tel Aviv, where Pasolini – after spending all morning travelling through countryside 'modern and very similar to Italy' – finds a scene which corresponds to his biblical archaic vision, a peasant separating wheat from chaff. While Pasolini observes the scene in satisfaction, Don Andrea references its parallels to Matthew 3:12, where John the Baptist addresses the Pharisees.

The scene is framed initially in medium shot – the 'shepherd' an image of pre-industrial, archaic purity Pasolini is seeking – before cutting to a long shot, with the peasant farmer in the centre and Pasolini and Don Andrea observing right of centre. Modernity soon contaminates sound and image in ironic juxtaposition. The scene is shot just off the road, which can be seen in the immediate background of the long shot. While Pasolini articulates his satisfaction at the 'archaic' scene, a 1950s car passes directly behind them, a signifier of modernity puncturing the fictitiously idealized (and orientalized) pastoral scene. This scene also recalls the quote from *After the Last Sky* (1986)

Figure 4.1 Archaic contamination as Orientalist cliché in *Sopralluoghi in Palestina* (Pier Paolo Pasolini, 1965). ©Arco Film.

from the previous chapter, in which Said cautions of orientalist cliché attaching itself to such images.

The biblical congruence of face, place and gesture that Pasolini hoped to find dissipates from this point on, with Pasolini's archaic, biblical land revealing itself to be irredeemably modern. The scene above is the first of several where Pasolini frames the non-Jewish figures in Palestine-Israel through a distinctly orientalist gaze. 'Archaic', 'savage' and 'primitive' all occur in descriptions of Arab-Palestinian and Druze populations, as Pasolini scans their faces in search of correspondence with his preconceived image. This burying of images beneath language has a long history in the Holy Land; freeing these images from Pasolini's discourse is one of the problems Ayreen Anastas will debate in *Pasolini Pa* Palestine*.

Pasolini's way of seeing frames the landscape, to paraphrase Walter Benjamin, as one of pathological modernity embedded with shards of archaic time. Just three minutes into the documentary we find Pasolini again lamenting the disjuncture between reality and expectation, as towards Nazareth he encounters 'un paesaggio contaminato dalla modernità', which translates as 'a landscape contaminated by modernity'. This notion of modernity corrupting a pure, archaic essence runs through Pasolini's broader aesthetics, and therefore Pasolini's evolving concept of contamination – as both an aesthetic and ideological process – requires some explication.

Critical and ideological contamination in Pasolini

The concept of contamination in Pasolini, as documented (Steimatsky 2008; Forgacs 2019), constitutes a specific aesthetic practice, a mixing of high and low styles and voices to produce new aesthetic experiences. These function as 'a creative kind of dirtying, one that worked to "pull up" the low and "pull down" the high' (Forgacs 2019: 22). This is witnessed in Pasolini's early feature filmmaking, in the contamination of Bach and Vivaldi with the Roman *borgate* (working-class suburbs) in *Accattone* (Pasolini 1961) and *Mamma Roma* (Pasolini 1962), respectively, and the contamination of contemporary music with scripture in *The Gospel According to St. Matthew*.

Much of the focus on Pasolini's use of contamination frames it as a productive, creative force, a dialectics which provokes new forms of thought. In his article 'Dirt and Order in Pasolini', David Forgacs makes an important distinction, tracing an evolution in Pasolini's work from positive contamination to negative (Forgacs 2019: 23). Whereas the former is a stylistic and formal approach to artistic dirtying, the latter – a turn towards contamination in an almost biological sense – emerges as a thematic rather than formal response to a cancerous moral corruption of purity by ideological forms, be they Fascism or capitalist modernity. It is this move from contamination to corruption that Forgacs highlights in Pasolini's work predominantly (but by no means exclusively) after the late 1960s, illustrated in allegorical forms of corruption in *Porcile* (*Pigsty*) (Pasolini 1969) and *Salò o le 120 giornate di Sodoma* (*Salò, or the 120 Days of Sodom*) (Pasolini 1975) (Forgacs 2019: 23).

Following Forgacs, it is my contention that this primarily aesthetic repulsion towards ideological contamination marks *Sopralluoghi in Palestina* as distinct from the other *Appunti* films, which use critical contamination to pose political questions and self-critique. This is most explicit in *Appunti per un'Orestiade Africana* (*Notes Towards an African Orestes*) (Pasolini 1970), which contains elements of self-reflexivity (the opening scene questioning the cinematic self) and critical contamination (questions of Statehood and justice framed through a resituating of the *Oresteia*) to think through ideological contamination (the loss of the archaic aspect of the non-aligned world). In contrast, contamination in *Sopralluoghi in Palestina* is precisely this negative thematic form, expressed as a corrupt form of modernity dirtying archaic forms which, for Pasolini, emerge very occasionally as 'wreckage' (both the 'biblical' world and the 'Arab' world are framed in these terms). This is taken as a justification for his decision to displace the Gospel to a South Italy more authentically archaic but with the analogical potential for political critique.

Pasolini, Palestine and the pan-South

Upon hearing Pasolini's doubts over representing the Holy Land and rectifying the discordance between his imagination and the landscape itself, Don Andrea proposes the idea of displacing the film elsewhere, albeit for different reasons. Seemingly drawing on the incompatibility of the Holy Land with the plastic arts, he advises Pasolini, 'No image can be created here. It has to be absorbed and reinvented elsewhere. The specific purpose should be this: condense and absorb the spirit. Then, possibly, relive it, rebuild it, invent it perhaps; in another setting, another place.'

For Pasolini, this reinvention elsewhere is informed by his own interpretation of Marxist and Gramscian thought, seeing the social relations and disparity of wealth in Palestine-Israel analogously through his own European framework. This approach compels him to see in the non-Jewish populations of Palestine an echo of the 'European lumpenproletariat', those set outside of history within Pasolini's own context. It cannot be understated how central a theme this is throughout his work, from his early poetry to his late documentaries. Pasolini's own reformulation of Gramsci's Southern Question imagines a political and cultural 'South' far beyond the borders of Italy. This is what Giovanna Trento terms 'the Pan-South (*Panmeridione*)' (Trento 2012: 59). This concept is thought of topologically rather than geographically, as shifting points of place and language in a network comprising 'peasantry, dialects, pre-modern societies, Rome's sub-proletarian suburbs, rural Friuli, urban Naples, the Arab world, and sub-Saharan Africa' (Trento 2012: 60). Behind this thinking lies what Noa Steimatsky terms 'the persistence of archaic forms in the contemporary world' (Steimatksy 2008: 133). These archaic forms include landscapes, gestures and language which remain outside the homogenizing, industrializing forces of late Capitalist modernity. It is in such archaic remnants – 'a heap of wheat, the gestures of a farmer, and, most prominently, in the pagan, pre-Christian faces extolled by Pasolini in Druze villages or among tribes of Bedouins in the desert' – that Henrik Gustafsson identifies Pasolini's analogical method (Gustafsson 2015: 207).

Beyond Pasolini's use, these ideas of the archaic and the *archē* (origin) have a complex philosophical history, which needs contextualizing.

Locating the archaic

In Aristotelian thought, the *archē* is a founding principle or concept, which is logically bound to a *telos*, or end goal, a principle crucial to both Hegelian and Marxist philosophy. Pasolini, with an understanding of both Greek mythology and Marxian thought, has a nuanced and complex understanding of the archaic, which for him signifies more of a geographical and linguistic notion than a temporal understanding. Rather than historical reconstruction, he is concerned with transposing remnants of the past to analogously critique contemporary social and industrial relations. Pasolini expands on this, stating that 'Southern Italy allowed me to make the transposition from the ancient to the modern world without having to reconstruct it archaeologically or philologically' (Stack 1969: 82). However, a different understanding of the archaic seeks to excavate concepts (such as 'Palestine') from a historical tradition which suppresses their heterogeneity and alternative meanings.

In *The Signature of Things*, Giorgio Agamben (2009) traces the concept of a 'philosophical archaeology', drawing on Kant's metaphysics and Foucault's genealogy. The work of philosophy, and thus philosophical archaeology, is not just concerned 'with what has been, but also with what ought to and could have been' (Agamben 2009: 82). It is precisely this that gives this form of archaeology a curious temporality of a future perfect or, as Agamben terms it, a future *anterior*. Philosophical archaeology thus seeks to strip a concept of its historical tradition and open it to contingency, seeking not a historical object but a 'field of bipolar currents' through which past and present inform one another (ibid.: 110).

Reading Pasolini's archaic method as a pan-South *topos* allows for a thinking which can both transpose the Gospel into the Italian South and imagine 'Christ as an intellectual in a world of the poor available for revolution' as contemporaneously analogous to a revolutionary and archaic potential in the Italian South which can resist the hegemonic North (Stack 1969: 78). This same method can transpose Hellenic ideas of emergent justice and democracy to the postcolonial African continent.

One might argue that Pasolini's specific understanding of archaic method and subsequent act of displacement in *Sopralluoghi in Palestina* 'freed' him from both capitalist development and an overdcoded sacred space to create an analogy physically remote from the state, industrial modernity or official religious sites. However, I would argue that by framing his non-Jewish characters in his film as signifiers of 'an archaic Arab world', his romantic primitivism and discursive formations construct a reductive 'Image of Palestine' within (Western) historical tradition. Taken in and of itself, without the accompanying analogical force of *The Gospel According to St. Matthew*, *Sopralluoghi in Palestina* remains a closed text, in which the 'Arab world' is a homogenized 'spirit' trapped in an image.

The 'Note' that is not: Pasolini, the postcolonial and *struttura da farsi*

An unresolved political tension structures Pasolini's documentary in a way distinct from his *Appunti* films (whose titles indicate their experimental, open, *da farsi* (literally, 'to be made') approach). Elements of *Sopralluoghi in Palestina* suggest that Pasolini recognizes the class disparities in Palestine-Israel as analogous to those he sees in South Italy, Africa and India. Nonetheless, the tendency to uncritically reproduce founding political myths (a barren landscape linked with Arabness) and silence images of Palestinian and Arab subjects beneath orientalizing discourse makes this work particularly open to critical dialogue.

By contrast, *Notes Towards an African Orestes* contains a crucial challenge to Pasolini's somewhat paternalistic romanticism of his subjects. Towards the end of the film's first quarter, Pasolini is in a classroom presenting his ideas for a retelling of the Oresteia in Africa to a group of students in Rome. Articulating both the view that Ancient Greek society is similar to that of what he terms 'African tribal civilization', and that Orestes's discovery of justice and democracy is correlative to what has happened in contemporary postcolonial Africa, he poses the question of whether to set the film in the current day or the Africa of 1960. The first student entertains Pasolini's question, even citing a somewhat Pasolinian contamination of the African continent with the character of European modernity. Upon asking whether other students agree, however, he encounters robust critique of his Eurocentric assumptions and imprecise language. Firstly, he is told, Africa is a continent and not a country. Thus, to speak of a universal experience from the Mediterranean to the southern tip, or the Atlantic to the Indian Ocean makes no sense. Secondly, argues another student, thinking in terms of 'tribalism' is how Europe subjugated the African continent. This dialogue constitutes some of the experimental 'openness' of the

Appunti films, with Pasolini taken aback by the diversion away from his question into pointed challenges to some of his assumptions.

Whereas Pasolini's universalist assumptions about 'Africa' and 'Africans' are challenged and critiqued as part of the open construction of *Notes Towards an African Orestes*, similar universalist assumptions about 'Arabs' in *Sopralluoghi in Palestina* remain uncontested, leaving no space for Arab or, more specifically, Palestinian intellectual or cultural life beyond the frame of an 'ancient, archaic Arab world'. The unresolved tension between the Pasolini of the postcolonial Notes, and the Pasolini of orientalist location scouting in *Sopralluoghi in Palestina*, is perhaps what makes that documentary such a fertile object of engagement for both Ayreen Anastas and Basma Alsharif.

From Bethlehem to Basilicata: An *archē*-ology of repetition in *Pasolini Pa* Palestine* (Ayreen Anastas 2005)

In the philosophical (and Agambian) sense of the archaic, Ayreen Anastas employs a properly *archē*-ological approach in *Pasolini Pa* Palestine* (2005), one which opens Pasolini's work to contingency. This approach functions on multiple levels. It uncovers lost potential, unexplored paths and missteps in retracing *Sopralluoghi in Palestina*; it challenges the assumptions about and negations of Palestinian (and Arab) experience in Pasolini's original journey; finally, it remaps it to uncover the contemporary geopolitical reality of occupation.

Pasolini Pa* Palestine is a response to the filmmaker which proceeds in the spirit of Pasolini's *da farsi* approach, interrogating what Pasolini failed to see through the dual blind spots of both personal perspective and historical circumstance. Forty years after Pasolini's original, failed journey, Anastas attempts a repetition. This approach to repetition as a philosophical process is clarified by Anastas (2006: 478), who references the Heideggerian notion of *Wiederholung* (understood as repetition/retrieval) in her own description of the work. This idea sees the act of repetition itself as revealing new possibilities within the original work. The film is, by Anastas's own admission, an attempt to actualize the potential in Pasolini's abandoned trip by examining both paths not taken, and moments lost to historical circumstance.

The title of the film seems to acknowledge the ambiguous status of Pasolini's *Appunti* legacy, with the *Pa** an acknowledgement of the politically engaged but paternalistic Western filmmaker. This sound also suggests both a bi-directional stutter and an interruption; the latter travels back as mode of corrective dialogue to Pasolini's 1963 search, while the stutter indicates the staccato contemporary journey fragmented by the geopolitical impossibilities of occupation. Anastas makes an explicit reference to the film's essayistic openness when pondering the title of the film in its closing credits: 'Notes … Re Sites of Thoughts … or Notes … for a New Testament' she wonders, before settling on *Pasolini Pa* Palestine*. The 'Pa', Anastas states, could refer back to 'father', or forward to 'Palestinian Awakening'. This statement's double consciousness appears to open the present to a radical, secular revolutionary spirit of self-production of the past. The spirit here lies in the nascent moments (and experimental images) of the Palestinian revolution, now lost as mere commodity images which sustain the bureaucracy of another 'Pa', the Palestinian Authority.

At fifty-one minutes, the film occupies a near-identical duration to Pasolini's documentary. In the journey's repetition, the voices are multiplied from a dialogue to a quartet, two male and two female. Ayreen Anastas is 'the director' and Karam Tannous is credited as 'the voice' (sometimes heard in dialogue with Anastas). Suhail Shadoud and Haissam Zaina play the roles of Pasolini and Don Andrea, respectively. A tension between place and language conditions the film throughout. There is a desire to respect and imitate the cartography of Pasolini's journey, while his non-localizable terms such as 'the Arab World' and 'the spirit' trigger diversions and detours.

This is illustrated in the film's five-minute opening, which repeats abortive attempts to recreate the opening of *Sopralluoghi in Palestina*, in which the farmer separates the wheat from the chaff. The original scene takes place close to the Jordanian border (which Pasolini describes as 'the archaic spirit of the ancient Arab world') but far from the Galilee (the archaic place of the Gospel passage). These dichotomies of proximity and distance, place and spirit are played with throughout *Pasolini Pa* Palestine*. The first scene opens in Bethlehem with a close-up of a woman's hands separating grain as Shadoud paraphrases Pasolini in exclaiming luck at finding 'an image of an authentic biblical world' among a 'landscape of settlements' (explicitly replacing 'modernity'). Shadoud then further infuses Pasolini's words with geopolitical contemporaneity, referring to 'a shrinking landscape of arbitrary borders and barriers' which means Galilee (as it was for Pasolini) 'is still far from here'. The West Bank is 'near to the Arab World in spirit' and thus provides, Shadoud notes with irony, a scene 'typical for the archaic Arab world'.

At this point comes Anastas's first interjection: 'Stop! Stop!' she exclaims over a split screen of the edit suite and Pasolini's original scene. With a sense of critical irony which will condition the repetitions throughout, she states that 'for the repetition to happen we need to follow the original path'. The scene's location (Bethlehem) and domestic setting are 'corrected'. Bethlehem comes at the end of Pasolini's journey, and the setting should be more pastoral to reflect the original scene's aesthetic. The scene restarts with Anastas's command: 'Let's try again.' This next iteration relocates the coordinates ('We are in the Golan Heights, 70km from Damascus … Not far from here lies the cease-fire line') and frames a 'pastoral' scene of agricultural workers in a field. Anastas interjects again: 'The Golan is also wrong! The Galilee, not the Golan!' These proper nouns (the West Bank, the Golan, the Galilee) politicize Pasolini's original terms, connecting a topology of occupation (the former two) to a topology of loss (the dispossessed Arab villages of the Galilee).

Unexplored paths and lost pasts

The slippages of place and language throughout *Pasolini Pa* Palestine* indicate its central concern; the act of repetition uncovers possibilities within the original text which were either unforeseeable or unnoticed. Regarding the unforeseeable, the cartography which lies beyond the horizon of Pasolini's visibility is that of the 1967 occupation and its borders. Thus, the West Bank and Golan Heights become contemporary (geo)politicized markers of Pasolini's 'Arab world'. A landscape 'contaminated by modernity' in 1963 is translated into a landscape 'contaminated by settlements' in 2005. The unnoticed is expressed in *Pasolini Pa* Palestine*'s subtle critiques of the touristic naivety of the original text. These come in the second segment of the trip (Lake Tiberias), where Shadoud (as Pasolini) switches from repeating Pasolini's original words to lamenting 'repeating the same mistakes' 40 years later. The first of these is the decision to travel in the unbearable heat of summer 1963 rather than spring, a time of year 'when I could have gotten a lot more out of this landscape'. The route taken is also lamented. Shadoud's Pasolini notes that the archaic landscapes Pasolini would find in and around 1960s Matera in fact could have been found in the villages around Hebron at that time. Hebron reoccurs in a later scene. A Jerusalem-based Italian architect shows Anastas stills from the location scouting process of Franco Zeffirelli's *Gesù di Nazareth* (*Jesus of Nazareth*) (1977) and highlights their aesthetic suitability for Pasolini's Gospel.

This sequence also laments the impact of the occupation and Second Intifada on these villages and their architecture. The villages around Hebron thus constitute an element of unrealized potential for Anastas. A landscape then undiscovered by Pasolini is now lost to destruction and ruin.

A loss of different kind is expressed in the attempt to recreate Pasolini's kibbutz scene. In the original film, the kibbutz scene is its sole participatory interview. It is discussed as a model of collective living, with communitarian approaches to labour and childcare presented as an idealistic model. The contemporary repetition, eventually abandoned, sees Anastas and a German kibbutz resident discuss the loss of this ideal. The resident laments a more transactional relationship in contemporary kibbutizim, with a number being privatized and workers renting space while working elsewhere (the interviewee rents a bungalow in the kibbutz a four-minute walk from where he works). The 1963 scene is one of the few occasions where Pasolini finds a collective, communitarian aspect within a modern, increasingly capitalist State. The loss of these principles in the 2005 scene reflects this time an aspect not missed by Pasolini (in the manner of the architecture of Hebron), but lost in Israel's continuing drift from the radical, socialist aspects of its societal structures. Cumulatively, these scenes demonstrate the film's unstable, *archē*-ological temporality. It opens the original work to that which *will* have been and *could* have been.

Beyond the 'Image of Palestine'

Alongside the diversions in language necessitated by the repetitions, the film makes an explicit break with Pasolini's physical journey at the eighteen-minute mark. As the filmmakers traverse Lake Tiberias, from where Pasolini in 1963 observes 'Ancient Gadara where now Syrian soldiers fire on the Jews',[3] Anastas interjects, correcting 'Gadara' first to 'Occupied Golan' and then 'the Golan Heights', again reflecting the geopolitical reality of the 1967 borders. At this point, Shadoud signifies a break with Pasolini's journey (on to Nazareth) and their own (into the Golan Heights). This is justified as desire to move 'beyond the image'. Shadoud's statement is juxtaposed with Pasolini's footage of 'unusable' images of 'savage, pre-Christian' faces he finds in Beersheba, which correspond in his orientalist perspective to those in the Druze villages. Shadoud's follow-up words are superimposed on Pasolini's original scene and interrupt that scene's commentary. Moving beyond the image, claims Shadoud, entails freeing these images from Pasolini's words, or 'the sound that masks a certain image', a phrasing which echoes the Godardian 'turning down the volume' of *Ici et ailleurs* (1976). This scene signifies a move beyond Pasolini's original image at two levels. Firstly, it stages a crucial intervention into the geopolitical realities of occupation (Israel's Arab population living not as citizens but as 'occupied subjects') and conducts an interview on both the history of and daily life in the Golan Heights. Secondly, this intervention rearticulates what Pasolini was unable to fully realize (the daily lives of his Arab documentary subjects rather than their 'faces' or 'spirit') or foresee (the post-1967 geopolitical reality).

In this desire to move beyond the image, *Pasolini Pa* Palestine* prefigures a contemporary struggle in Palestinian filmmaking – to reconfigure the image of resistance and decolonize the image of Palestine in order to imbue both with a resistance of image. Anastas's contrapuntal engagement with the archive to create new, critically resistant images through juxtaposition and dialogue with old makes *Pasolini Pa* Palestine* an early example of an essayistic engagement with Palestinian archival images. It is perhaps Pasolini's lack of essayistic engagement in *Sopralluoghi in Palestina*, when compared with his more consciously 'open' *Appunti* films, which gives it the status of an object to be (re)made through repetition and retrieval, as Basma Alsharif will demonstrate 12 years after Anastas.

Letter from Gaza: Location scouting for Palestine in *Ouroboros* (Basma Alsharif 2017a)

The 'Image of Palestine' presented as mere 'wreckage of the biblical world' in Pasolini's documentary is one which Basma Alsharif both interrogates and inverts in her 2017 film *Ouroboros*, by turning this Holy Land framing of Palestine back on Matera, while simultaneously locating hidden traces of Palestine in the fabric of other colonial histories. Structurally, its cyclical movement links locations from the 'here' of Gaza to the 'elsewhere' of Los Angeles, the Mojave Desert, Basilicata and Brittany. These locations, while ostensibly beginning and ending with Gaza, exist as a laterally connected network. The film's form folds them into one another, implicating a network of places and histories in what Alsharif terms Gaza's 'perpetual present' (Alsharif 2017b). The film's broader temporal structure shifts between inter-titles: dawn, noon, dusk and night. Like the film itself, these shifts have little concern for linearity. There is, in a manner echoing *Pasolini Pa* Palestine*, a thematic concern for repetition and restarts, which are hinted at in the film's title. The Ouroboros is an ancient Egyptian symbol of a snake eating its own tail, representing a cycle of destruction and creation.

Ouroboros opens with an extraordinary, uncanny scene signifying convergent contemporary crises. A vertical drone shot frames the sea, held static above the Mediterranean as the waves break away from the shore, rolling back into the water. The drone-shot visual is matched by an aural drone of a hurdy-gurdy playing a repetitive hypnotic tone. The simultaneously beautiful and unsettling image of waves receding back into the sea appears to suggest a paradoxical image of crisis and hope. The strangeness of waves un-breaking suggests ecological crisis alongside the physical near impossibility of reaching Gaza, while simultaneously creating a spatial expansiveness in a territory of extraordinary geopolitical striation.

The film's following sequences survey the topography of Gaza, which is vertically shot through digital drone cameras. These scenes employ smash cuts to move between the post-2014 scenes of destruction to contemporary Gaza City. The drone photography is accompanied by the aural drone of a hurdy-gurdy, whose significance will become clear in the film's closing scenes in a Breton Chateau. The film's temporal shifts and architectural transitions between dilapidation, destruction and renewal position Gaza as a threshold space. In *After the Last Sky* (1986), Edward Said frames this threshold of creation and ruin as innate in Palestinian architecture, writing that 'each Palestinian structure presents itself as a potential ruin' (Said 1986: 38). Gaza's image appears in contrapuntal tension, between the 'here' of a quiet tour of Alsharif's grand family home, and the 'elsewhere' of the cold, digital drone-eye which striates an opaque, militarized space more familiar to the Western gaze.

Colonialism in a minor key

Colonialism, permanence and ruin intersect in contrapuntal movements throughout the film. In its next movement, the film leaves Gaza, in a topographic and aesthetic shift, but not before introducing its 'narrative' voice, which both occasions the first transition to North America, and introduces the film's de-territorialization of language. The US segments examine the legacy of slavery and the marginalization of Indigenous culture. The film's spoken interjections are sparse, but when they come, act as interruptions of a major language. A monologue on loss is delivered in Chinuk Wawa, while overlaid in English in embossed white subtitles. The film's two monologues bookend the film, as do the two Gaza sequences over which they lay.

The use of Chinuk Wawa, a creole language that emerged from pidgin and is a combination of Chinook, Nuu-chaa-nulth, English and French, serves multiple purposes. Having evolved as a trade language between Native Americans and settlers, it subsequently dwindled from 100,000 speakers in the nineteenth century, to just 640 in the current day, having once been on the threshold of extinction.[4] This movement mirrors the hegemony of English as a colonizing language; from Empire, via trade to information flows. Chinuk Wawa also has the benefit of opacity, being a language that is alien to a majority of the audience, be they English or Arabic speakers. This refusal to allow a linguistic pathway between language and image embraces the practice of dis-identification at work in constructing a defamiliarizing audiovisual image of Gaza, one which both implicates and frustrates the viewer. Crucially, the wider role language plays in the film is that of de-territorializing, or perhaps more accurately, *displacing* a major language. This process is illustrated most acutely in the film's relation between sub-titling and narration in the Gazan house scenes. The use of English subtitles goes beyond translation, becoming a graphic feature of these scenes. This draws the eye from the mise en scène to the relationship between spoken and written language. English, looming in upper cased embossed white font, is foregrounded to the point of conspicuousness. The 'disjunction between content and expression' that Deleuze and Guattari (1983: 20) see in the de-territorialization of utterances is amplified here in the defamiliarizing layering of emboldened English vowels over the unfamiliar consonant-heavy sounds of Chinuk Wawa. The act of displacement occurs in this disjunction between text and sound. The text is foregrounded to the extent that it detaches itself from the mise en scène in a way more familiar with inter-titling than sub-titling, rendering its use of English both conscious and constructed, occasioning a rejection of its naturalization as a global lingua franca engendered by colonialism and Imperial trade. The fact that Chinuk Wawa both grew in prominence as a contact language through trade and exchange and was driven to near extinction by the disequilibria of those forces reinforces its subversive element when spoken back to the English text.

Interruption and subversion of the dominant, majoritarian language is a thread that runs through the film, linking the temporal and spatial folds as its shifts through its five locations. The one constant human presence outside of the Gaza sequences is the artist, Diego Marcon, a near silent 'seer' who wanders through time and space. His own act of linguistic interruption occurs in the Mojave Desert, but he initially appears in the film's first movement beyond Gaza, marked by the transition from digital to 35mm. While this gives the film a less clinical colour palette, the sense of the uncanny is maintained using temporal distortions. Retaining the reverse motion photography of the Gazan house tour, Macron first appears walking backwards along a sidewalk, before entering the house of a young Los Angelian couple. The couple seem pleasantly surprised by this arrival, while in the midst of preparing soup. The use of discontinuity editing, through a jump cut, sees the sudden appearance of a full house, seemingly rehearsing dialogue for a play. This somewhat disjointed recital continues, before cutting to a scene in which the ostensible 'leader' of the group (seen below, in the beige gown) performs a song.

The violent juxtaposition of expression and content pervades that still domestic scene as the tall, African American man launches into a bass-baritone rendition of the opening two verses of 'Dixie':

> Oh, I wish I was in the land of cotton
> Old times there are not forgotten
> Look away! Look away!
> Look away! Dixie Land
>
> In Dixie land where I was born in
> Early on one frosty mornin'
> Look away! Look away!
> Look away! Dixie Land

The song was written in 1859, and was performed for Minstrel shows before being adopted as an unofficial anthem of the Confederate States during the Civil War (McWhirter 2012: para. 3). The re-appropriation of a song of racist caricature, which became an anthem to anti-abolitionist secessionists, echoes the subversion of the acoustic space of colonialism enacted in Kamal Aljafari's *Port of Memory* (2009) in Chapter 2, where a Hebrew lament of Mizrahi oppression in Jaffa is 'haunted' by the discursively erased figure of the Palestinian. It is these topologies of colonialism, and the barbarism that lies beneath, which connect these discrete locations and orient them around Gaza.

Between the Negev and the Mojave: The desert and 'frontier' culture

Alsharif's own topological movement between the coordinates of colonialism and exile moves from the biblical image of Matera to the desert, specifically, the Mojave Desert. Within Alsharif's own structural logic of destruction and renewal, ruin and permanence, the Mojave Desert is a potent symbol of endings. However, the idea of the desert as something to be conquered and overcome looms large in the mythology of Zionism and the Westward Expansion of the United States through the idea of Manifest Destiny.

In fact, in the latter half of *Sopralluoghi in Palestina*, Pasolini notes the plight of the Bedouin in the Negev, a desert he refers to as 'being conquered day by day by the Israelis'.

The notion of settling, or striating the desert is one that has a strong resonance in the Israeli imagination, one involved in the construction in Zionist mythology of the Sabra[5] as a figure both tough and hardy yet at home in the harsh non-European environment, while retaining the allegorical capacity to 'bloom' in the desert. Ella Shohat (2010: 31) has identified this trend in early Israeli filmmaking, a mastering of the land which both provides continuity with biblical Israel and a 'dramatic rupture with the Diaspora Jew'. As such, the Bedouin of the Negev pose a challenge to the logic of the Israeli State: a state founded on a notion of an end to wandering and diasporic experience. 'Monotheism', writes Laura Marks (2015: 150), 'cannot tolerate nomads'. Zionism's need to both settle Palestine and striate the desert stems from a similar intolerance. Alongside this allusion to 'conquering', Pasolini highlights the Kibbutzim outside of Nazareth as constituting 'zones "colonized" by Jews', an allusion to the seemingly paradoxical synchronic postcolonial coloniality of the State, as recognized by Joseph Massad (2000). However, it is also another manifestation of the modern which Pasolini finds so abhorrent, with modern buildings looking 'institutionalized' and trees a product of 'reforestation'.

The dual drives of territorial expansion and frontier culture which define settler-colonial societies make the continuities between the Mojave, the Negev and Gaza clear. W. J. T. Mitchell highlights these continuities when reflecting on desert landscapes and the Holy Land in the second section of his 2000 essay 'Holy Landscape: Israel, Palestine and the American Wilderness'. In this second section, subtitled 'The Desert, the Idol and the Iconoclast', Mitchell reflects on the desert landscapes of his childhood in Nevada, asking,

> What does it have to do with Palestine? What does the American wilderness, with its Judeo-Protestant 'errands' – wanderings, ordeals, treks across the desert in search of the Promised Land – have to do with Palestine? Everything clearly. Since the beginning, Americans have been turning toward their own Western frontier as a wilderness to be traversed in search of a promised land, a Zion. (Mitchell 2000: 201)

It is in that very frontier culture, the construction of a wilderness to be traversed, that triggers a sense of déjà vu upon Mitchell's first visit to Israel. It is also such a frontier culture that projects emptiness onto spaces necessarily rendered as 'wilderness' so as to be settled and 'civilized'. The marginalization, orientalization, and elision of Native Americans historically in the North American cinematic gaze, particularly in Hollywood, can be seen as bound up with the frontier mentality, an uncritical 'rough energy and optimism' (ibid.) romanticized and integral to building ideology. These are the same founding myths Ella Shohat traces at the nascence of Israeli cinema, the Yishuv cinema in the decade preceding the founding of the state. Focussing on case studies of *Oded the Wanderer* (Hayeem Halamichi, Nathan Axelrod, 1933) and *Sabra* (Aleksander Ford, 1933), Shohat (2010) charts the emergence of the heroic pioneer narrative and aesthetic, where the figure of the Sabra is a civilizing, benevolent presence, correlative to yet distinct from[6] the European colonial imagination, and also reliant on the production of emptiness characteristic of settler-colonial societies (Veracini 2011). The frontier culture that underpins settler colonialism is rendered cinematically in the presence of the settler surviving and thriving in the desert. An inversion of this occurs in the striking opening sequence of the Mojave Desert passage. The sequence opens with an extreme long shot of a lone figure set against the empty plain, with the red, lunar-like mountains of the Mojave rising in the distance.

The shot is evocative of the visual language of the Western, blurring the figure-ground relation in such a way as to suggest an almost symbiotic relationship, a continuum between harsh landscape and those who settle it. Perhaps the most famous example of such a shot is the opening scene of *The Searchers* (John Ford, 1956) in which Ethan Edwards (John Wayne) emerges from the desert, a barely discernible figure on a horse, entirely at home alone in the desert. Alsharif's shot in *Ouroboros* inserts a Native American figure into the mise en scène, the figure of Bo Gallerito, a Mescalero Apache actor, and a defamiliarizing presence in this particular frame.

The use of Chinuk Wawa and the evocation of the Mojave as analogous to the Negev constructs a counterpoint with the work of Mahmoud Darwish, and its use in English in Jean-Luc Godard's *Notre Musique* (2004). Darwish's 1992 poem 'The Red Indian's Penultimate Speech to the White Man' stages Chief Seattle's 1855 speech to the Governor of Washington Territory, a lament for the changing of worlds from indigenous to settler. Darwish's poem addresses the Native American experience as analogous to the Palestinian one and, in directly addressing Columbus, the work fits into his wider thematic concerns with 'the two "1492s"' (Shohat 2006: 209), the beginning of European colonialism and the end of Muslim and Sepharidc Jewish presence in the Iberian Peninsula. Perhaps the most contrapuntal reading of the Native American nineteenth-century experience with contemporary settler colonialism in the Palestinian context occurs explicitly in the poem's seventh stanza, which reads:

> There are dead who sleep in rooms you will build
> there are dead who visit their past in places you demolish
> there are dead who pass over bridges you will construct. (Darwish 2009 [1992a]: 77)

These words echo Darwish's laments for the ghosts of Deir Yassin and Kafr Qāsim which occur throughout his work. The poem appears on screen in *Notre Musique* (2004), Jean-Luc Godard's Dantesque symphony to twentieth-century legacies of colonialism and war. The film's three movements consist of Hell, Purgatory and Heaven. The second movement is the bulk of the film, and Darwish himself appears both as commentator on the opening images of destruction and interlocutor with an Israeli journalist on Palestine/Israel in an extended scene. His poem itself appears staged in the destroyed remains of Sarajevo's National Library. The poem is delivered accusingly by two Native Americans to a bureaucratic figure who is processing books to be burned, itself a restaging of the fate of the library at Serb forces' hands. The poem references the address to Columbus to meet 'as two strangers of one time and one land' (ibid.: 70), reference that ties Palestine and Israel to the conquest of the Americas and to Bosnia, a complex linking of erasure of war and possible reconciliation in a city, like Darwish's Granada, of Islamic culture in Europe.

Unlike Alsharif's use of Chinuk Wawa to tell a transnationally connected history of colonialism through Palestine, *Notre Musique* puts the Arabic words of a Palestinian poet in a language not used in the original 1855 address, as Dyer and Mulot note in their reading of Darwish in translation in Godard:

> Because the Native American characters recite the poem in English, the implication is that the man burning the books represents the 'white man' of Chief Seattle's address. It is nevertheless important to keep in mind that Chief Seattle's 1855 speech had not been in English; it was conveyed to its white audience through a translation from its original Duwamish into Chinook, which was then translated into English. (Dyer and Mulot 2014: 80)

It is worth recalling at this point the way in which Alsharif uses embossed English sub-titling over Chinuk Wawa in Gaza to interconnect notions of linguistic and cultural erasure; it might be argued Godard's juxtaposition of book burning with linguistic erasure of both Arabic and Duwamish performs a similar gesture of linking colonial histories of loss through Palestine.

Conrad and Pasolini: A contrapuntal reading

Ouroboros's penultimate movement involves a transition from an inversion of the visual logic of settler colonialism, to an interruption of colonial history through a disjuncture between language and image. The scene opens with two characters standing impassively outside a small, dilapidated white building. This scene takes place in the small, austere, library on the edge of the Mojave.[7] A young woman sits at the table and begins reading aloud from Conrad's *Heart of Darkness*, while the Italian man (Diego Macron) who shifts seamlessly through Alsharif's topological network paces restlessly around her. She reads from the final passage of the book, where Marlow lies to Kurtz's fiancée when asked to relay his final words. Mid-passage, the man interrupts the recital with an offer of a magic trick, a trick attempted unsuccessfully several times.

The interruption of Conrad's words, and the coloniality of those words creates an interesting parallel with Alsharif's own dialogue with Pasolini. Conrad's work has been the focus of severe criticism in the field of postcolonial studies, most notably by Chinua Achebe (1988) in his essay 'An Image of Africa: Racism in Conrad's Heart of Darkness', in which he argues that Conrad's depiction of Africa as non-European 'darkness' is irredeemably racist and Eurocentric. Said's (1994, 2003) contrapuntal reading of Conrad both recognizes his contemporary attempts to critique colonialism and the historical limits and blind spots occasioned by Conrad's inability to 'see' the non-European. Crucially, this contrapuntal approach opens currents between Conrad and responses from Naipaul and Salih, the result of which is 'not only that Salih and Naipaul depend so vitally on their reading of Conrad, but that Conrad's writing is further actualized and animated by emphases and inflections that he was obviously unaware of, but that his writing permits' (Said 2003: 25). Intentionally or not, *Ouroboros*'s engagement with Conrad and Pasolini is a contrapuntal one, in that each of those figures had a critical relationship with their own contemporary moment, yet both were unable to fully see the figure of the non-European, a blind spot necessitating the contemporary response through both critique and dialogue, which *Ouroboros* offers in its linguistic interruption of Conrad's words, and its creation of a mythic 'image' of Basilicata as a response to Pasolini's 'image' of Palestine.

Ouroboros's penultimate movement shifts from the arid, dusty landscapes of the Mojave to the lush verdant gardens of a Bretagne chateau. This move is made via a transition from the failed magic trick in the Mojave with the inter-title TRY AGAIN, a command that both echoes the film's essayistic structure and also conveys the solitude of exile, a solitude articulated by Edward Said's own reflections on the ontology of exile in his essay 'Reflections on Exile'. Said's essay conveys the loneliness of exilic wandering, observing that 'in a very acute sense exile is a solitude experienced outside the group: the deprivations felt at not being with others in the communal habitation' (Said 2000: 140). Marcon's solitary wanderer is a conduit for Alsharif's own exilic loneliness and wanderings through Kuwait, France and the United States. The transition between the Mojave and Brittany alludes to another of the film's undercurrents of loss – that of a lost love and threshold of remembrance and forgetting which involves starting again. After the inter-title TRY AGAIN, we see Marcon and a woman together in a moonlit landscape, looking into each other's eyes. Marcon leans in and whispers something; a second inter-title 'WHAT NOW?' fills the screen. At this point, the film 'starts' again, as a camera tracks up the entrance to a Bretagne chateau. This fleeting episode of love, witnessed in fragments during the LA scenes, is left behind to fade as yet another structure that presents as a potential ruin.

The move to the Bretagne chateau creates an architectural juxtaposition with the liminality of the Mojave and the potential ruin of Gaza. Here stands a monument to architectural permanence, a grand fifteenth-century chateau, enriched and preserved over half a millennium. Alsharif's camera, surveying the grandeur and peacefulness of this site, invites questions as to the here/elsewhere forces that preserve and enrich some structures while others become ruins. This is the latent index of barbarism within any cultural 'treasure' that Walter Benjamin identifies in *On the Concept of History*, writing,

> For in every case these treasures have a lineage that he cannot contemplate without horror. They owe their existence not only to the great geniuses who created them, but also to the anonymous toil of others who lived in the same period. There is no document of culture that is not at the same time a document of barbarism. (Benjamin 2006: 392)

The index of colonial history carried within this Bretagne chateau tells a history of the oppressed, which situates its architectural permanence in relation to sites of erasure such as the Mojave and Gaza within the wider colonial topology that structures the film. Between the sixteenth and nineteenth centuries, nearby Nantes was France's largest slave trading port, and it is the dynamics of exploitation and colonialism behind the edifices of the opulent architecture both in and around the metropole which this sequence examines.

From drone-ear to drone-eye: Returning to Gaza

The film comes full circle, its 'return' to Gaza taking place in the interior of the chateau. A couple sit in a large drawing room while slowly the aural drone which accompanied the film's opening sequence returns. This escalates in volume as the camera gradually pans left to reveal the hurdy-gurdy player. An extremely slow dissolve superimposes the visual and the aural drone, as the sights and sounds of colonial France merge with the drone-eye of Gaza which opened the film.

This graphic match of sound and image brings the film to its end and beginning, Gaza, in a perpetual state of destruction and renewal, and implicates Europe's colonial history in Gaza's present. The film ends in a double movement,

Figure 4.2 The convergence of visual and aural drone in *Ouroboros* (Basma Alsharif, 2017a). ©Momento Films.

a contraction and expansion of all the sound and images that have come before, as the film's five locations and multiple histories merge in a musical coda, structured to a techno beat. As Diego Marcon dances, destruction, renewal, desert and verdant landscape create dialectical images which both situate Gaza and Palestine relationally and also explode histories of colonization that have sought to ossify and isolate Gaza specifically as an image of stasis, but Palestine more generally as a reductive, overcoded 'Image of Palestine'.

Letters to Levi, letters to Pasolini: Location scouting in Basilicata

While Palestine/Gaza is the trace which links the other locations' histories to a colonial present, the most explicit engagement with Palestinian representation and image comes in its Basilicata section, the film's third movement in its cycle. Alsharif's own dialogue with Pasolini in *Ouroboros* is perhaps more critical than Anastas's in *Pasolini Pa* Palestine*. Highlighting the parallels between the process of location scouting and colonial exploration, she claims that creating an image to correspond to the mind's eye and overlaying that image on a site involves 'inherently exploiting the landscape and population there' (Alsharif 2017a). Clarifying her own engagement with the south of Italy by way of Pasolini's in Palestine-Israel, she inverts Pasolini's image of opacity to 'look at Matera as an image, what it symbolises in regards to its history and what it represents today: the serene pastoral landscapes, the preserved ancient city' (Alsharif 2017a).

Alsharif's engagement with Basilicata extends beyond Pasolini to the work of Carlo Levi, specifically his 1945 memoir *Cristo si è fermato a Eboli* (*Christ Stopped at Eboli*). This documents his experience of internal exile after his banishment from Turin to Basilicata in the 1930s for his anti-fascist activism. Levi documents his own estrangement, along with the stark poverty of the South in contrast with the industrial North. The book itself, perhaps foreshadowing Pasolini's own displacement of the Holy Land to Basilicata, is rich with descriptions of Lucania (now Basilicata) as a land at the threshold of the sacred and the cursed. It is a place outside time, history and the State and a place of failed transcendence with 'pain residing forever in earthly things' (Levi 2000 [1947]: 12). Grassano, the town to which Levi was first exiled, is described as 'a streak of white at the summit of a bare hill, a sort of miniature Jerusalem in the solitude of the desert' (Levi 2000: 13).

Between Basilicata and Bethlehem 137

Figure 4.3 Matera as commodity image in *Ouroboros* (Basma Alsharif, 2017a). ©Momento Films.

In a scene from the Basilicata section of *Ouroboros*, the lone figure of Diego Marcon wanders through the Basilicatan countryside, smoking a cigarette as the words of Levi's experience of open incarceration drift across the screen.

This juxtaposition of text and image works as a poetics of exile on several levels. Firstly, from Alsharif's own perspective, being raised in Kuwait and France to Gazan parents, the scene resonates with the filmmaker's feeling of estrangement in all three. Further, the status of Gaza since 2005, no longer occupied from within but de facto occupied from without,[8] is effectively that of an open prison. The passage itself is taken from Levi's initial impression upon arriving in Gagliano (Aliano) and noting the unease he felt at being unfree in a landscape which conveyed openness. The juxtaposition of text, image and context conveys the intersection between exile, occupation and inequality that links Gaza to Basilicata, a link which led Alsharif away from Pasolini towards Levi. There is an 'irony' to this which Alsharif (2017b) admits, in that it was Pasolini who led her to Basilicata in the first place. Speaking of the impact of *Christ Stopped at Eboli* on her, she states, 'I was completely floored by Levi's descriptions of the villagers in the Southern Italian town: it was as though he were describing Gaza today' (Alsharif 2017a). Perhaps a blind spot of Alsharif's critique of Pasolini is that the marginalization of one culture by another was in fact a crucial factor leading Pasolini to analogously reconstruct the class relations of Palestine-Israel in Southern Italy. The structures and lore Levi and Pasolini

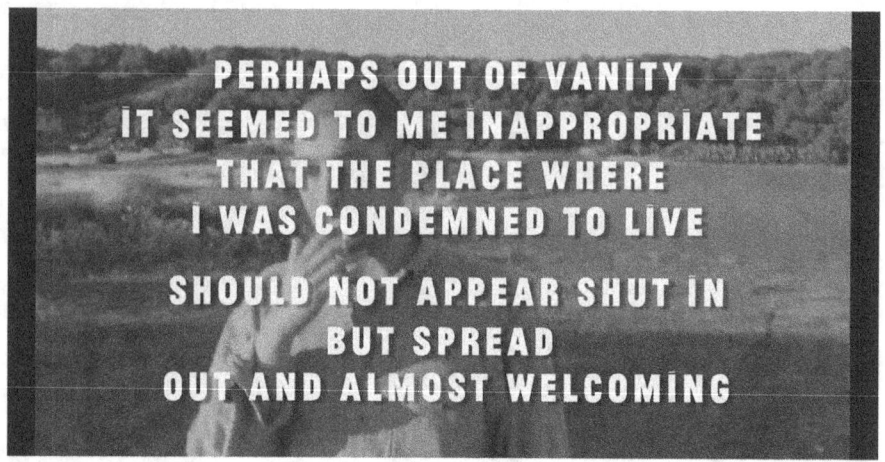

Figure 4.4 Exilic estrangement: Levi in Gaza in *Ouroboros* (Basma Alsharif, 2017a). ©Momento Films.

both recognize as conditioning the South which they witness bear striking resemblances to one another. The resemblance is most acute between a morality of common fate borne more of nature than religion for Levi, and a morality not founded on evangelism for Pasolini. When Pasolini sees in the margins of 1963 Israel a space where 'Christ's preaching has not been heard … even from afar', we see correlative figures in Levi's Lucania of 1935: 'Christ never came this far, nor did time, nor the individual soul, nor hope, nor the relation of cause to effect, nor reason, nor history' (Levi 2000 [1947]: 12). Pasolini explicates this lack of evangelism, through which he links Palestinian and Southern Italian faces by explaining a morality conditioned neither by State nor Church, claiming, 'It isn't founded on love but on honour; … If there is piety, it's because it's there, not because it's supposed to be there. You can see this better in the Arabs than in Southern Italians' (Stack 1969: 75). These threads connect Pasolini's Basilicata to Levi's Lucania and Basma Alsharif's Gaza. The contemporary Gaza Alsharif sees in the pages of Levi's 1935 Lucania/Basilicata is a correlate of the Basilicata Pasolini saw in the Palestinian remnants of 1963 Israel.

In the way these two works engage with, critique and are informed by Pasolini's documentary, they add a crucial contrapuntal voice to open up Pasolini's original work. Looking beyond its original context to the contemporary geopolitical reality of Palestine, these films interrogate the blind spots in Pasolini's representation of the people and the land yet manage to uncover productive similarities and new insights through this process of critique.

Da farsi and a dialectical image of Palestine

A contrapuntal reading of *Sopralluoghi in Palestina* – through *Pasolini Pa* Palestine* and *Ouroboros* – achieves two aims. Firstly, it 'opens' the documentary in the spirit of Pasolini's own *da farsi* approach. Situating the work relationally goes some way to meeting the aims of open, anti-colonial dialogue within that approach. Secondly, such a reading, by both repeating and resituating Pasolini (and Levi), reveals the potential and contingency in the original works: the missed landscapes, lost pasts and contemporary resonances (such as those which connect Levi's Basilicata to Alsharif's Gaza) that can be awakened.

Anastas's *Pasolini Pa*Palestine* articulates a conversation with Pasolini between 1963 and 2005, in a voice unheard of in Pasolini's own film: female and Arabic. It also attempts detours and diversions around his original route, necessitated by the shifting cartographic reality. The structure of Basma Alsharif's *Ouroboros* resembles an atonal, contrapuntal ensemble, through its connections with other histories (both political and cinematic), its tensions between colonialism, postcoloniality, exile and home, and its themes of emergence and disappearance. In seeking traces of Palestine in the American West, French colonial architecture and the South of Italy, Alsharif's film in fact constructs a Palestinian *topos* as a condition, a stubborn reminder (or remnant) of presence in those histories and geographies that have forgotten it. This approach in fact bears a resemblance to Pasolini's own construction of a pan-South *topos*, which connects the condition of Europe's marginalized South to the Global South. Crucially, however, Alsharif's perspective looks out *to* Europe *from* a Palestine producing itself.

These images and moments combine to create an open, multi-directional image, where lateral and temporal connections intersect, creating not an archaic 'Image of Palestine' but, more accurately, what Walter Benjamin might term a *dialectical* one. In both *On the Concept of History* (1940) and *The Arcades Project* (1982) (Benjamin's magnum opus of his mature thought, unfinished at his death) the notion of an image at a standstill, one that allows for a different conception of historical experience, is a crucial one. Benjamin's most sustained theoretical description of the dialectical image comes in Convolute N of the Arcades Project, writing, 'For while the relation of the present to the past is a purely temporal, continuous one, the relation of what-has-been to the now is dialectical: is not progression but image, suddenly emergent. – Only dialectical images are genuine images (that is, not archaic)' (Benjamin 1999 [1982]: 106 [N2a,3]).

In this way, Benjamin's dialectical image renders visible Agamben's *archē-ological* method, which excavates an earlier work not as a static, past artefact but as a dynamic process which shapes and is shaped by the present. The dialectical image treats the 'what-has-been' (and what *could* have been) and 'the now' as co-present coordinates in a topological field in which 1930s Basilicata can dwell in contemporary Gaza, and Pasolini's journey is made and remade in the West Bank.

Pasolini's work both shapes and is shaped by responses from Anastas and Alsharif, constructing a bi-directional dialogue in which an Italian male voice is counterbalanced by Arabic female ones. A contrapuntal *reading* of Pasolini's *Sopralluoghi in Palestina* similarly situates it relationally with Levi, Alsharif and Anastas. These four texts interact across an archaic/contemporary axis and a reality/image one. The intersection of these axes through the connective properties of the texts forms what I term a 'dialectical image of Palestine'. Visually, such an image might be imagined thus:

This approach highlights the continuities and discontinuities of place and language emergent in a contemporary Palestinian cinema characterized by dialogue with a cinematic and textual archive, from which it constructs contrapuntal, dialectical images of contemporary criticality. These images examine the intersection of myth, image, representation and ruin from which a totalizing 'Image of Palestine' emerges. It is just such an intersection which underpins *Sopralluoghi in Palestina*. Yet Pasolini's compulsion to displace the Holy Land by analogy left space between those images he abandoned. This space is where Anastas and Alsharif were able to produce themselves.

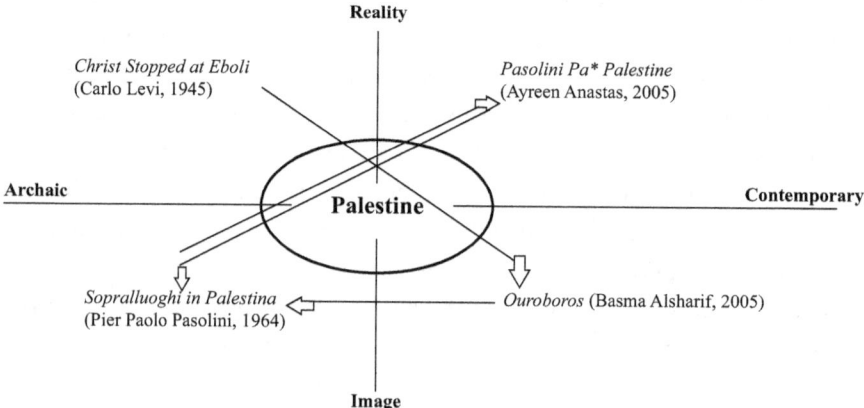

Figure 4.5 A dialectical cinematic image of Palestine. ©Robert George White.

Coda: Basma Alsharif, Edward Said and post-Palestinian futures

When reflecting on the assigning of the adjective 'post-Palestinian' to her work in light of its exploring the world through Palestine, that is, Palestinian elsewheres, Alsharif recalls its first use, summoning the 'What Now?' interrogative of *Ouroboros*:

> It was Eyal Sivan who first called my work 'Post-Palestinian' at the 59th Flaherty Seminar in 2013 ... This definition allowed me to realize that my perspective is based on an acceptance of the possibility that Palestine may never become a state, that the right of return will never be acknowledged, and that I am interested in what comes next, what we do now. (Alsharif 2015)

Alsharif shares with Edward Said an ambiguous 'luxury' of distance from the images with which they engage. Said was estranged from the locations Jean Mohr photographed in *After the Last Sky*. Alsharif's exilic estrangement from Gaza manifested itself in both a physical absence from the location[9] (like Said), and in the quality of images themselves. Unlike the rest of the film, which is shot on 35mm, the Gaza sequences are shot on digital, which gives them a sharpness, detachment and lack of warmth in comparison to the film images that come between them.

In sharing the exilic estrangement of *al-ghurba*, Basma Alsharif and Edward Said also share the 'double vision' that is the 'privileged affliction' of exile. That is, a double movement, from subject to object, proximity to distance. Speaking of the sense conveyed by Jean Mohr's photographs, of Palestinian seeing themselves 'at once inside and outside our world' (Said 1986: 6), Said goes on to describe the similar double movement, or shifts between first, second and third person in his approach to writing *After the Last Sky*, stating that as abrupt as these shifts are, I feel they reproduce the way 'we' experience ourselves, the way 'you' sense that others look at you, the way, in your solitude, you feel the distance between where 'you' and where 'they' are (ibid.).

Alsharif's own approach to her film essay follows a similar logic, a Palestine at once intimate and distant from what she terms her 'removed perspective from the cause' (Alsharif 2018). In a 2018 interview, reflecting on the 'post-Palestinian' identification, she elaborates on the ebbing and shifting of hope in the wake of the series of assaults on Gaza and how her own distance from it led to a reframing, claiming, 'And so my hope shifted away from Palestine, because

I have this luxury in the diaspora, and towards connecting it to other histories I saw Palestine reflected in' (ibid.). It is the privileged affliction of the 'luxury' of distance that allows both Alsharif (through text and moving image) and Said (through text and still image) to explore this lateral relation as means through which to discuss ideas around exile, displacement, colonialism and erasure. It is to this post-Palestinian future, perhaps more accurately an archaeology of the present, that this book will now turn.

5

Towards a post-Palestinian cinema: Imagining states of being beyond the status quo

Staging 'post': Thinking Palestine beyond the fossilized present

As the previous chapter closed on the work of Basma Alsharif, it is apt that these concluding comments examine a consciousness referenced in her work: namely, a post-Palestinian one. The prefix 'post' is a contentious one in scholarship on Palestine, for obvious reasons. Joseph Massad's essay 'The "Post-Colonial" Colony: Time, Space, and Bodies in Palestine/Israel' highlights the problematic 'synchronicity of the colonial and the postcolonial (as discursive and material relations) in Palestine/Israel' (Massad 2000: 312). Massad's deliberately provocative and paradoxical title stresses the anomaly of Israel emerging as a State in a moment of anticolonial struggle, thus aligning itself with this movement, despite Zionism itself aligning with earlier European colonial (and settler-colonial) values. The very act of naming transforms the power relations of how the space is understood. Exploring these contours, Massad asks,

> What constitutes the difficulty in naming it [Palestine/Israel] in relation to colonialism? Can one determine the coloniality of Palestine/Israel without noting its postcoloniality for Ashkenazic Jews? Can one determine the postcoloniality of Palestine/Israel without noting its coloniality for Palestinians? Can one determine both or either without noting the simultaneous colonizer/colonized status of Mizrahic Jews? How can all these people inhabit a colonial/postcolonial space in a world that declares itself living in a postcolonial time? (ibid.)

Anna Ball works with a parenthetical 'post' to approach Massad's problem of synchronicity, explaining, 'I sometimes use the term "(post) colonial" (rather than simply "colonial", "post-colonial" or "postcolonial") ... in contexts where I wish to denote something of the ambivalent synchronicity of Palestine's colonial conditions and postcolonial desires' (Ball 2012: 6).

Massad's aforementioned reference to a putative 'postcolonial time' is one Patrick Williams and Anna Ball reformulate to place when exploring the postcolonial 'nowhere' of Palestine in the academy, with reference to a discipline 'which has, up until now, failed to address it, namely postcolonial studies' (Williams and Ball 2014: 128). This failure, they argue, stems from both the fact that 'Palestine is not yet "post-" the "colonial"' and 'the restrictions on what Said (1984: 27) termed "permission to narrate" Palestine's story as a colonized nation' (ibid.).

Post-Palestinian appears (on the surface) an even more contentious label in a context where a struggle for either equal rights or a state is as yet unrealized. However, as the coda of the previous chapter intimated, the cultural thinking behind this 'post' signifies (following Habiby) a 'pessoptimistic' temporality: an untimely and simultaneous after *and* not yet, contained in Alsharif's question: What now? Before examining examples of this post-Palestinian 'turn' it is worth retracing our steps to see how an atonal cinema anticipates this turn.

The right to remain out of place: A transnational atonality

Throughout this book I have argued that the atonal cinema under study articulates a transnationally networked Palestinian image of contrapuntal criticality. This is at once an image of Palestinians elsewhere and of Palestinian elsewheres. It looks for these elsewheres in the transnational connections of its past, prompted by the (re)discovery in the last decade of its transnationally scattered revolutionary archive. However, as we saw in the case of Ayreen Anastas and Miguel Littín, this transhistorical and transnational dialogue with revolutionary moments and global texts predates this (re)discovery. Alsharif's question (what now?) is the same one Anastas implies in *Pasolini Pa* Palestine* when contemplating a 'Palestinian Awakening'. The 'what now?' is also the 'where now?'

In the post-Oslo, post-Intifada moment, from the deeply ambiguous 'luxury' of distance (outside the Occupied Territories) which the atonal filmmakers in this book contemplate Palestine, Palestinian elsewheres are also the necessary transnational connections of its present. If, as Alsharif fears, the right of return never materializes, then what of Adorno and Said's demand? What of the right to remain out of place, to stand away from home so as to look at it anew? What might one see *from* elsewhere, *of* elsewheres?

A suggestion of sorts comes in the form of an essay John Collins wrote around the time of Anastas's dialogue with Pasolini. In 'From Portbou to Palestine and Back' (2006), Collins looks at Palestine from Portbou, the small coastal town on the French/Spanish border which was the final resting place of Walter Benjamin. An olive tree next to the cemetery and the vastness of the Mediterranean prompt him to look from Benjamin to a Palestine to which Benjamin's friend Gershom Scholem emigrated, but he did not. Collin's piece imagines what Benjamin might have made of the Jewish home and its State in its current form. However, it also looks to an idea of Palestine far larger than its current or historical territory: a Palestine which leaves traces in Europe, from the shores of the Mediterranean which connect it, to the olive tree, to Marwan, the Spanish-Palestinian songwriter Collins finds in Madrid. Marwan's Palestine 'is a locus of defeat and injustice ("the amputated land of my grandfather"), but he also refuses to claim that this experience is unique' (Collins 2006: 78). Citing songs which link Palestinian injustice and proximity to violence to experiences of Brazilians in the favelas and Nicaraguan's struggle against an ossified and corrupt revolutionary government, Collins notes that 'For Marwan, Palestine is bigger than Palestine' (ibid.).

A Palestine bigger than Palestine. This is precisely the contemporaneity of Alsharif's question, a question that prompted her to look for traces of Gaza in Levi's south Italy, traces of Palestine in US frontier culture, traces of Palestinian potential ruins in a Bretagne chateau. It is a transnational Palestine that, in spite of the stasis and hopelessness of the present moment, blasts the archive out of the continuum of history, treating it as an active source not just for a contemporary resistance of image but for a contemporary solidarity and a shared commonality with other struggles. Before we return to the post-Palestinian present, this notion of archival practice requires some reflection in light of emerging work on the Palestinian cinematic archive.

Future anteriors: Reflections on *archē*-ology and the archive

In her most recent book, *Becoming Palestine* (2021) (published as I write this), Gil Hochberg argues for the existence of an 'archival imagination' among contemporary Palestinian artists, with the aim of 'reclaiming' the archive as a site of contemporaneity rather than a historical object. Countering a notion favoured by historians that archives entail discovery or revelation of the unknown, she contends, 'It is indeed time to realize that archives hide very little, and that the secrets of the archive are usually open secrets, and hence hardly secrets at all' (Hochberg 2021: viii).

The framing of the archive as a site of colonial power to be interrogated informs Rona Sela's recent work. *Looted and Hidden – Palestinian Archives in Israel* (Sela 2017) engages with Palestinian cinematic images looted from the 1982 PLO archives and hidden in Israeli military archives, but also film and photographic images of Palestinian life in the Mandate. Sela's film attempts to render visible the partitioning of the Palestinian image from the history of Zionist historiography so as to undermine both its political efficacy and legitimacy. Sela, a curator and researcher at Tel Aviv University, treats the archive as an instrument of colonial power, and sees her role as revealing its hidden bounty of Palestinian cultural production. This type of archival practice perhaps corresponds to Hochberg's notion of the (official state) archive as a holder of open secrets already known to those within the tradition of the oppressed. However, Sela's film is quite open that it is an engagement with the *Israeli* archives of hidden Palestinian life to render visible to other *Israelis* the ideology of such practices, in the tradition of the New Historians.[1]

Constructing the archive in a manner privileged in history as a discipline and the nation-state as an institution is perhaps an understandable position against which to propose a rearticulation of the archive 'as a source of a *yet-to-come future*' (ibid.: 14). However, the somewhat hegemonic formulations of both archive and archaeology Hochberg is working with (or rather against) ignore the potentialities already present within existing formulations of these concepts. This historicized framing of the archive as a primarily past-oriented, documenting exercise with which contemporary artists break somewhat simplifies the relationship artists such as Emily Jacir, Annemarie Jacir and Mohanad Yaqubi have with the Palestinian revolutionary archive, as Nadia Yaqub claims:

> Efforts to recover Palestinian archives from materials scattered around the world are not merely nostalgic projects. These efforts are laden with meaning in the context of Palestinian post-Oslo politics. Such works may seek not just to document but to actively recover the points of commonality that linked leftist movements of the past. (Yaqub 2018: 200)

This recovery of points of lost commonality/paths not taken is, as I have argued, a crucial aspect of contemporary filmmakers' engagement with the Palestinian revolution and the broader context of a revolutionary politics within which

Palestine was transnationally located. Just such an engagement informed Ayreen Anastas's and Basma Alsharif's *archē*-ological, contrapuntal reading of a postcolonial Pasolini, (re)locating traces of Palestine in south Italy. Similarly, Miguel Littín's diasporic Palestinian consciousness was awakened by the transnational reach of the Palestinian revolution, fortified among the artists and activists of the non-aligned movement in Algeria and sustained in and beyond his exile from Chile. It is the loss of the emancipatory politics of revolution and the partial loss/diasporic scattering of the archive in 1982, along with the fossilized politics of the present, which, I have argued, drive the Palestinians elsewhere featured in this book to seek Palestinian elsewheres. In doing so, they rearticulate the transnational moments of self-production the early years of the revolution and its contemporaries occasioned.

In speaking of 'the teleology of revolution (loss, return, and recovery)' (Hochberg 2021: x), Hochberg argues that an archival nostalgia seeks to recover (and redeem) a time before the rupture of the Nakba. As she sees it, 'There remains today a strong discursive preoccupation with redemption and recovery as the incentive to enter the archive' (ibid.: 14). Yet, she argues, 'these recovery projects tend to reinforce the status of the of the archive as a tomb – a temple of the past and a source for cultivating limited and highly restricted identities based on a "shared past"' (ibid.).

However, the atonal cinema examined in this book, far from treating the Palestinian revolution as a static historical archive, grasps the historical currents of the nascent Palestinian revolution and its cinema of self-production; the *archē*-ological impetus of the resistance of image *within* atonal cinema seeks to liberate the overcoded Palestinian image and restore this revolutionary signification as reflexive, critically engaged and transnationally connected. This is not a movement nostalgic for the institution of the Palestinian revolution, but rather one which harnesses that spontaneous, iterative and nascent force of Palestinians producing themselves through images. As such, it is an archival practice that is always already contrapuntal, putting the open images of the Palestinian revolution in dialogue with the present moment.

The emergence (in the most recent works of my selected corpus) of an engagement with an archival practice as both a cinematic 'struggle of visibility' to see one's own image (Yaqubi 2017), and an *archē*-ological uncovering of how Palestinians can produce and circulate images of themselves for themselves I argue, reinforces the two main forms of resistance underpinning my analysis of atonal cinema. That is, the aforementioned resistance *of* image and resistance *to* partition, both of which articulate a capacity to imagine the political otherwise inherent in this atonal cinema and also in the post-Palestinian turn gestured to in the recent work of Basma Alsharif, Larissa Sansour and Elia Suleiman.

The post-Palestinian consciousness in these filmmakers' works builds on the 'resistance of image' identified in the dissonant criticality of the atonal cinema identified in this book and, I argue, conveys not a sense of a temporal 'after' but rather a call to think *beyond* what Gil Hochberg terms 'the limits of the separatist imagination' (Hochberg 2007: 140), to imagine the politics of the present otherwise. This comes from a contemporary political impasse predicated on the idea of partition which persists despite its logical impossibility. This refers, on the one hand, to the aforementioned architectural impossibility of partitioning the West Bank, as described in Eyal Weizman's evocation of a 'hollow land' (Weizman 2007). On the other, it refers to a cultural partitioning which is equally impossible. The resistance to this partition refuses the division of Arab and Jew, Palestine and Israel into East/West Eurocentric binaries, but instead is nostalgic for and recognizes Palestinian (and Muslim) culture in Southern Europe and the Americas: the *al-Andalus* of Darwish's poetic memory; the archives of the Palestinian revolution's filmmaking in Rome's *Archivio Audiovisio del Movimento Operaio e Democratico* (AAMOD);[2] the traces of Pasolini Anastas and Alsharif found in Basilicata; the diaspora in Chile. A transnational Palestinian culture which is both in and of the West feels particularly vital at a time when the 'Question of Palestine' in the West – politically speaking – is still (and increasingly) a taboo one.

Imagining liberation beyond the national: The revolutionary archive and the post-Palestinian present

The sixth chapter of Nadia Yaqub's *Palestinian Cinema in the Days of Revolution* (2018), a comprehensive and sustained historical study of the filmmaking of the Palestinian revolution, situates the legacy of the revolution within twenty-first-century Palestinian filmmakers' work. It cites both efforts within the last decade to recover and digitize elements of the 'lost' Palestinian film archive (Yaqub 2018: 199) and films that incorporate archival material from this period, or as is the case with *When I Saw You*, borrow from the mise en scène of revolutionary cinema (ibid.: 201). While the book's broader thesis diverts from my own – that a resistance of the image in the selected films can be traced back to the image questioning inherent in early Palestinian revolutionary cinema – Yaqub's book does identify what it terms a 'post-national movement' emerging in contemporary Palestinian cinema, perhaps significantly, in experimental short filmmaking. Citing the video art of Basma Alsharif and Sama Alshaibi, she claims that '[their] relationship to the cause is characterized by distance. Their engagement with questions of national identity, state building, and the right to return to Palestine is shaped by a keen awareness of what is and is not politically possible in this historical moment' (ibid.: 218).

Questions of distance and political (im)possibility are crucial ones, as it is from the distance of elsewhere that the recent work of Basma Alsharif, Larrisa Sansour and Elia Suleiman seeks to connect a globalized Palestine to a Palestinianized globe: connecting Palestine's colonial past and present to other analogous experiences at a time when state-based 'solutions' crash against the rocks of the 'One State Reality', against which Sophie Azeb posits the 'no-state solution' in which Palestinians 'make space, not states' (Azeb 2019: 23). The task of imagining the present otherwise – at a time when the political status quo seemingly forecloses alternatives – is one with which this post-Palestinian turn grapples. The remainder of this chapter will examine how this post-Palestinian turn manifests, briefly examining the work of Basil Khalil, before focussing on Larissa Sansour and Elia Suleiman's temporal and spatial rearticulations of a post-Palestinian present.

Basil Khalil's inverted states of the absurd

British-Palestinian filmmaker Basil Khalil's work responds to the post-Palestinian condition with an elevated sense of the absurd, creating imaginative geographies which invert spatial ordering to critique the fossilized present reality.

Thus the discordant realties of partitioned co-existence are inverted for a logic of co-dependence in his absurdist encounter between orthodox settlers and Palestinian Carmelite nuns, *Ave Maria* (2015). This short film deals with a family of settlers whose car crashes into the Virgin Mary statue outside an enormous, fortress-like convent in the West Bank. The disembodied head of the statue lies prone in a blood-like pooling of oil, the first of several scenes in which the limits of religious tolerance are tested. The competing laws of religious dogma create a series of absurd encounters, as the accident happens both on the dawning of *Shabat* and during the nuns' (near perpetual) vow of silence. Despite the settlers' predicament and need of help, there is an initial insistence on deference to the laws of *Shabat*, such as in a scene where Moshe attempts to call a friend to be rescued from 'Arab territory', and insists Sister Marie makes the call for him, breaking her vow of silence. She dials the number, but leaves the phone on the table, forcing Moshe to eventually relent and pick up the receiver. Such compromises occur throughout the film, as a fractious camaraderie develops to achieve their goals: a return to silence and the settlement, respectively.

Khalil's forthcoming feature (currently in post-production), *A Gaza Weekend* (2022), takes the reality of the security wall which keeps Gaza one of the most isolated and controlled strips of land on Earth and puts it in an unspecified future where said isolation makes it a haven after a viral epidemic ravages Israel. Ironically delayed by Covid-19, the film imagines an Israeli state embargoed by the UN by land, air and sea and a Gazan taking a job smuggling Israelis through tunnels into Gaza and to the port, complicated by a delay which leaves a British-Israeli couple stranded in his basement.

Such inverted imaginings hold a mirror up to both the ideal and messy reality of co-existence and perpetual state of emergency that deems occupations and blockades a 'security necessity'. Khalil's comedic mirror effect allows an inverted image of this world to be critically reflected on.

Larissa Sansour's heterotopian non-futures

The work of Larissa Sansour emerges in a fossilized present, wary of teleological nationalist thinking which binds an *archē* to a *telos*. It doesn't so much imagine either utopian or dystopian Palestinian futures, as borrow the visual grammar of science fiction to require us to look at the world as it is in order to allow us to think how it might be otherwise. Sansour was born in East Jerusalem and resides in London (via Denmark and the United States). Sansour's work blends live action and digital images to construct imagined 'post-Palestinian' landscapes, the science fiction framing suggesting a temporal 'post', but instead primarily drawing on a spatial thinking of architectural and archaeological practices to reflect heterotopian presents. In 'Of Other Spaces', Foucault defines heterotopias as 'something like counter-sites, a kind of effectively enacted utopia in which the real sites, all the other real sites that can be found within the culture, are simultaneously represented, contested, and inverted' (Foucault 1986: 24).

Sansour's 2012 work *Nation Estate* takes Eyal Weizman's 'politics of verticality' (2007: 12–16) – the attempts to partition Palestine-Israel both horizontally and vertically thus layering two national claims to the same space on top of each other – to its logical, extreme. A Palestinian State is imagined not horizontally but rather inverted, as vertically partitioned from Israel. The Nation Estate of the title imagines a Palestinian state as a heterotopic site of decontextualized, fragmentary symbols and signifiers of Palestinian-ness, a museum of the symbols of the Palestinian archipelago if you will, contained across the floors of a single, looming high-rise block.

The floors are accessed by key/ID card and elements of Palestinian sites occupy vertically partitioned floors, given proper names such as Bethlehem, Jerusalem and Hebron. The problem of partitioning the Temple Mount/Haram al-Sharif is 'solved' by its existence in two places at once. It is both rendered on the Jerusalem floor of the building, while the original remains visible through the window of the tower block, a 'Jerusalem without Palestinians'. Although this duplication seems absurd, it in fact echoes political proposals articulating a vertical partition in an attempt to 'solve' the Euclidian impossibility of partitioning Israel's three dimensions from Palestine's. Eyal Weizman explains that during the 2000 Camp David Summit, Clinton suggested a vertical partitioning of the Temple Mount/Haram al-Sharif, explaining that 'Palestinians would control the surface of the Haram al-Sharif, the Dome of the Rock and Al-Aqsa mosque on top of it, while Israeli sovereignty would extend

Figure 5.1 A vertical politics of partition in *Nation Estate* (Larissa Sansour, 2012). ©Larissa Sansour.

Figure 5.2 Bethlehem as museum-piece in *Nation Estate* (Larissa Sansour, 2012). ©Larissa Sansour.

to the "depth of the ground" underneath, where the temples were presumed to have lain' (Weizman 2007: 14). The artwork imagines if not exactly the death of the two-state 'solution', then its coming-into-being as an always already living death, a museum of Palestinian signifiers as synthetic representation, securely out of the field of visibility of Israel in which Bethlehem becomes, like the other sites of the building, a mere heritage exhibit.

The past that will have been: *In the Future They Ate from the Finest Porcelain* (2016)

Sansour's more recent piece, *In the Future They Ate from the Finest Porcelain* (2016) again exists in some indeterminate retro future (as suggested by the temporal ambiguity in the title), rendered here as a seemingly post-apocalyptic site in which a representative (self-described as a 'narrative terrorist') of civilization (perhaps lost, but this remains ambiguous) drops porcelain into the desert landscape in the hope that future archaeologists might discover it as evidence of that civilization's existence on the land. The piece both satirizes and interrogates the political uses of archaeology to reinforce present territorial claims. The juxtaposition of the imagery of science fiction (the plates are dropped as bombs from spaceships), Palestinian signifiers (the porcelain is decorated with the imagery of the *kefiyyeh*) and figures from Palestine's colonial past (figures dressed in the outfits from both the British Mandate and Ottoman

Figures 5.3 and 5.4 Interrogating the politics of archaeology at the threshold of disappearance in *In the Future They Ate from the Finest Porcelain* (Larissa Sansour, Søren Lind, 2016). ©Larissa Sansour and Søren Lind.

Figure 5.4

periods) creates a densely layered visual language of colonialism and erasure alongside the politics of myth in creating the concept of a people.

While the film works as a critique of the nationalist weaponizing of architecture in Palestine-Israel, it also asks, like Alsharif's works, difficult questions as to coming to terms with loss, imagining a post-Palestinian future as an archive to be discovered as evidence of having been.

In her own reading, Hochberg describes the film in terms of an inversion of the practice of archaeology, namely 'the replacement of "digging" (the archaeological defining activity) with "burying" in Sansour's film: the burial of fake archaeological findings for future discoveries' (Hochberg 2021: 34). As with a positioning of the archive as a guardian of the past from which to depart, archaeology here is framed in terms of how it is used as a science to reinforce nationalist claims in order to propose a 'new counterarchaeological manner' in Palestinian visual art (ibid.). However, a more accurate description of how archaeology functions more broadly in Palestine-Israel and its cinema is not through digging/burying, but through the lens of concealing/uncovering, a logic of haunting Hochberg (2015) applies to the role of ruins in the Israeli literary imagination. Just such a logic of archaeological concealment is exemplified in Eyal Weizman's observations on the use of mythical facades in Jewish settlements on the outskirts of Jerusalem. Tracing the architectural development of outer Jerusalem neighbourhoods, Weizman follows the evolution of stone as a political symbol, first as a structural element, and latterly, a 6-cm-thick 'stick-on signifying element for creating visual unity between new construction and the Old City' (Weizman 2007: 30). In this way, Weizman highlights the dual meaning that the *archē* holds for nationalist projects: not merely as an 'origin' to be excavated and 'revealed' but also a specular surface of false continuity, giving the modern a veneer of the mythic.

Similarly, the subsuming of Palestinian architectural ruins into the taxonomy of Israel's archaeological practices attempts to conceal the spectre of Palestinian presence in Israel – a repression doomed to fail – as witnessed in the work of Kamal Aljafari and Annemarie Jacir in Chapter 2 of this book. In those particular examples, the fact that a Hebrew song of Mizrahi loss can be haunted by a Palestinian and the ruins of a Palestinian village passed off as 'biblical' haunted by a Palestinian assumed to be an American Jew uncovers the historical intimacy of Levantine cultures that both Israeli and Palestinian nationalisms purposefully conceal.

This also points to an alternative practice of archaeology as a conceptual uncovering, close to Said's thinking of a Palestinian (and subaltern) archaeology as 'opened to the existence of other histories and a multiplicity of voices' (Said 2003: 50). Said's thinking of archaeology here draws on his own contrapuntal readings of Freud's archaeological excavations of Jewish identity opening it out to its non-Jewish origins in *Moses and Monotheism* (1939). In fact, what Said infers from Freud's 'excavation' of identity resonates with Giorgio Agamben's (2009) concept of 'philosophical archaeology' examined in Chapter 4, that which seeks the *archē* as 'not properly a past but a moment of arising; however, access to such can only be obtained by returning back to the point where it was covered over and neutralized by tradition' (Agamben 2009: 105). It is only through the completion of a philosophical archaeology that an *archē* will be revealed, thus it is a regression that reveals a past that will have been, a past that has been concealed and thus not lived through. In this link between archaeological regression and traumatic repression, Agamben engages with Cathy Caruth's work on trauma in *Unclaimed Experience*, in order to trace the currents that link memory and forgetting to perception of the present. 'The point of archaeology,' Agamben tells us, 'is to gain access to the present for the first time, beyond memory and forgetting, or rather, at the threshold of their indifference' (ibid.: 106). The problem of excavating the present from the forces of memory and forgetting is the focus of Sansour's most recent work.

It passes but it does not pass away: Larissa Sansour's *In Vitro* (2019)

In Vitro (2019) follows Larissa Sansour's loose 'trilogy' on Palestinian elsewheres, *A Space Exodus* (2009), *Nation Estate* (2012) and *In the Future They Ate from the Finest Porcelain* (2015). Each of those films imagined the coming-into-being of a Palestinian state as an act of virtual impossibility: an 'exodus' to the moon, a vertically partitioned state museum in Jerusalem and a time travelling archaeological resistance group. This concern with questions of fossilized presents and future archives is most fully developed in her most recent work.

In Vitro takes place in an underground bunker in Bethlehem (in which an enormous orchard is being cultivated) a number of years after an ecological disaster, which is rendered in an extraordinary opening sequence. A slow, reverse tracking shot reveals an eerily still Bethlehem. A quiet street is suddenly flooded with rushing crude oil, filling the street and eventually the entire frame. This extraordinary moment of ecological crisis recalls the opening of Basma Alsharif's *Ouroboros* (2017), in which the tide breaks backwards from the shore of Gaza. In a similar vein to that film, in which Gaza existed as a 'perpetual present', this Bethlehem is occupied by the present as an oppressive present absence. The film's two protagonists, Dunia and Alia, form a generational counterpoint: Dunia, an ageing, bedridden scientist, and Alia, a cloned version of her daughter. This counterpoint is formalized in the film's structure, which partitions the frame in two, a technique used for both single shots and for split screens. The latter are used regularly to partition the enormous underground space and the

Bethlehem scenes of the past, while the former reveal the underground orchard in its totality. These split screens also arrange the dialogue, alternating between front and side profile as Dunia and Alia put forward their counter-generational views on nostalgia, memory and the nation. These dialogues revolve around the Saidian notion of the problem of the present, which is spatialized as a vast, black, spherical void in the basement of the underground bunker.[3] This problem of the present is very much the problem of the post-Palestinian present, in which memories of exile and deferred return stand in tension with an uncertain yet-to-come. Alia, as a clone, is filled with this 'congentital exile' and seeks a clean break with it. Dunia, despite seeing the clones as the guardians of something restorative, is also acutely aware of this blocked present, as the following monologue illustrates:

> This present barely exists. You were born into purgatory. Like past generations in this place. They all tried to redeem this present. Lit it up with old stories and promises of thing to come. But the void only grows. Soon it's so imposing and violent it devours everything in its way.

The past, in both the general inherited memories of exile but also the specific historical weight of Bethlehem, overcodes this present. When Alia bemoans the abstraction of loss (we see images of Dunia and her child before the disaster and grainy, archival images of historic Bethlehem), she laments that, if and when she goes above ground, 'all I will see is a ghost town'. This brings the reply from Dunia that 'Bethlehem was always a ghost town. The present upstaged by the past'. It is just such an overwhelming past that must be destroyed to begin anew. The extraordinary opening scenes of Bethlehem ablaze with oil fires suggest just such a clean break with the weight of the past, a point Sansour clarifies: 'It was important to begin with these oil spills gushing through the city and into the Church of the Nativity. For me, all of Bethlehem's iconographies and structures had to be dismantled before the dialogue could start' (Sansour 2021).

The film continues to mark a generational distinction in attitudes towards the past, with Alia rejecting Dunia's past 'out there', contrasting it with the fossilized eternity of the bunker: 'The only past I know is here. Everything else is just a fairytale', she claims. When Dunia retorts that such tales forge nations, Alia's response lays waste to the iconography of nationhood, much in the same way the fire laid waste to the iconography of Bethlehem:

> I don't care about your nations. Their stories, their rituals, the repetition of imagery. This struggle, this land, these seasons. Memory channelled by a

handful of tropes. These scents, this fabric, this history reduced to symbols and iconography. A liturgy chronicling our losses. These plagues. These disasters. This exodus.

Such a cynical view of this assemblage of signifiers of national identity echoes both Sansour's own *In the Future They Ate from the Finest Porcelain* (2016) and the thought of Elia Suleiman. The former satirizes the facts on the ground of nationalist archaeology to maintain the fiction of a homogenous people. With regard to the latter, Suleiman's own work (particularly *Divine Intervention* (2002)) and views are highly sceptical of the straitjacket of national identity. Citing the Israeli state's co-option of hummus and falafel as symbols of the national cuisine, Suleiman sees the construction of essentializing identities as the preserve of 'not necessarily those who are under occupation, but those who are into occupation' (Suleiman 2016). Citing the overemphasis of certain symbols of Palestinian identity – food, embroidery, *keffiyehs* and dancing *dabke* – as a restrictive if understandable 'counter-effect' of occupation, Suleiman proposes a more elastic identification with a commitment to liberation, unburdened by national iconography.

The refrain of the oil spill towards the end of *In Vitro* seems to signify the local/global anxieties of the film. These hold that the icons and symbols of the national must burn to start anew, but also that Palestine's long history of colonialism is globally connected – an extractive world system built on fossil fuels – and the twilight of the Anthropocene brings not a need to redeem a national identity but rather a new ecology. It is away from identity and towards Suleiman's more elastic identification of post-Palestinian elsewheres this chapter now turns.

'It might as well be elsewhere': *It Must Be Heaven* (Suleiman 2019)

Elia Suleiman's most recent feature, *It Must Be Heaven* (2019), is both a logical continuation of his preceding Nazareth/Jerusalem trilogy and a logical departure. As a continuation, the first thirty minutes take place in a familiar Nazareth of absurd, quotidian vignettes, much like the opening thirty minutes of *The Time That Remains* (2009). However, while that film regressed back to the Nakba to tell a personal history of that city, this one departs spatially, moving out from Palestine-Israel in order to escape Palestine elsewhere but, in the post-Palestinian manner of Basma Alsharif, only finding Palestinian elsewheres.

Much like his previous works, the absurd vignettes are punctuated by moments of banal violence and pathos. Just such an example of the banality of state violence occurs at the thirty-minute mark, as Suleiman's 'E.S.' drives to Haifa airport. E.S. sees a police patrol car in his rear-view mirror, which draws closer before pulling alongside. The two military police officers in the front swap sun glasses with each other, admiring themselves in the rear-view mirror. In the back seat sits a blindfolded, still woman, strikingly evocative of Ahed Tamimi.[4] A melancholic E.S. looks on, before accelerating away from this casual flaunting of state oppression.

The preceding scene is one of immense pathos in the context of Suleiman's previous works. Suleiman's first feature, *Chronicle of a Disappearance* (1996), closed on an image of his parents sleeping in front of the television, and ended on a dedication: 'To my parents, my only homeland.' *Divine Intervention* (2002) is marked by his father's passing and *The Time That Remains* (2009) is in part an elegy to his father and an homage to his mother, who features in the contemporary Nazareth scenes. The scene in question in *It Must Be Heaven* begins with Suleiman planting a lone olive tree in the garden, before cutting to a stoic removal company (whose ironic brand name in Arabic reads 'Smile') loading up boxes, a wheelchair and a walker: the last remnants of his parents in their absence. With this 'homeland' now lost, E.S. departs, first for Paris (the director's home) and then New York.

The world he finds beyond Palestine-Israel is a globalized Palestine, a world John Collins (2011) (following Paul Virilio) sees as structured by a logic of militarized acceleration, of securitization and 'dromology'.[5] This is a world in which Palestine is the laboratory of an 'emerging global homeland security economy' (Collins 2011: 17). This globally securitized world manifests in a starkly empty Paris of poverty and racialized policing, in which police frequently outnumber citizens: measuring and controlling the café terrace E.S. drinks at, following an elderly woman along a metro platform and pursuing two Arab men on roller blades. Suleiman's unintentional arrival on Bastille Day means a near silent city is punctuated by militarized bursts of sound: jets overhead, tanks rolling through deserted streets and the sound of hooves from the Republican Guard's Cavalry Regiment. In New York, the sound of militarized skies again permeates the atmosphere, as E.S. finds himself surveilled by a helicopter overhead. A trip to the bodega sees the space function as a synecdoche of US gun culture, as aisles are rendered impassable by every shopper's open-carry of an increasingly bewildering array of firearms, from handguns to bazookas.

While this scene appears surreal on the surface, in the legislative and cultural context of 2022 it feels darkly prophetic for the wider country.

The two major set pieces in Paris and New York reflect a stubborn and persistent framing of the proper noun 'Palestine' in Western discourse. In Paris, this manifests in a meeting with a film producer, who declares his sympathy with the Palestinian cause, while – cautious to avoid an overtly orientalizing gesture – acknowledging that his production company does not want a film that would be 'too didactic or exotic about Palestine'. Nonetheless, Suleiman is informed, 'this project doesn't correspond to our editorial policy in the sense that it takes place in Palestine but it might as well be elsewhere. It could even take place here.' This scene embodies the fundamental structural tension in the film: On the one hand, E.S. cannot leave Palestine behind, its militarized traces structure the post-9/11 West and thus home rumbles in his wake. On the other, any attempt to uncouple his Palestinian-ness from 'the cause' – an image of Palestine as an image of resistance – or construct a Palestinian identification that doesn't correspond to such a set of fixed signifiers is rejected as a homogenous 'elsewhere' by those sympathetic only to a Palestine as an idea of perpetual struggle/resilient suffering.

Conversely, in the New York sequence the danger of the mere existence of the proper noun 'Palestine' in the anglophone West is revealed as a scandalous taboo. This is depicted in a scene in which a female performance artist in central park, dressed in white with angel wings attached, drops her coat and turns slowly to reveal a top fashioned from the Palestinian flag. This act triggers the immediate sound of sirens, as the NYPD give chase with a blanket, attempting to suppress this display of 'public indecency'. Such a visual metaphor will be familiar to intellectuals and artists who work on Palestine in the anglophone West: from the experiences of Edward Said and his Palestinian contemporaries at Columbia, to the 2017 cancelling of the premiere of a stage production of Ghassan Kanafānī's *Returning to Haifa* (2000), to the UK education secretary banning schools from sending students to the Tottenham Palestine Literary Festival in 2011. In a context where the two-State solution remains the stated foreign policy goal of the United States and the UK, to bring 'Palestine' into visual or discursive being in the anglophone West is still the forbidden montage par excellence.

The film ends, perhaps appropriately, on a 'pessoptimistic' note in a club in Haifa, the resting place of Emile Habiby. Habiby, author of *The Secret Life of Saeed the Pessoptimist* (1974), is perhaps the most enduring cultural figure of Palestinian presence within Israeli society. Haifa, a port city with a complex historical memory of Arab-Jewish, Palestinian and Israeli co-presence, like Lod and Acre, is often lauded as a 'model' of co-existence. This ideological model is challenged when Palestinian citizens of Israel express solidarity with those in the Occupied Territories, or express a desire for meaningful equality. Despite this difficulty, in the post-Palestinian imagination it retains a kernel of transformative post-national promise. In this cathartic and hedonistic club scene Suleiman sees a new generation of globally networked, post-Palestinian subjects whose struggle is one born as much of affiliation as filiation, a generation 'now conscious that Palestine is a concept of gender equality, a concept of being progressive, and a concept of building identifications with all injustices in the world' (Suleiman 2021). That is, a Palestine bigger than Palestine.

Notes

Introduction: Writing back – Edward Said, contrapuntalism and the 'Image of Palestine'

1 My use of the hyphen here in contemporary usage for the geopolitical space follows Edward Said, Mahmoud Darwish, Ella Shohat and Gil Hochberg in refusing the very discursive parameters which construct Arab and Jew, Palestine and Israel as politically and culturally partitionable figures. I use this term for the cultural space which not only recognizes the 'Two-State Solution' as a chimera but also resists the 'One-State Reality' that is the political status quo. References to the State of Israel are to its current political/legal entity, while references to Palestine-Israel refer to the cultural impossibility of the continued partition project of the State and the cinema (particularly – but far from exclusively – the Cinema of the Interior examined in Chapter 2) which overtly haunts this partition project.

2 In *The World, the Text, and the Critic* (1983), Said speaks of the tension that pulls the secular critic between two poles: 'One is the culture to which critics are bound filiatively (by birth, nationality, profession); the other is a method or system acquired affiliatively (by social and political conviction, economic and historical circumstances, voluntary effort and willed deliberation)' (Said 1983: 25). Said's own 'affiliations' were subject positions he moved through by virtue of his exilic critical distance.

3 This lack of hierarchy is evolutionary. Early (Renaissance) uses of counterpoint tended to relate to fixed melodic centre, the *cantus firmus*, whereas from the Baroque period the style evolved to free counterpoint, the relation between these independent tones.

4 It is worth noting that the music terms Said is working with – counterpoint, tonality, atonality – have a meaning embedded in and particular to Western music and culture. The chromatic scale around which tonal music is organized consists of twelve equal intervals a semitone apart, and twelve-tone equal temperament (ET) is the tuning system which is the foundation of Western classical music. In non-Western music cultures, microtonality (any tones which fall between the keys of a piano tuned in ET) is more common. In following Said and Adorno, I'm cognizant of the risk of being seen to impose a Western theoretical framework to Palestinian cinema. However, Said's own descriptions of *After the Last Sky* as

drawing on Adorno's atonality and the non-representational art of the Islamic world point to his own contrapuntal rhythms of non-belonging: A Palestinian in the West but not of it, affiliated to both while estranged from each. Said's own affiliative double consciousness of exile provides a model for the filmmakers in this book: Palestinians elsewhere often looking for Palestinian elsewheres, in the tradition of Said, Mahmoud Darwish and Anton Shammas.

5   In his early writings (1953–4), in which he is beginning to develop his system of orders, Lacan (1988: 66) states, 'The real, or what is perceived as such, is what resists symbolisation absolutely.' It is both the pre-linguistic state from which we are delivered and traumatic irruption through which language and symbolization fail. In his usage of *das Ding* Lacan draws on the work of Freud, noting the existence in German of two words for thing: *das Ding* and *die Sache*. While the latter conveys the representation of a thing in reality, the former for Lacan is 'the beyond-of-the-signified' (1988: 54) and as such characterized by 'primary affect'. It is thus within the register of the Real and, as such, irrupts into the Symbolic and the Imaginary as trauma.

6   When discussing Schonberg's approach to variation, Adorno (2006: 46) writes that 'all is identical, "the same". But the meaning of this identity is reflected as nonidentity. The initial material is fashioned so that holding it fast means at the same time transforming it.' This relationship between continuity and transformation is one Adorno comes back to, reflecting on the likeness of Schonberg's use of classical bourgeois music to that of contemporary materialist dialectic uses of Hegel, in that it both 'annuls and saves it' (ibid.: 48).

7   Originally delivered as a radio address a year before Adorno's death in 1969.

8   In his essay *What Is the Contemporary?*, Agamben references a note Roland Barthes made in his Colleges de France lectures: 'The contemporary is the untimely' (Agamben 2009b: 40).

9   The title alludes to Darwish's (1984) poem *Earth Presses against Us*. The poem was written two years after Darwish left Beirut and became a wandering exile, living in Cairo, Tunis and Paris. In its second line the poem expresses the corporeal experience of a body politic shattered by exile, with the words 'to pass through, we pull off our limbs' (2003: 9). The title of Said and Mohr's book is taken from the poem's middle section, which poses the rhetorical questions: 'Where should we go after the last border? Where should birds fly after the last sky?' (ibid.). This language of Darwish's late style enacts, as Said (1994a: 115) himself recognizes, a thinking beyond both the contemporary moment and finitude. That is, 'survival after the aftermath' (ibid.).

10 Said writes with a deep awareness of his own exilic position. Said, in conversation with W. J. T. Mitchell, defines narrative as 'speaking from a place' (1998: 26). The

places from which Said speaks in *After the Last Sky* (at a great physical distance from Palestine-Israel, laterally to Mohr's photography, critically to the nationalisms of both Israel and the Arab states) problematize a notion of a stable Palestinian identity, an instability reflected in Said's slippage between pronouns (1986: 6) and his textual de-centring of images of Palestine throughout the book.

11 Habiby's (1974) novel *Al-Waqāʾiʿ al-gharībah fī ʾkhtifāʾ Saʿīd Abī ʾl-Naḥsh al-Mutashāʾil* (*The Secret Life of Saeed the Pessoptimist*) combines the Arabic *mutafaʾil* (optimist) with *mutashaʾim* (pessimist) to form the portmanteau *mutashaʾil*. According to Said (1986: 26), this word 'repeats the Palestinian habit of combining opposites like *la* ("no") and *naʿam* ("yes") into *laʿam*.'

12 The filmmakers around which the chapters of this book on 'transnational' Palestine are structured have an atonal relationship with Palestine as both a place and idea, with the vast majority of them having lived, worked or grown up (in some cases all three) globally. Their distance from the cause is both temporal (the post-Oslo moment of political stasis) and spatial (not living, working or overtly focussed on representing life in the Occupied Territories). The filmmaking of the Occupied Territories in general and the West Bank in particular has been well documented in the context of 'roadblock movies' (Marks 2006; Gertz and Khleifi 2008; Dickinson 2016), filmmaking most associated with the Second Intifada but continuing thematically in the work of Hany Abu Assad, Khaled Jarrar and Rashid Masharawi, among others. The perspective of the atonal cinema examined in this book, with its criticality founded in a resistance of image, comes from a putative 'luxury' of distance, in which Palestinians *elsewhere* engage with images of Palestinian *elsewheres*.

Chapter 1

1 24 January 2003, to be precise.
2 The double genitive here suggests both the subject's adapting to survive, and the essential permanence of the status quo.
3 The PLO maintained a number of archives in Beirut during their exile there. Filmmaking materials were stored in the Palestine Cinema Institute Archive (PCI) archive. The whereabouts of this archive after the 1982 Israeli invasion of Lebanon remain unknown. However, as Nick Denes (2014) and Nadia Yaqub (2018) highlight, describing it as lost is somewhat misleading when multiple copies of films were distributed around the PLOs global networks. A diasporic scattering might be a more accurate term than loss, with copies of materials being found and digitized in Italy and Germany.

4   A note on usage. While throughout the book I use the term 'Third World' to describe the non-aligned movement, in its theoretical use I retain the original French, *tiers-mondisme* and *tiers-mondiste*. The Third World is a translation of the original French *tiers monde*, which was coined by economist Alfred Sauvy, retaining the revolutionary potential of *le tiers état* in pre-revolutionary France. While coined in Europe, the French term travelled out of Europe, with Frantz Fanon using it to express a subaltern revolutionary consciousness. Christoph Kalter notes that 'the othering implicit in the French term *tiers* – which carries connotations of "outsider" and can be translated as "other" instead of "third" – was foregrounded, but now reversed in its perspective. Instead of a Third World other, Fanon asserted a Third World self' (Kalter 2017: 120). For more on the genealogy of this term, see C. Kalter (2017) 'From global to local and back: The 'Third World' concept and the new radical left in France', *Journal of Global History*, 12(1): 115–36.

5   Vertov's notion of editing as a 'factory of facts' draws on the Latin route of 'fact' itself as a construct, *facere*, to make. Reality is thus something to be made and remade through cinema.

6   In a 1980 Cahiers du Cinema article, Godard (1985: 460; emphasis in original) claims that 'cinema isn't one image *after* another, it is one image *plus* another forming a third – this third being formed in the moment of viewing the film' ('Le cinéma ce n'est pas une image après l'autre, c'est une image plus une autre qui en forment une troisième, la troisieme étant du reste formée par le spectateur au moment où il voit le film.')

7   Edward Said highlights the relative temporariness and lack of severity of this term when contrasted with the Nakba of 1948, and its suggestion of a catastrophic deviation from continuity, arguing that *naksa* 'suggests nothing more radical than a relapse, a temporary setback, as in the process of recovery from an illness' (Said 2000: 47). There is an irony here considering the 'temporary permanence' of settlement building and the contemporary political impasse, an irony Said was perhaps not unaware of as he moved away from the two-state solution towards the end of his life.

8   Literally 'between dog and wolf', when fading light makes the two figures indistinguishable. In Genet's use, the term signifies a betweenness of states, and corresponds to the fragility and ephemeral state he sees in the Palestinian fedayeen.

9   Foucault first uses this term in *Discipline and Punish* (1977) towards the end of the first chapter. When reflecting on why he is writing a history of the prison, he poses the rhetorical question: 'Why? Simply because I am interested in the past? No if one means by that writing a history of the past in terms of the present. Yes, if one means writing a history of the present' (Foucault 1977: 31). This marks a shift in Foucault's thinking towards the emergence of his genealogical method; that is, an

analysis (or uncovering) of how (often forgotten) historical struggles and power relations emerge in contemporary practices.

Chapter 2

1 Chad Emmet (1995: 64) notes that Nazareth received a lesser classification than Nazareth Illit in an Israeli Law passed to stimulate capital investment, which led to a disparity in both industrial development and unemployment rates.
2 A historical-legal condition of Palestinians within Israel and the subtitle of Suleiman's later film *The Time That Remains*, this concept will be unpacked later in the chapter.
3 Jacques Derrida is insistent on this disjointed temporality in *Specters of Marx*, claiming of the revenant: 'One cannot control its comings and goings because *it begins by coming back*' (Derrida 1994: 11).
4 Along with Ghassan Kanafānī, Emile Habiby is perhaps the best-known Palestinian novelist. He remained in Israel, helping found the Communist Party and sitting on the Knesset. His best-known work is his 1974 novel *Al-Waqā'i' al-gharībah fī 'khtifā' Sa'īd Abī 'l-Naḥsh al-Mutashā'il* (*The Secret Life of Saeed the Pessoptimist*). The literal translation of Habiby's novel: 'The strange events leading to the disappearance of the man known as father of the bad omen, the pessimist-optimist.'
5 Deir Yassin was a Palestinian village near Jerusalem, which was depopulated and the site of a massacre by the Irgun, a Zionist paramilitary group, on 9 April 1948. A psychiatric hospital, Kfar Shaul, now lies on the site of the former village.
6 While the translation here is literally exterior, it refers to those (like Said) in exile and who, during the PLO's early years, viewed Palestinians in the Israeli state with suspicion. This diminished as their steadfastness and increasing politicization was recognized, and the revolutionary optimism of exiled Palestinians after the Palestinian revolution dissipated.
7 When questioned at the 2019 London Film Festival on the appearance of Handala imagery in his most recent work, *It Must Be Heaven* (2019), Suleiman claimed any similarities with al-Ali were coincidental rather than an homage.
8 In contrast to other mixed cities in Israel, such as Lod, Ramle and Haifa, Nazareth is unique in having an Arab population – to the point of near exclusivity.
9 In English translations of Aristotle's *Politics*, 'faction' is commonly the English translation for *stasis*.
10 The shot and framing are an intertextual reference to the same gift shop featured in Suleiman's *Chronicle of a Disappearance* (1996), which was the locus of much of that film's 'activity'.

11 For Freud, disembodied corporeal elements betray a heightened uncanniness. He writes, 'Severed limbs, a severed head, a hand detached from the arm (as in a fairy tale by Hauff), feet that dance by themselves ... – all of these have something highly uncanny about them, especially when they are credited, as in the last instance, with independent activity' (ibid.: 150).

12 Aljafari notes in the establishing shot of Ramle that remaining families in Jaffa and Ramle in 1948 were given the houses of other Palestinians.

13 In Hebrew, literally 'Eastern' (Shohat 2010: 154).

14 Both Gil Hochberg (2007) and Ella Shohat (2006) describe this process at length, articulating how the spectre of anti-Semitic orientalism in Europe compels a form of orientalism to be re-produced in hegemonic Euro-Israeli culture. Essentially, they both argue, a form of pathological partitioning occurs so as to disassociate any trace of 'Arabness' from the national narrative.

15 At the 2013 Palestine and the Moving Image Conference, Aljafari explained the painstaking process of archiving the Palestinians (often friends and acquaintances) caught in the frames of Israeli and Hollywood Cinema shot in Jaffa (notably, *The Delta Force* (1986)), and how bringing these spectral figures to the foreground of a lost Jaffa would constitute his next feature – which would become *Recollection* (2015).

16 The second segment of the film documents al-Manshiyya – a neighbourhood that was occupied by the Irgun and razed in 1948, with much of the Arab population being forced to leave by sea to Gaza and Egypt, and some moving into the Ajami neighbourhood (Zochrot 2014).

17 The film's clearest forebear is Alexander Sokurov's *Russian Ark* (2002), a vertical history of Russia and Europe.

18 Gitai has spoken of this interruption in interviews at the release of the film. In a 2014 interview with Nienke Huitenga, he states, 'As a citizen of Israel, I think the relation between Jews and Arabs should not be interrupted. So when I translate this to my own language of film, to the syntax of cinema, I also don't want to interrupt' (Gitai 2014).

Chapter 3

1 While Naficy's 'Accented Style' is quite nuanced, there are numerous slippages in his distinctions between diaspora and exile. The Palestinian case is described as both a diaspora and exile at different points in the book. Despite this, some overly schematic distinctions put each category into rigid binaries, exemplified by the following: 'In short, while binarism and subtraction in particular accent

exilic films, diasporic films are accented more by multiplicity and addition' (Naficy 2001: 15). This chapter, in particular, but this book in general complicates a thinking of diaspora and exile centred on a homeland, which the very notion of the atonal challenges.

2   The exception to this being the work of Baeza (2014) and El Attar (2019).
3   While the Palestinian revolution would be sustained in South Lebanon and is conventionally considered to have ended in the Israeli invasion of Lebanon in 1982, its first 'death' in Jordan led to a hardened, institutionalized but factionally divided movement in Lebanon, which would be exiled (and its film archive largely destroyed) in 1982.
4   La Tierra Prometida (The Promised Land, 1973) documents the brief establishment of a socialist republic in Chile in 1932, focussing on a farmers' uprising in Palmilla. The film combines documentary and fiction, drawing on testimony of survivors and combining folksongs and restaged speeches. *Actas de Marusia* (Letters from Marusia, 1976) dramatizes a brutally suppressed miners' strike in 1925. Both films use popular memory as a strategy to critique the violent and accelerated demise of Allende's Popular Unity government.
5   Gabriel cites third cinema as both 'a soldier of liberation' alongside the gun in revolutionary struggles, but the recovery of popular memory as indicative of those other major regions where the battles have 'moved into the cultural front' (Gabriel 1989: 55).
6   The book is written by Marquez, a result of long, in-depth interviews with Littín, but uses the first person in a creative interpretation of Littín's words to describe the clandestine return of the director to Pinochet. Marquez clarifies that he has endeavoured 'to respect the narrator's way of thinking, which does not always coincide with mine' (Marquez 1986: xxx).
7   José Miguel Palacios notes, in films made in exile in the wake of the coup, 'Chilean exile cinema's almost ritualistic gesture of freezing the frames on leftist icons: fists, red flags, Allende's close up, the presidential palace in flames' (Palacios 2016: para. 52).
8   Young Palestinians in the First Intifada were known as the 'children of the stones' for their use of stones and slingshots; this Intifada being in marked contrast to the Second by the fact that it was largely unarmed. Barbara M. Parmenter, in her 1994 book *Giving Voice to Stones: Place and Identity in Palestinian Literature*, recognizes the symbolic power stone throwing had in subverting the biblical narrative of David, 'part of Israel's national mythology of a small community pitted against giants' (Parmenter 1994: 2).
9   As Stuart Elden explains in *Terror and Territory: The Spatial Extent of Sovereignty* (2009), 'those in control of a territory – states – can act in ways that those not in

control of territory cannot' (Elden 2009: xxx). By this logic 'to control a territory is to exercise terror; to challenge territorial extent is to exercise terror'. In other words, those with control over territory can act with relative impunity due to a state-based system of rules, while those without it, who attempt to resist or challenge such a system are 'necessarily coded as "terrorists"' (ibid.). As Elden suggests, the codifying of control *of* territory as legitimate, and *challenge to* it as illegitimate, structures a logic of legitimate/illegitimate violence within those parameters.

10 The struggle between Secularism and Political Islam in Palestinian politics, to a certain extent, mirrors that across postcolonial pan-Arabist states as Marxist national liberation movements within the Tricontinental Revolution gave way to rising Political Islam. Hamas were founded in 1988 and came to prominence in the First Intifada, with their popularity growing in the perceived stasis and surrender of the Oslo Accords. Fatah somewhat opportunistically borrowed their tactics in founding their own armed wing, the Al Aqsa Brigades, who would carry out suicide attacks during the Second Intifada.

11 This can be seen in media coverage of protests against evictions in East Jerusalem's *Sheikh Jarrah* neighbourhood (made possible by the same 1950 Law of Absentee Property described in Chapter 2), which received comparatively little attention until Hamas launched rockets into Israel. This action, justified by Hamas as a 'reaction', brought decontextualized calls to condemn Hamas and stop the violence, with events in East Jerusalem barely entering into the discussion as to why tensions had escalated at this point. This was illustrated starkly (but by no means exclusively) in Husam Zomlot's (Head of the Palestinian Mission to the United Kingdom) interview on BBC's Newsnight, 10 May 2021.

12 This laissez-faire approach is exemplified most explicitly in the closing lines of the 1947 Ministry of Information film, *Portrait of Palestine*, made in the final years of the mandate, and largely presenting the British as a benevolent presence absolved of any responsibility for what may transpire next. The voiceover states, 'The Jews claim Palestine as their ancient home. The Arabs have lived there for a thousand years. Palestine's problem is whether these two kindred races can be reconciled and can live and work together in peace.' Far from its benevolent self-presentation, the British Mandate oversaw, in Jerusalem and throughout what it would term the Holy Land, a programme of de-modernization and 'a language of biblical antiquity and religious sectarianism' (Wallach 2020: 18).

13 Levinas argues that the face-to-face encounter places an ethical responsibility on the self to the other, one which exceeds its capacity to respond. Levinas's face of the other invokes the biblical injunction 'thou shalt not kill' (Levinas 1985: 89). In this way, the face is the universal site of ethics (but crucially, not *politics*)

for Levinas. In a discussion of his ethics in the wake of the Shabra and Shatilla massacres in 1982, Levinas infamously withheld the status of the other to the Palestinian, marking a distinction between neighbour and enemy in the relation between the Palestinian and the Israeli, an ostensible conflation of the realm of ethics and politics, in which the alterity of the neighbour (ethics) makes way for a political relation of enmity (Schmitt 1996). As Levinas states, when neighbour becomes enemy 'alterity takes on another character, in alterity we can find an enemy' (Levinas 1989: 294).

14 Mer Khamis was born to Jewish mother, Arna Mer, and a Palestinian father, Saliba Khamis. This identification also recalls the de-totalizing identification of Edward Said as a Jewish Palestinian.

15 The theme of cultural intifada, resistance to occupation but all forms of oppression through the arts is one Mer Khamis returns to, and was embodied in his Freedom Theatre. He states, 'We believe that the third intifada, the coming intifada, should be cultural, with poetry, music, theatre, cameras, and magazines' (Mee 2021: 168). Mer Khamis's work and life feature in Udi Aloni's essay film, *Art/Violence* (2013), which begins with a recorded interview with Mer Khamis from 2006, in which he evokes an image of corporeal violence articulated by the occupation, claiming that 'Israel is destroying the neurological system of the society'. The response to this is primarily gestural, as Mer Khamis invokes a networked, multimedia artistic response to occupation. Nevertheless, the film articulates in its title the idea of art as a weapon of resistance, evoking the Third Cinema mantra that the camera 'becomes a gun' (Getino and Solinas 1969: 107).

16 Although Israel's settlements were dismantled in 2005 and its military formally disengaged, the UN still regards Gaza as occupied due to the extent of its infrastructural control (as the next chapter explains). While this disengagement was regarded externally as a potential step towards the two-State solution, the Israeli government saw it differently, as Dov Weisglass (Ariel Sharon's senior adviser) explained, stating that disengagement 'supplies the amount of formaldehyde that is necessary so there will not be a political process with the Palestinians' (Shavit 2004: n.pag).

17 Kafr Qāsim was the site of a massacre on 29 October 1956; forty-nine Arab civilians, unaware of a curfew announced on the eve of the Sinai war, were shot and killed by the Israel Border Police. The massacre remains unrecognized officially, and along with Deir Yassin, is both a common trope of Darwish's poetry and a constitutive element of Palestinian popular memory. The words in Littín's film (in Spanish) borrow from Darwish's 'Death for Nothing', the third poem in a collection of six, *Flowers of Blood* (1967), written in part as a response to the massacre.

Chapter 4

1. Not a point of historical origin but, following Agamben (2009), a field of meaning stretched between past and present.
2. Between 1968 and 1970, Pasolini made both *Appunti per un film sull'India* ('Notes for a Film about India') (1968) and *Appunti per un'Orestiade Africana* (*Notes Towards an African Orestes*) (1970). While both contain issues of representation (which a reflexive Pasolini sometimes acknowledges), they form part of Pasolini's Marxist, Fanon-influenced filmmaking practice, *struttura da farsi* (Caminati 2016: 136). This openness sees film as a 'structure to be made' conceived as an unfinished dialogue, a provocation to revolutionary action.
3. A reference to the frequent border skirmishes on the Israel/Syria border in the 1960s.
4. The publication of Chinuk Wawa: As Our Elders Teach Us to Speak It (University of Washington Press, 2012) is credited with revitalizing the language in the Pacific North-West.
5. Literally 'prickly pear', a plant that thrives in harsh landscapes but has a sweet interior. The term, arising in the 1930s, refers to Jews born in Mandate Palestine (or Israel after 1948), as opposed to those who had immigrated. The modern Hebrew term comes from the Arabic *sabr*, meaning perseverance.
6. Distinct from, in that the Zionist project didn't have the dynamic of exploitation and enrichment between colony and metropolis that characterized European colonialism, with these rather being 'located in the self same place' (Shohat 2010: 40).
7. The actual location being California State University's Desert Studies Center Research Library.
8. Israel still retains control of Gaza's airspace and maritime space, and controls six of Gaza's seven land crossings.
9. In an interview with Gustavo Beck, Alsharif (2017b) clarifies that she 'remotely directed the scenes in Gaza'.

Chapter 5

1. The New Historians were a group of historians (including Benny Morris, Ilan Pappé and Avi Shlaim) in Israel in the 1980s who challenged prevailing orthodoxies in Israeli state history (such as Israel's role in the Nakba and its portrayal as an abandonment rather than an expulsion) through access to newly declassified documents in the Israeli military and government archives.

2 Rome's *Archivio Audiovisio del Movimento Operaio e Democratico* (AAMOD) is where Emily Jacir and German filmmaker Monica Maurer (who worked with the PFU) would discover and restore Italian films made in solidarity with the Palestinian revolution and, most significantly, restore the rushes of *Tel al Zaatar* (Mustafa Abu Ali, Pino Adriano, Jean Chamoun, 1977), 'the only Palestinian and Italian co-production, a collaboration between the Palestinian Cinema Institution and Unitlelefilm' (Jacir 2013: para. 12). Jacir's archival research was in wider project tracing the concurrent decline of the Italian Left and loss of the Palestinian revolution, and tracing their prior points of intersection.
3 This void is Sansour's own installation *Monument for Lost Time* (2019) which, along with *In Vitro*, formed part of the *Heirloom* show at the 2019 Venice Biennale.
4 Ahed Tamimi is a Palestinian activist who made global headlines as a 16-year-old in December 2017, when she was detained and sentenced to eight months in prison for slapping an IDF soldier during a protest against settlement expansion in Nabi Salih, her village.
5 Dromology is a theory Paul Virilio develops in *Speed and Politics* (1986 [1977]). Literally the science of speed, it investigates how acceleration impacts on the infrastructures and movements of modernity. Collins sees dromatic violence in the use of technologies of speed, power and control that allow the Occupation of the Palestinian Territories to continue apace (Collins 2011: 87).

References

Abu Artema, A. (2018) 'Interview: The Palestinian Who Sparked March of Return with a Facebook Post'. Interviewed by Mustafa Abu Sneineh for *Middle East Eye*, 8 June [online] Available online: http://www.middleeasteye.net/news/Gaza-great-march-return-Israel-Ahmed-Abu-Artema (accessed 15 July 2018).

Abu-Manneh, B. (2016) *The Palestinian Novel: From 1948 to the Present*. Cambridge: Cambridge University Press.

Abugattas, J. (1982) 'The Perception of the Palestinian Question in Latin America', *Journal of Palestine Studies*, 11(3): 117–28.

Acta General de Chile (1986) [Film] Dir. Miguel Littín, Chile, Cuba, Spain: Alfil Uno Cinematografica.

Adorno, T. (1989 [1964]) 'Progress', in G. Smith (ed.), *Benjamin: Philosophy, Aesthetics, History*, 84–101, Chicago: University of Chicago Press.

Adorno, T. (1996 [1966]) *Negative Dialectics*, trans. E. B. Ashton. London: Routledge.

Adorno, T. (2005 [1969]) 'Resignation', in *Critical Models: Interventions and Catchwords*, trans. H. W. Pickford, 289–93, New York: Columbia University Press.

Adorno, T. (2006 [1949]) *Philosophy of New Music*, trans. R. Hullot-Kentor. Minneapolis: University of Minnesota Press.

Agamben, G. (2000 [1993]) 'Beyond Human Rights', in G. Agamben (ed.), *Means without End: Notes on Politics*, trans. V. Binetti and C. Casarino, 15–26, Minneapolis: University of Minnesota Press.

Agamben, G. (2009a) *The Signature of All Things*. New York: Zone Books.

Agamben, G. (2009b) 'What Is the Contemporary?', in G. Agamben (ed.), *What Is an Apparatus? and Other Essays*, trans. D. Kishik and S. Pedatella, 39–54, Stanford: Stanford University Press.

Agamben, G. (2015) *Stasis: Civil War as a Political Paradigm*. Edinburgh: Edinburgh University Press.

Aljafari, K. (2010) 'This Place They Dried from the Sea: An Interview with Kamal Aljafari'. Interviewed by Nasrin Himada for *Montreal Serai*, 28 September. Available online: http://montrealserai.com/2010/09/28/this-place-they-dried-from-the-sea-an-interview-with-kamal-aljafari/ (accessed 23 July 2016).

Aljafari, K. (2016) 'Kamal Aljafari: Unfinished Balconies in the Sea'. Interviewed by Nathalie Handal for *Guernica*, 18 February. Available online: https://www.guernicamag.com/kamal-aljafari-filming-ghosts-and-unfinished-balconies/ (accessed 10 August 2020).

Alsharif, B. (2015) 'Basma Alsharif by Aily Nash: Working with, and through, Conflict'. Interviewed by Aily Nash for *Bomb Magazine*, 12 March. Available online: https://bombmagazine.org/articles/basma-alsharif/ (accessed 6 January 2018).

Alsharif, B. (2017a) 'An Endless Cycle: Basma Alsharif Discusses "Ouroboros"', *MUBI Notebook*, 9 August. Available online: https://mubi.com/notebook/posts/an-endless-cycle-basma-alsharif-discusses-ouroboros (accessed 6 January 2018).

Alsharif, B. (2017b) '*Ouroboros* and the Cycle of Violence: An Interview with Basma Alsharif'. Interviewed by Justine Smith. *Senses of Cinema*, (85). Available online: http://www.sensesofcinema.com/2017/feature-articles/basma-alsharif-interview/ (accessed 6 January 2018).

Alsharif, B. (2018) 'Interview with Basma Alsharif'. Interviewed by Helen Mackreath for *The White Review*. 30 June. Available online: http://www.thewhitereview.org/feature/interview-basma-alsharif/ (accessed 30 August 2018).

Ana Arabia (2013) [Film] Dir. Amos Gitai, France, Israel: Agav Films.

The Anabasis of May and Fusako Shigenobu, Masao Adachi, and 27 Years without Images (2013) [Film] Dir. Eric Baudelaire, France: Rai 3.

Anastas, A. (2006), 'Setting in Motion', *Rethinking Marxism*, 18(4): 476–523.

Anidjar, G. (2003) *The Jew, the Arab: A History of the Enemy*. Stanford: Stanford University Press.

Ashcroft, B., Griffiths, G. and Tiffin, H. (2002 [1989]) *The Empire Writes Back: Theory and Practice in Post-Colonial Literatures*. 2nd edn. London: Routledge.

Ave Maria (2015) [Film] Dir. Basil Khalil, Palestine, France, Germany: Incognito Films.

Azeb, S. (2019) 'Who Will We Be When We Are Free? On Palestine and Futurity', *Funambulist*, (24): 22–7.

Baeza, C. (2014) 'Palestinians in Latin America: Between Assimilation and Long-Distance Nationalism', *Journal of Palestine Studies*, 43(2): 59–72.

Ball, A. (2012) *Palestinian Literature and Film in Postcolonial Feminist Perspective*. New York: Routledge.

Barthes, R. (1993) *Camera Lucida*. London: Vintage.

Bartine, D. (2015) 'The Contrapuntal Humanisms of Edward Said', *Interdisciplinary Literary Studies* 17(1): 59–85.

Barenboim, D. and Said, E. (2004) *Parallels and Paradoxes: Explorations in Music and Society*. New York: Vintage.

Bayoumi, M. (2005) 'Reconciliation without Duress: Said, Adorno, and the Autonomous Intellectual', *Alif: Journal of Comparative Poetics*, (25): 46–64.

Bazin, A. (1967) *What Is Cinema? Volume 1*, trans. Hugh Gray. Berkeley: University of California Press.

Bazin, A. (2003 [1958]) 'Bazin on Marker', trans. D. Kehr, *Film Comment*, 39(4): 44–5.

Benjamin, W. (1999 [1982]) *The Arcades Project*, trans. H. Eidland and K. McLaughlin, Cambridge: Belknap.

Benjamin, W. (2006) *Selected Writings Vol. 4 1938-1940*. Cambridge: Belknap.
Blaine, P. (2013) 'Representing Absences in the Postdictatorial Documentary Cinema of Patricio Guzmán', *Latin American Perspectives*, 40(1): 114–30.
Brennan, T. (2021) *Places of Mind: A Life of Edward Said*. London: Bloomsbury.
Butler, J (2004) *Precarious Life: The Powers of Mourning and Violence*. London: Verso.
Caminati, L. (2016) 'Notes for a Revolution: Pasolini's Postcolonial Essay Films', in E. Papazian and C. Eades (eds), *The Essay Film: Dialogue, Politics, Utopia*, 127–44, London: Wallflower.
Caminati, L. (2019) 'Filming Decolonization: Pasolini's Geopolitical Afterlife', in L. Peretti and K. Raizen (eds), *Pier Paolo Pasolini, Framed and Unframed: A Thinker for the Twenty-First Century*, 63–77, New York: Bloomsbury.
Caruth, C. (1996) *Unclaimed Experience*. Baltimore: Johns Hopkins University Press.
El Chacal de Nahueltoro (1969) [Film] Dir. Miguel Littín, Chile: Cine Experimental de la Universidad de Chile.
Chaudhuri, S., and Finn, H. (2003) 'The Open Image: Poetic Realism and the New Iranian Cinema', *Screen*, 44(1): 38–57.
Chronicle of a Disappearance (1996) [Film] Dir. Elia Suleiman, Palestine, Israel, France, Germany, USA: Dhat Productions.
Cohen, H. (2002) 'The Internal Refugees in the State of Israel: Israeli Citizens, Palestinian Refugees', *Palestine-Israel Journal*, 9(2), Middle East Publications, Available online: http://www.pij.org/details.php?id=159.
Collins, J. (2006) 'From Portbou to Palestine and Back', *Social Text*, 24(4): 67–85.
Collins, J. (2011) *Global Palestine*. New York: Columbia University Press.
Crónicas Palestinas (2001) [Film] Dir. Miguel Littín, Chile: Pepe Torres.
Dabashi, H. (2012) *Elia Suleiman's Cinema as the Premonition of the Arab Revolutions*. [online] aljazeera.com. Available online: https://www.aljazeera.com/indepth/opinion/2012/04/20124151301368419.html (accessed 25 February 2020).
Dabashi, H. (2020) *On Edward Said: Remembrance of Things Past*. La Vergne: Haymarket Books.
Daney, S. (1999) 'Before and After the Image', *Discourse: Journal for Theoretical Studies in Media and Culture*, 21(1): 181–90.
Darwish, M. (2003) *Unfortunately, It Was Paradise: Selected Poems*, trans. M. Akash and C. Forché, Berkeley: University of California Press.
Darwish, M. (2009 [1992]) 'Eleven Planets at the End of the Andalusian Scene', in M. Darwish (ed.), *If I Were Another*, trans. F. Joudah, 57–68, New York: Farrar, Straus and Giroux.
Darwish, M. (2009 [1992a]) 'The "Red Indian's" Penultimate Speech to the White Man', in M. Darwish (ed.), *If I Were Another*, trans. F. Joudah, 69–77, New York: Farrar, Straus and Giroux.
Darwish, M. (2009 [2005]) 'Counterpoint: For Edward Said', in M. Darwish (ed.), *If I Were Another*, trans. F. Joudah, 183–92, New York: Farrar, Straus and Giroux.

Darwish, M. (2010) *Absent Presence*, trans. M. Shaheen, London: Hesperus Press.

Darwish, M. (2012) '"Exile Is So Strong Within Me, I May Bring It to the Land": A Landmark 1996 Interview with Mahmoud Darwish'. Interviewed by Helit Yeshurun, *Journal of Palestine Studies*, 42(1): 46–70.

Deleuze, G. (1989) *Cinema 2*, trans. H. Tomlinson and R. Galeta. London: Athlone

Deleuze, G., and Guattari, F. (1983). What Is a Minor Literature?, *Mississippi Review*, 11(3): 13–33.

Denes, N. (2009) 'The Precarious Life of the Palestinian Image: Reflections in the Wake of Gaza', *Vertigo*, 4(3): 26–7.

Denes, N. (2014) 'Between Form and Function', *Middle East Journal of Culture and Communication*, 7(2): 219–41.

Derrida, J. (1994) *Specters of Marx: The State of the Debt, the Work of Mourning and the New International*. New York: Routledge.

Derrida, J. (2002) 'Spectographies', in J. Derrida and B. Stiegler (eds), *Echographies of Television*, trans. J. Bajorek, 113–34, London: Polity.

Derrida, J. (2015) 'Cinema and Its Ghosts: An Interview with Jacques Derrida'. Interviewed by Antoine de Baecque and Thierry Jousse. *Discourse*, 37(1): 46–70.

Dickinson, K. (2016) *Arab Cinema Travels: Transnational Syria, Palestine, Dubai and Beyond*. Basingstoke: Palgrave Macmillan.

Divine Intervention (2002) [Film] Dir. Elia Suleiman, France, Germany, Morocco, Palestine: Arte France Cinéma.

Dyer, R., and Mulot, F. (2014) 'Mahmoud Darwish in Film: Politics, Representation, and Translation in Jean-Luc Godard's *Ici et ailleurs* and *Notre musique*', *Cultural Politics*, 10(1): 70–91.

El Attar, H. (2019) 'Restoring Narratives: Third-Generation Palestinian Chileans and Cinema', *Review: Literature and Arts of the Americas*, 52(2): 185–90.

Elden, S. (2009) *Terror and Territory: The Spatial Extent of Sovereignty*. Minneapolis: University of Minnesota Press.

Elden, S. (2013) *The Birth of Territory*. Chicago: University of Chicago Press.

Emmelhainz, I. (2019) *Jean-Luc Godard's Political Filmmaking*. London: Palgrave Macmillan.

Emmett, C. (1995) *Beyond the Basilica: Christians and Muslims in Nazareth*. Chicago: University of Chicago Press.

Ezra, E., and Rowden, T., eds (2006) *Transnational Cinema: The Film Reader*. New York: Routledge.

Fanon, F. (1965) *A Dying Colonialism*, trans. H. Chevalier, New York: Grove Press.

Film Socialisme (2010) [Film] Dir. Jean-Luc Godard, 2010, Switzerland, France: Vega Film.

Forgacs, D. (2019) 'Dirt and Order in Pasolini', in L. Peretti and K. Raizen (eds), *Pier Paolo Pasolini, Framed and Unframed: A Thinker for the Twenty-First Century*, 11–34, New York: Bloomsbury.

Foucault, M. (1977) *Discipline and Punish: The Birth of the Prison*, trans. Alan Sheridan. London: Penguin Books.
Foucault, M. (1986) 'Of Other Spaces', *Diacritics*, 16(1): 22–7.
Friedman, Y. (2010) 'Palestinian Filmmaking in Israel: Negotiating Conflicting Discourses'. Unpublished PhD thesis, University of Westminster.
Freud, S. (2003) *The Uncanny*, trans. David McLintock. London: Penguin.
Gabriel, T. (1989) 'Third Cinema as Guardian of Popular Memory: Towards a Third Aesthetics', in J. Pines and P. Willemen (eds), *Questions of Third Cinema*, 53–64, London: BFI Publishing.
García Márquez, G. (1987) *Clandestine in Chile: The Adventures of Miguel Littín*, trans. A. Zatz. New York: New York Review.
Genet, J. (2003 [1986]) *Prisoner of Love*, trans. B. Bray. New York: New York Review Books.
Genet, J. (2004) *The Declared Enemy: Texts and Interviews*, trans. B. Bray. Stanford: Stanford University Press.
Gertz, N., and Khleifi, G. (2008) *Palestinian Cinema: Landscape, Trauma and Memory*. Edinburgh: Edinburgh University Press.
Getino, O., and Solanas, F. (1969) 'Toward a Third Cinema', *Tricontinental*, (14): 107–32.
Gitai, A. (2014) 'Interview with Amos Gitai'. Interviewed by Nienke Huitenga for *wzzzt.com*, 17 July. Available online: https://wzzzt.com/2014/07/17/interview-with-amos-gitai/ (accessed 3 November 2016).
Godard, J. L. (1985) *Jean-Luc Godard par Jean-Luc Godard*. Paris: L'Étoile et Cahiers du cinema.
Graham, S. (2004) 'Constructing Urbicide by Bulldozer in the Occupied Territories', in S. Graham (ed.), *Cities, War, and Terrorism: Towards an Urban Geopolitics*, 192–213, Oxford: Blackwell Publishing.
Guattari, G. (2000 [1989]) *The Three Ecologies*, trans. I. Pinar and P. Sutton. London: Athlone.
Gustaffson. H. (2015) 'Remnants of Palestine, or, Archaeology after Auschwitz', in H. Gustafsson and A. Grønstad (eds), *Cinema and Agamben: Ethics, Biopolitics and the Moving Image*, 207–32, New York: Bloomsbury.
Haberman, C. (1992) 'Israel Expels 400 from Occupied Lands; Lebanese Deploy to Bar Entry of Palestinians', *The New York Times*, 18 December. Available online: https://www.nytimes.com/1992/12/18/world/israel-expels-400-occupied-lands-lebanese-deploy-bar-entry-palestinians.html (accessed 15 June 2019).
Habashneh, K. (2020) 'Plan B – Filming Revolution, Building Solidarities' [Recorded panel]. Palestine Film Institute Pavilion, Cannes Film Festival, Cannes, France. 26 June. Available online: https://www.palestinefilminstitute.org/filming-revolution-building-solidarities (accessed 30 November 2021).
Habiby, E. (2010 [1974]) *The Secret Life of Saeed the Pessoptimist*, trans. S. Jayyusi and T. Le Gassick. London: Arabia Books.

Haifawi, Y. (2018) 'The Political Program of the Campaign for One Democratic State in Historic Palestine', *mondoweis.net*. Available online: https://mondoweiss.net/2018/08/political-democratic-palestine/?fbclid=IwAR2hSgK-PhVZa3e9PKuFDJXxmWN7o25iRwA4Ygyr80rrBrGGZ1pQA7vx2QQ (accessed 13 October 2018).

Hammer, J. (2005) *Palestinians Born in Exile: Diaspora and the Search for a Homeland*. Austin: University of Texas Press.

Harbord, J. (2007) *The Evolution of Film: Rethinking Film Studies*. Cambridge: Polity Press.

Harrison, O. (2018) 'Consuming Palestine: Anticapitalism and Anticolonialism in Jean-Luc Godard's *Ici et ailleurs*', *Studies in French Cinema*, 18(3): 178–91.

Higbee, W., and Lim, S. (2010) 'Concepts of Transnational Cinema: Towards a Critical Transnationalism in Film Studies', *Transnational Cinemas*, 1(1): 7–21.

Hilal, J. (2007) 'Relations between Palestinian Diaspora (al-shatat), Palestinian Communities in the West Bank, and Gaza Strip', *Migration and Refugee Movements in the Middle East and North Africa*. The American University in Cairo, Egypt, 23–25 October. Available online: https://documents.aucegypt.edu/Docs/GAPP/Jamil_Hilal.pdf (accessed 12 September 2017).

Hochberg, G. (2007) *In Spite of Partition: Jews, Arabs and the Limits of Separatist Imagination*. Princeton: Princeton University Press.

Hochberg, G. (2015) *Visual Occupations: Violence and Visibility in a Conflict Zone*. Durham: Duke University Press.

Hochberg, G. (2021) *Becoming Palestine: Toward an Archival Imagination of the Future*. Durham: Duke University Press.

Ici et ailleurs (1976) [Film] Dir. Anne-Marie Miéville and Jean-Luc Godard, France: Gaumont Films.

In the Future They Ate from the Finest Porcelain (2015) [Film] Dir. Larissa Sansour and Søren Lind, UK, Denmark, Palestine, Qatar: Iambic Dream Films.

In Vitro (2019) [Film] Dir. Larissa Sansour and Søren Lind, UK, Denmark, Palestine: Spike Island.

It Must Be Heaven (2019) [Film] Dir. Elia Suleiman, France, Qatar, Germany, Canada, Turkey, Palestine: Nazira Films.

Jacir, A. (2017a) 'Annemarie Jacir on the Tensions of shooting "Wajib" in Nazareth'. Interviewed by Melanie Goodfellow for *Screendaily*, 15 December. Available online: https://www.screendaily.com/features/annemarie-jacir-on-the-tensions-of-shooting-wajib-in-nazareth/5125051.article (accessed 10 October 2018).

Jacir, A. (2017b) 'Wajib – an Interview with Annemarie Jacir'. Interviewed by Jeremy Elphick for *4:3*, 7 September [online]. Available online: https://fourthreefilm.com/2017/09/wajib-an-interview-with-annemarie-jacir/ (accessed 10 October 2018).

Jacir, E. (2013) 'Emily Jacir: Letter from Roma', *Creative Times Reports*, 3 September 2013 [online]. Available online: https://creativetimereports.org/2013/09/03/emily-jacir-letter-from-roma/ (accessed 12 May 2021).

Kanafānī, G. (2000) *Palestine's Children: Returning to Haifa & Other Stories*. Boulder, CO: Lynne Rienner.

Kalter, C. (2017) 'From Global to Local and Back: The "Third World" Concept and the New Radical Left in France', *Journal of Global History*, 12(1): 115–36.

Karpat, K. (1985) 'The Ottoman Emigration to America, 1860–1914', *International Journal of Middle East Studies*, 17(2): 175–209.

Lacan, J. (1988) *The Seminar of Jacques Lacan: Book 1 Freud's Papers on Technique, 1953–1954*. Cambridge: Cambridge University Press.

Levi, C. (2000 [1947]). *Christ Stopped at Eboli*, trans. F. Frenaye, London: Penguin.

Levinas, E. (1985) *Ethics and Infinity: Conversations with Philippe Nemo*. Pittsburgh: Duquesne University Press.

Levinas, E. (1989) *The Levinas Reader*, S. Hand (ed.). New York: B. Blackwell.

Levy, L. (2012) 'Nation, Village, Cave: A Spatial Reading of 1948 in Three Novels of Anton Shammas, Emile Habiby, and Elias Khoury', *Jewish Social Studies*, 18(3): 10–26.

Limbrick, P. (2012) 'Contested Spaces: Kamal Aljafari's Transnational Palestinian Films', in T. Ginsberg and A. Mensch (eds), *A Companion to German Cinema*, 218–48, Oxford: Blackwell.

Littín, M. (1976) 'Interview with Miguel Littín', in M. Chanan, *Chilean Cinema*, 53–65, London: BFI Publishing.

Littín, M. (2014 [1976]) 'Film Makers and the Popular Government Political Manifesto', in S. Mackenzie (ed.), *Film Manifestos and Global Cinema Cultures: A Critical Anthology*, 250–2, Berkeley: University of California Press.

Littín, M. (2020) 'Plan B – Filming Revolution, Building Solidarities' [Recorded panel]. Palestine Film Institute Pavilion, Cannes Film Festival, Cannes, France. 26 June. Available online: https://www.palestinefilminstitute.org/filming-revolution-building-solidarities (accessed 30 November 2021).

Looted and Hidden – Palestinian Archives in Israel (2017) [Film] Dir. Rona Sela, Israel.

Magome, K. (2006) 'Edward Said's Counterpoint', in S. Nagy-Zetmi, (ed.), *Paradoxical Citizenship: Edward Said*, 67–74, Lanham: Lexington Books.

Malm, A., and the Zetkin Collective (2021) *White Skin, Black Fuel: On the Danger of Fossil Fascism*. London: Verso.

Marks, L. (2000) *The Skin of the Film*. Durham: Duke University Press.

Marks, L. (2006) 'Asphalt Nomadism: The New Desert in Contemporary Arab Cinema', in M. Lefebvre (ed.), *Landscape and Film*, 125–47, New York: Routledge.

Marks, L. (2015) *Hanan al-Cinema*. Cambridge: MIT Press.

Massad, J. (2000) 'The "Post-Colonial" Colony: Time, Space and Bodies in Palestine/Israel', in F. Afzal-Khan and K. Seshadri-Crooks (eds), *The Pre-occupation of Postcolonial Studies*, 311–46, Durham: Duke University Press.

McWhirter, C. (2012). 'The Birth of "Dixie". *The New York Times*, 31 March [online] Available online: https://opinionator.blogs.nytimes.com/2012/03/31/the-birth-of-dixie/ (accessed 10 June 2018).

Medien, K. (2019) 'Palestine in Deleuze', *Theory, Culture & Society*, 36(5): 49–70.

Mee, E. B. (2012) 'The Cultural Intifada: Palestinian Theatre in the West Bank', *TDR: Drama Review*. [Online], 56(3): 167–77. Available online: https://doi.org/10.1162/DRAM_a_00194.

Mitchell, W. J. T. (2000) 'Holy Landscape: Israel, Palestine, and the American Wilderness', *Critical Inquiry*, 26(2): 193–223.

Montage Interdit (2012) [Web Archive] Dir. Eyal Sivan, Israel: Momento Films.

Moore-Gilbert, B. (2018) 'Palestine, Postcolonialism and Pessoptimism', *Interventions*, 20(1): 7–40.

Mulvey, L. (2006) *Death 24x a Second: Stillness and the Moving Image*. London: Reaktion Books.

Muslih, M. (1987) 'Arab Politics and the Rise of Palestinian Nationalism', *Journal of Palestine Studies*, 16(4): 77–94.

Naficy, H. (2001) *An Accented Cinema*. Princeton: Princeton University Press.

Naficy, H. (2006) 'Palestinian Exilic Cinema and Film Letters', in H. Dabashi (ed.), *Dreams of a Nation: On Palestinian Cinema*, 90–104, London: Verso.

Nation Estate (2012) [Film] Dir. Larissa Sansour, Palestine, Denmark.

Los Náufragos (The Shipwrecked) (1994) [Film] Dir. Miguel Littín, Chile, France, Canada: ACI Comunicaciones.

Nervus Rerum (2008) [Film] Dir. The Otolith Group, Palestine, UK: LUX.

Notre Musique (2004) [Film] Dir. Jean Luc Godard, France, Switzerland: Avventura Films.

Off Frame AKA Revolution Until Victory (Kharij al-Itar: Thawrah Hatta al-Nasr) (2016) [Film] Dir. Mohanad Yaqubi, Palestine, France, Jordan, Lebanon, USA, UK: Idioms Film.

Ouroboros (2017) [Film] Dir. Basma Alsharif, Palestine, Qatar, France, Belgium: Idioms Film.

Palacios, J. M. (2015) 'Chilean Exile Cinema and its Homecoming Documentaries', in R. Prime (ed.), *Cinematic Homecomings: Exile and Return in Transnational Cinema*, 147–63, New York: Bloomsbury Academic.

Palacios, J. M. (2016) 'Resistance vs Exile: The Political Rhetoric of Chilean Exile Cinema in the 1970s', *Jump Cut*, (57). Available online: https://www.ejumpcut.org/archive/jc57.2016/-PalaciosChile/index.html (accessed 12 August 2021).

Palestina: Imágenes Robadas (Palestine's Stolen Images) (2017) [Film] Dir. Rodrigo Vázquez, UK: Bethnal Films.

Parmenter, B. (1994) *Giving Voice to Stones: Place and Identity in Palestinian Literature*. Austin: University of Texas Press.
Pasolini Pa* Palestine (2005) [Film] Dir. Ayreen Anastas, Palestine.
Peteet, J. (2007) 'Problematizing a Palestinian Diaspora', *International Journal of Middle East Studies*, 39(4): 627–46.
Port of Memory (2009) [Film] Dir. Kamal Aljafari, Germany, France, UAE, Palestine: Novel Media.
Rascaroli, L. (2008) 'The Essay Film: Problems, Definitions, Textual Commitments', *Framework: The Journal of Cinema and Media*, 49(2): 24–47.
Recollection (2015) [Film] Dir. Kamal Aljafari, Palestine: Novel Media.
Reid, J. (2012) 'The Neoliberal Subject: Resilience and the Art of Living Dangerously', *Revista Pléyade*, (10): 143–65.
The Roof (2006) [Film] Dir. Kamal Aljafari, Germany: Filmstiftung Nordrhein-Westfalen.
Route 181: Fragments of a Journey in Palestine-Israel (2004) [Film] Dir. Michel Khleifi and Eyal Sivan, Belgium, France, Germany, UK: Momento.
Said, E. (1983) *The World, the Text, and the Critic*. Cambridge: Harvard University Press.
Said, E. (1984) 'Permission to Narrate', *Journal of Palestine Studies*, 13(3): 27–48.
Said, E. (1986) *After the Last Sky*. London: Vintage.
Said, E. (1992 [1979]) *The Question of Palestine*. New York: Vintage Books.
Said, E. (1994a) *Culture and Imperialism*. New York: Vintage.
Said, E. (1994b) 'On Mahmoud Darwish', *Grand Street*, (48): 112–15.
Said, E. (1994c) *The Politics of Dispossession*. London: Chatto & Windus.
Said, E. (1995) *Peace and its Discontents: Essays on Palestine in the Middle East Peace Process*. London: Vintage.
Said, E., and Mitchell, W. J. T. (1998) 'The Panic of the Visual: A Conversation with Edward W. Said', *boundary 2*, 25(2): 11–33.
Said, E. (2000) *Reflections on Exile*. Cambridge: Harvard University Press.
Said, E. (2003) *Freud and the non-European*. London: Verso.
Said, E. (2005) *Power, Politics and Culture: Interviews with Edward Said*, G. Viswanathan (ed.). London: Bloomsbury.
Said, E. (2006 [2003]) 'Preface', in H. Dabashi (ed.), *Dreams of a Nation: On Palestinian Cinema*, 1–5, London: Verso.
Salt of this Sea (Milh Hadha al-Bahr) (2008) [Film] Dir. Annemarie Jacir, Palestine, Belgium, France, Spain, Switzerland: Philistine Films.
Sansour, L. (2021) 'Larissa Sansour: Filming a Vanishing Present'. Interviewed by Nadine Khalil for *Ocula*, 20 January [online]. Available online: https://ocula.com/magazine/conversations/larissa-sansour-filming-a-vanishing-present/ (accessed 10 November 2021).
Schmitt, C. (1996) *The Concept of the Political*. Chicago: University of Chicago Press.

Schulz, H. (2005) *The Palestinian Diaspora*. London: Routledge.

Schwabe, S. (2018) 'Paradoxes of Erasure: Palestinian Memory and the Politics of Forgetting in Post-Dictatorship Chile', *Interventions*, 20(5): 651–65.

Shammas, A. (2002) 'Autocartography: The Case of Palestine, Michigan', *Palestine-Israel Journal*, 9(2), *Middle East Publications*. Available online: http://www.pij.org/details.php?id=154 (accessed 12 August 2018).

Shatz, A. (2013) 'The Life and Death of Juliano Mer-Khamis', *London Review of Books*, 35(22): 3–11.

Shavit, A. (2004) 'Top PM Aide: Gaza Plan Aims to Freeze the Peace Process', *Haaretz*, 6 October. Available online: https://www.haaretz.com/1.4710372?v=1651761393311 (accessed 5 December 2021).

Shehadeh, R. (1982) *The Third Way, a Journal of Life in the West Bank*. London: Quartet Books.

Shohat, E. (2006) *Taboo Memories, Diasporic Voices*. Durham: Duke University Press.

Shohat, E. (2010) *Israeli Cinema*. 2nd edn. London: I.B. Tauris.

Sivan, E. (2013) 'Montage Interdit. A Conversation with Eyal Sivan'. Interviewed by Interview by Neja Tomšič for *anti-utopias*, 20 January. Available online: https://anti-utopias.com/editorial/montage-interdit-a-conversation-with-eyal-sivan/ (accessed 10 August 2020).

Sopralluoghi in Palestina (1965) [Film] Dir. Pier Paolo Pasolini, Italy: Arco Film.

Stack, O. (1969) *Pasolini on Pasolini: Interviews with Oswald Stack*. London: Thames and Hudson.

Steimatsky, N. (2008) *Italian Locations: Reinhabiting the Past in Postwar Cinema*. Minneapolis: University of Minnesota Press.

Stites Mor, J. (2022) *South-South Solidarity and the Latin American Left*. Wisconsin: University of Wisconsin Press.

Suleiman, E. (2000) 'A Cinema of Nowhere', *Journal of Palestine Studies*, 29(2): 95–101.

Suleiman, E. (2003) 'Notes from the Palestinian Diaspora: An Interview with Elia Suleiman', *Cineaste*, 28(3): 24–7.

Suleiman, E. (2003a) 'The Occupation (and Life) Through an Absurdist Lens', *Journal of Palestine Studies*, 32(2): 63–73.

Suleiman, E. (2010) 'A Different Kind of Occupation: An Interview with Elia Suleiman'. Interviewed by Sabah Haider for *The Electronic Intifada*, 1 February. Available online: https://electronicintifada.net/content/different-kind-occupation-interview-elia-suleiman/8654 (accessed 2 April 2016).

Suleiman, E. (2016) 'Elia Suleiman: Hope and Action Despite Pessimism'. Interviewed by Daniel Tkatch for *Political Critique*, 5 September. Available online: http://politicalcritique.org/world/2016/filmmaker-suleiman-hope-and-action/ (accessed 3 January 2017).

Suleiman, E. (2021) '"Palestinanisation is Everywhere: Elia Suleiman on It Must Be Heaven': Hope and Action Despite Pessimism'. Interviewed by Nick Chen for *Sight and Sound*, 15 June. Available online: https://www.bfi.org.uk/sight-and-sound/int erviews/elia-suleiman-it-must-be-heaven-palestine-paris-global-violence (accessed 18 December 2021).

Tawil-Souri, H. (2014) 'Cinema as the Space to Transgress Palestine's Territorial Trap', *Middle East Journal of Culture and Communication*, 7(2): 169–89.

Telmissany, M. (2010) 'Displacement and Memory: Visual Narratives of *al-Shatat* in Michel Khleifi's Films', *Comparative Studies of South Asia, Africa and the Middle East*, 30(1): 69–84.

Telmissany, M., and Schwartz, S. (eds) (2010) *Counterpoints: Edward Said's Legacy*. Newcastle upon Tyne: Cambridge Scholars.

They Do Not Exist (1974) [Film] Dir. Mustafa Abu Ali, Palestine: Palestine Cinema Institute.

The Time That Remains (2009) [Film] Dir. Elia Suleiman, France, Belgium, Italy, UK, UAE, Palestine, Israel: Nazira Films.

Traverso, A. (2010) 'Dictatorship Memories: Working through Trauma in Chilean Post-Dictatorship Documentary', *Continuum*, 24(1): 179–91.

Trento, G. (2012) 'Pier Paolo Pasolini and Pan-Meridional Italianness', in L. Di Blasi, M. Gragnolati and C. F. E. Holzhey (eds), *The Scandal of Self Contradiction: Pasolini's Multistable Subjectivities, Geographies, Traditions*, 59–83, Vienna: Verlag Turia + Kant.

La Última Luna (2005) [Film] Dir. Miguel Littín, Chile, Mexico, Spain: Latido Films.

Veracini, L. (2011) 'Introducing', *Settler Colonial Studies*, 1(1): 1–12.

Wajib (2017) [Film] Dir. Annemarie Jacir, Palestine, France, Colombia, Germany, UAE, Qatar, Norway: Philistine Films.

Waldman, G. (2009) 'Violence and Silence in Dictatorial and Postdictatorial Chile. The Noir Genre as a Restitution of the Memory and History of the Present', *Latin American Perspectives* 36(5): 121–32.

Wallach, Y. (2020) *A City in Fragments: Urban Text in Modern Jerusalem*. Stanford: Stanford University Press.

Wayne, M. (2001) *Political Film: The Dialectics of Third Cinema*. London: Pluto Press.

Wehr H. (1994) *A Dictionary of Modern Written Arabic*. Ithaca: Spoken Language Services.

Weizman, E. (2007) *Hollow Land*. London: Verso Books.

Willemen, P. (1989) 'The Third Cinema Question: Notes and Reflections', in J. Pines and P. Willemen (eds), *Questions of Third Cinema*, 1–29, London: BFI Publishing.

Williams, P., and Ball, A. (2014) Where is Palestine?, *Journal of Postcolonial Writing*, 50(2): 127–33.

Yaqub, N. (2018) *Palestinian Cinema in the Days of Revolution*. Austin: University of Texas Press.

Yaqubi, M. (2017) 'Off Frame A.K.A. Revolution until Victory: An Interview with Director Mohanad Yaqubi'. Interviewed by Ivan Čerečina for *4:3*, 3 April. Available online: https://fourthreefilm.com/2017/04/off-frame-a-k-a-revolution-until-vict ory-an-interview-with-director-mohanad-yaqubi/ (accessed 14 May 2018).

Zochrot (2014) 'al-Manshiyya Neighborhood', *zochrot.org*. Available online: https://www.zochrot.org/villages/village_details/56077/en?alManshiyya_Neighborhood_ _Yaffa_ (accessed 24 March 2020).

Zurayk, C. (1956) *The Meaning of Disaster*, trans. Bayly Winder. Beirut: Kayat

Index

Adorno, Theodor, 1–2, 5, 14, 24, 60
   atonal counterpoint, 6–8
   Negative Dialectics, 7
   Philosophy of New Music, 6
   Said, Edward, 8–10
   Schoenberg, Arnold, 6
affiliation, 1, 3, 160
After the Last Sky, 2, 4–5, 9–10, 13–19, 64, 97, 105, 127, 141, *see* Said, Edward
Agamben, Giorgio, 11–12, 23, 67, 82, 114, 120, 140, 154–5
   philospohical archaeolgy, 120, 140, 154–5
   remnant, 82
   Stasis, 67
   topology, 23, 114
   What Is the Contemporary?, 11
al-Andalus, 60–1, 148, *see* Darwish, Mahmoud
Aljafari, Kamal, 15, 20, 24–5, 60, 72–82, 85–6
   Adorno, Theodor, 24, 60
   Lorca, Federico Garcia, 60
   Port of Memory, 76–9
   Recollection, 79–82
   The Roof, 72–6, 86
Alsharif, Basma, 24, 27, 114
   Levi, Carlo, 136–8
   Ouroboros, 126–142, 155
   post-Palestinian, 27, 141, 144
Anastas, Ayreen, 41, 114, 117, 136, 139–40, 144
   Pasolini Pa* Palestine, 122–6
Arab-Jew, 59, 61, 65, 78, 83–6
archival nostalgia, 96, 147
archival practice, 31, 41–2, 59, 145–7
archive, 21, 25, 31, 41–4, 46, 51, 53, 56, 79, 82, 85, 112, 145–8
   Palestine Film Archive, 31, 44, 51, 56, 85, 148
atonal counterpoint, 5–6, 9, 13
atonal music, 5–7

atonality, 1–2, 5–10, 14, 21–2, 30, 144
   Deleuze, Gilles, 21

Barthes, Roland, 10, 17–18, 80
   studium and punctum, 17–18
Baudelaire, Eric, 53–7
   The Anabasis of May and Fusako Shigenobu, Masao Adachi, and 27 Years without Images, 53–57
Bazin, Andre, 42–3, 53, 72
   horizontal montage, 34
Benjamin, Walter, 4, 8, 117, 134, 145
   dialectical image, 139–40

Collins, John, 12, 41, 104, 145, 158
contrapuntal method, 2, 8, 44, 57
contrapuntal reading, 5, 9–10, 27, 82, 132–3, 139, 147, 154
counterpoint, 2–5, 9, 13, 19, 31, 34, 131

al-dakhil, 17, 25, 64, 70, 76, 78, 83–4, 90
Darwish, Mahmoud, 102, 106–7, 131, 148
   Absent Presence, 63
   Arab-Jew, 60
   contemporary critical distance, 12
   Lorca, Federico Garcia, 60–1
   Said, Edward, 3, 13
Deleuze, Gilles, 25, 34, 95, 128
   atonal cinema, 21
   minor cinema, 22
   Palestine, 23
Derrida, Jacques, 79, 81–2, 86
   haunting, 72

estrangement, 19, 69, 89–90, 136–7, 141, *see* al-ghurba
exile, 24, 87–91, 134, 156
   Adorno, Theodor, 9, 14
   Aljafari, Kamal, 86
   Littín, Miguel, 97–8

manfa, 89
Suleiman, Elia, 60

First Intifada, 18, 73, 96, 102
forbidden montage, 34–6, 42–3, 45–6, 159
Foucault, Michel, 120
  heterotopia, 19, 150
  history of the present, 53, 104

Genet, Jean, 29, 32, 38, 46, 53
  Palestinian revolution, 39–40
Gertz, Nurith and Khleifi, George, 30, 62, 88
al-ghurba, 69, 89–91, 141
Gitai, Amos, 16, 62, 105
  Ana Arabia, 83–5
  Arab-Jew, 83–6
Godard, Jean-Luc, 41, 51, 53, 57, 114, 126, 133
  Deleuze, Gilles, 21
  Ici et ailleurs, 32–9
  montage, 34–5
  Notre Musique, 32, 45, 131–2
  Palestinian revolution, 25
  Sivan, Eyal, 42–3
  Yaqubi, Mohanad, 43–6

Habiby, Emile, 17, 62, 73, 110, 144, 159
haunting, 62–5, 85–6
Hochberg, Gil, 22, 62–6, 86, 153–4
  archive, 145–8
  partition, 61

image of resistance, 25, 29–32, 51, 126, 159

Jacir, Annemarie, 41, 46, 78, 85, 100
  Suleiman, Elia, 69–72
  Wajib, 69–72
  When I Saw You, 46–53

Khalil, Basil, 149–50
Khleifi, Michel, 26, 42, 61, 86, 90

Levi, Carlo, 114, 136–40, 145
Littín, Miguel, 87–8, 94–8, 147
  Acta General de Chile, 98–100
  Cronicas Palestinas, 102–7
  La Ultima Luna, 107–11
  Los Naufragos, 100–2

transversal consciousness, 111–12
Lorca, Federico Garcia, 60–1

manfa, 89–90, *see* exile
Mitchell, W. J. T., 4–5, 13–14, 116, 130
Mohr, Jean, 2, 39, 64, 97, 103, 141
  After the Last Sky, 13–18

Nakba, 11, 42, 63, 68, 85, 90–1, 107, 147
naksa, 46, 91, 107

Palestinian Authority, 12, 23, 25, 31, 38, 40, 44, 123
Palestinian diaspora, 26, 87, 89–91
  in Chile, 91–4
  al-shatat, 89–90
Palestinian revolution, 48, 56, 66, 67, 68
  The Anabasis of May and Fusako Shigenobu, Masao Adachi, and 27 Years without Images., 53–7
  Genet, Jean, 39–40
  Godard, Jean-Luc, 25, 33 9
  Off Frame AKA Revolution Until Victory, 44–6
  When I Saw You, 46–53
Pasolini, Pier Paolo, 27, 41, 113–14, 147
  contamination, 118
  Ouroboros, 130, 136, 138
  pan-South, 114, 119, 139
  Pasolini Pa* Palestine, 122–6
  Sopralluoghi in Palestina, 115–22
  struttura da farsi, 121–2, 139
PFU (Palestine Film Unit), 25, 31–3, 41, 44, 49–51
  Abu Ali, Mustafa, 33, 44–6, 51, 112
philosophical archaeology, 120, 140, 154–5, *see* Agamben, Giorgio
PLO (Palestine Liberation Organization), 2, 25, 33, 38, 40, 45, 50, 53, 93
postcolonial studies, 1, 84, 133, 144
postcolonial theory, 3, 19, 61
post-Palestinian, 24, 27, 141, 143, 145, 148–50, 156, *see* Alsharif, Basma

resilience, 30–1, 41, *see* image of resistance

Said, Edward, 2, 24, 30, 38, 44, 64, 69, 89, 105, 127

Index

Adorno, Theodor, 8–10
affiliation, 1, 3, 160
After the Last Sky, 13–18, 103
atonality, 6–8
contemporaneity, 10–11
counterpoint, 2–6
Culture and Imperialism, 3–4, 8–10
Freud and the Non-European, 74
late style, 2, 8, 10
The Question of Palestine, 41
Palestinian cinema, 19
Sansour, Larissa, 150–7
  In the Future They Ate from the Finest Porcelain, 152–5
  In Vitro, 155–7
  Nation Estate, 150–2
Second Intifada, 30, 41, 65, 70, 88, 102, 104, 125
Shammas, Anton, 22, 73
Shohat, Ella, 1, 30, 61, 86, 130, 132
  Arab-Jew, 78, 84

Sivan, Eyal, 61, 86, 112, 141
  Montage Interdit, 42–4
Suleiman, Elia, 12, 14, 24, 41, 59–60
  Chronicle of a Disappearance, 65–6
  Divine Intervention, 66–7
  It Must Be Heaven, 157–60
  Jacir, Annemarie, 69–72
  The Time That Remains, 68–9
sumud, 29, 107, *see* image of resistance

Telmissany, May, 5, 90–1

Weizman, Eyal, 148, 151–2, 154

Yaqub, Nadia, 44, 146, 148–9
Yaqubi, Mohanad, 23, 41, 43
  Off Frame AKA Revolution Until Victory, 44–6

Zurayk, Constantine, 10–12

www.ingramcontent.com/pod-product-compliance
Lightning Source LLC
Chambersburg PA
CBHW052045300426
44117CB00012B/1984